Old-Time Music Makers of New York State

A YORK STATE BOOK

SIMON J. BRONNER

OLD-TIME MUSIC MAKERS
OF
NEW YORK STATE

SYRACUSE UNIVERSITY PRESS

First Edition
87 88 89 90 91 92   1 2 3 4 5 6

Published with support from the Pennsylvania State University at Harrisburg.

The paper used in this publication meets the minimum requirements of American National
Standard for Information Sciences—Permanence of Paper for Printed Library Materials, ANSI
Z39.48-1984. ∞™

Library of Congress Cataloging-in-Publication Data

Bronner, Simon J.
    Old-time music makers of New York State/Simon J. Bronner. — 1st ed.
      p. cm. — (A York State book)
    Bibliography: p.
    Includes discographies.
    Includes index.
    ISBN 0-8156-0216-2 (alk. paper):
      1. Country music—New York (State)—History and criticism.
2. Country musicians—New York (State)—Biography. 3. Folk dance
music—New York (State)—History and criticism. 4. Fiddle tunes—
New York (State)—History and criticism. I. Title.
ML3524.B75 1987
784.5'2'009747—dc19   87-21003   CIP   MN

For
RODERICK ROBERTS

Simon J. Bronner is Associate Professor of Folklore and American Studies at the Pennsylvania State University at Harrisburg. He is the author of *Grasping Things: Folk Material Culture and Mass Society in America, Chain Carvers: Old Men Crafting Meaning,* and *American Folklore Studies: An Intellectual History.*

Contents

Musical Transcriptions

Tables

Illustrations

Preface

WHAT ABOUT MUSICIANS who play the old fiddle tunes?" I asked. "Can I find them up here?" I was in Cooperstown, New York, close to the heart of the state, and I was talking to an elderly neighbor who recalled upstate village life. She cocked her head and laughed when I asked my questions about music. "Why there are millions of them," she exclaimed. Then she realized something and in a serious tone she advised, "But they're a well-kept secret, I guess. Most folks think the only fiddlers are in Nashville, but we had 'em here as long as I remember. Times are different now, but you can still hear them old-time music makers if you know where to look."

I looked in barn dances out in the countryside, in fire halls, in "hotels" (euphemisms for rural bars), and in senior citizens' centers. I found a rich legacy of music that these musicians held in common. It was not exactly folk music, because many of the songs were from commercial recordings or sheet music. It was not exactly country music, because the tunes and styles that the musicians used typically predated the development of commercial country music. It was probably best called old-time music. Indeed, this was the label given to the music by newspapers after the turn of the century.

Old-time music combined Anglo-Celtic fiddle tunes, square dance numbers, play-party tunes, Victorian parlor songs, native American and British ballads, sacred songs, and minstrel songs. It was "old-time" because it symbolized old-time rural values for an era after World War I when everything seemed modern. In New York State especially, old-time music meant the traditional country dance music that was the primary source of entertainment in the farm communities for more than a hundred years. The champion of old-time music was the country fiddler. This musician was the center of community entertainment throughout the nineteenth century. With his old familiar tunes and a style that recalled the mother country, the American country fiddler could lead dances, lighten the load at work bees, delight the young, and raise conversation at the general store.[1]

This book introduces some old-time musicians. It brings forth their music, their lives, their towns, and their times. You'll meet Ken Kane, Floyd Woodhull, Lyle Miles, John Dingler, Milo Kouf, Les Weir, Charley Hughes, Grant Rogers, and John McDermott. If these names are not as familiar to a national audience as their counterparts in Kentucky and Tennessee, it is not because they had no impact on their communities. They shared in a cultural process that was sweeping through rural America. They shared in the realignment of rural America to a metropolitan, industrial nation. Now more than entertainment and a social bond, their music was a symbol of a idealized past way of life; it often brought up for questioning the place of older values in the new alignment.

New York State musicians did not share in the commercialization of the music that hit regional centers such as Nashville, Wheeling, and Atlanta. To be sure, Floyd Woodhull and John McDermott recorded for major labels, but their main connection to their region was through performances on stage and on radio. Learning from nineteenth-century masters of their trade, Woodhull and McDermott and their old-fashioned music enjoyed great popularity throughout upstate New York from the early twentieth century to World War II. After the war, younger musicians like Ken Kane and John Dingler worked in their villages and organized barn dances to carry on the tradition inherited from the previous generation. But by the 1970s their audiences had dwindled. Where barn dances had brought rural people together in the lonely winters, cable TV kept many in their warm homes, and snowmobiles and improved road vehicles allowed others to bypass the dances for their socializing. The old communal institutions gave way to individualistic commercial entertainment.

Still Kane and others played for their families and friends. This is where I found them and interviewed them. To their stories and songs, I added accounts of old-time music found in newspapers, local histories, and archives. I compiled discographies, band chronologies, and musical transcriptions and collected photographs and illustrations. From these varied sources, I reconstructed a cultural history of a region in transition.

The present volume is the first book-length cultural analysis of old-time musicians in New York State. My purpose is not to inventory every old-time musician who performed in New York. Rather, I sought to describe musicians from my experience who told of the Yorker tradition. I have included samples of their tunes to illustrate the old-time repertoire and the contributions of York State musicians to it.

While you can find some dissection of texts in my notes, my narrative addresses the more human and cultural side of the music. *Country Music, U.S.A.* (1968) by Bill Malone set the stage for this kind of work by giving serious analysis to the evolution of country music from folk and old-time musical roots. Malone, however, overdrew the southern connection to old-time music, and state surveys by Charles K. Wolfe and Ivan M. Tribe for Kentucky, Tennessee, and West Virginia underscored that bias.[2] I add to the cultural analysis begun in these works and contribute the first survey in the North as a basis for later comparison. This book is meant to be exploratory. It is meant to open up a regional music for questioning and to invite deeper forays into the legacies of other musicians and other regions.

Using the example of New York's old-time musical legacy, I find the background of country music to be a more complicated story than the outline that has been previously drawn in works such as Malone's of a national musical foliage growing from a single southern root. Looking into the old-time music of regions such as New York State reveals the varieties of development and the fullness of the cultural reservoirs that fed the later popularity of a national country music.

The Yankee musical heritage was one of many country musics that grew out of the widespread British Isles inheritance in America. Paying particular attention to discographies and biographies, photographs and illustrations, accounts of stage and radio performances, community histories and regional collections, I argue that the story of old-time music is not a simple plot of a nationalization of southern music, as Malone has called its development into country music, but rather it is a saga of a complex regionalization, and later commercialization, out of the folkways of nationwide rural experience.

The book moves from the sources of old-time music in the colonial period to the adaptation of the music to the present. The narrative weaves historical and cultural background with the stories and performances of the musicians. With the call to "Strike Up a Familiar Strain," the first chapter begins with a background of the region's early traditional music—roots of the music in the eighteenth and nineteenth centuries and several pivotal figures in the transformation of this music into the commercial period of the twentieth century, most notably Alva Belcher and John McDermott. The famous car-maker Henry Ford also had a hand in continuing the nineteenth-century legacy of country fiddlers into the 1920s. Henry Ford conducted a campaign to revive old-time music and he endorsed Yankee fiddlers like Mellie Dunham on the image of rural entertainment in an industrializing nation. Related to Ford's sponsorship of fiddling contests and old-time dance parties was a spate of old-time recordings made on Edison Records. I especially discuss the contributions that early Yankee recording stars for Edison Records such as John Kimmel, Jasper Bisbee, and John Baltzell made to the northern rural market. After introducing this development of old-time music in the Northeast, I compare it with the prevalent ideas on the development of commercial country music from old-time music in the South.

The second chapter, "It Just Leaned Naturally Toward a Farmer of Hillbilly Image," discusses the character of old-time music during the second quarter of the twentieth century. During that time, the hillbilly image dominated the performance of old-time music. It was a way of making fun and it also raised questions by a younger generation about the effects of modernization on a rural way of life. The quote giving the chapter its title is taken from Floyd Woodhull, leader of the best-known old-time music band in New York. I trace the story of this family band from its folk roots in the nineteenth century to its triumphant performances and recordings in the 1940s, and finally to its decline in the 1950s. Along with the Woodhulls, other well-known York State hillbilly bands are discussed—the colorful Hornellsville Hillbillies, Ott's Woodchoppers, and North Country Hillbillies. In these hillbilly bands we can see the weave of family and rural values into the fabric of old-time music. The experience of these bands also shows the ways that basic patterns in the rural culture of New York State changed as the midcentury mark approached.

The third chapter takes us to the generation in old-time music that spanned the three decades after World War II. The theme of the chapter is taken from the words of Charley Hughes, "brings you back don't it?" Charley had avidly taken up the "western" music that took over from hillbilly music in the 1950s. At home, he had been reared on the old fiddle tunes played by his father and uncles. Charley's popular band, the Westernaires, played the new western hits but they also included the old-time Yankee tunes in their sets. The music brought them back to their homes, their families, and their communities as they used to be.

Ken Kane is a figure who retained his old-time music at home. He recalled the meaning of this music that seemed so much a part of where he lived on his youth and then on his older years when ripples of change had altered the region and its music. The music like the life that Ken led depended on family and community bonds. It depended on the carrying on of tradition in a rooted communal society. Ken made choices about the life he led and the music he played that reflected on the changing conditions of the region and the nation. Ken is not alone in his experience, as discussion of Les Weir, Grant Rogers, John Dingler, and Milo Kouf—other heirs to the Yorker old-time music tradition—will show.

My interest in the subject began in 1971 when I was an undergraduate at the State University of New York at Binghamton, New York. The sounds of old-time fiddle and guitar frequently wafted through campus, and they raised much talk about sources and styles. Through the prodding of musical friends in Binghamton such as Ruth Slovik, Margaret Erickson, Bill Healy, and Michael Beebie, and the scholarly guidance of Sam Chianis and Wilhelm Nicolaisen, I first sought out home-grown traditions. I began to research old-time music in earnest when I moved to Cooperstown in 1974. I owe Roderick Roberts there for putting me on the trail and for sharing with me his expertise on folk and country music. An extensive field trip during 1976 through the South, with an extended stay in Mississippi (funded by the National Endowment for the Arts), opened my eyes to continuities and variations in northern and southern old-time music. As director of the Archive of New York State Folklife during 1976 and 1977, I conducted interviews with figures involved with old-time music in New York State, and I organized the available material on New York State's old-time music, benefiting especially from the collections of old-time music left by Sam Eskin to the New York State Historical Association and from the counsel of Norman Cazden who at the time was compiling his compendium of folk songs from the Catskills. While at Indiana University from 1977 to 1981, I added comparative material to my collection from the Archives of Traditional Music and the Folklore Institute.

During the years that followed, I published several articles on the subject which reached specialists in country music research. I might have let the matter rest there, but teaching at the Pennsylvania State University at Harrisburg, I faced students eager to know more about old-time music and I found that they were particularly curious about the field work that I did in the Northeast. After I arrived at Penn State another pivotal moment was my meeting with the dean of tune-seekers, Samuel Bayard. He impressed upon me that more could be said, especially in regard to the instrumental music and dance tradition that I found. I also was moved by many young musicians in the area who were taking up old-time music anew and asking about the old masters. In the interim, I published books on folk crafts that made me think more about old-time musicians as crafts-people whose lives and products hold a significant symbolism in the midst of a rapidly changing culture.[3]

I undertook this book, then, to tell the story of an important source of old-time musical craft in New York State. I hoped to reach a wider audience and to expand the arguments that I had made earlier. Research funds from the Pennsylvania State University at Harrisburg helped me to complete the book in 1986.

Two special musicians who inspirited my work on this book are Pamela deWall and Henry Koretzky of Harrisburg, Pennsylvania. Pamela deWall completed the transcriptions of musical selections and was among the first to comment on my cultural analysis. A brilliant fiddler as well as a student of American culture, she helped me to listen more closely to what the music as well as the musicians were saying. Henry Koretzky taught me a great deal about the techniques of old-time music. Besides giving me the benefit of his deft playing, he made available his tremendous record and magazine collection and encouraged me to tune up my writing instrument.

I owe thanks to faculty at Penn State for supporting my work. John Patterson, coordinator of the graduate program in American Studies, infected me with his love of folk music. My colleague Michael Barton played the role of Doubting Thomas and forced me to hone my arguments. William Mahar, when he was not busy being head of the Humanities Division, donned his musicologist's cap to comment on my work. He made me feel confident that the story of this music was significant in American studies; he understood that New York was worth the trouble.

My work also benefited from the contributions of the excellent staff at Penn State at Harrisburg. Donna Horley handled my correspondence with great efficiency and Darrell Peterson gave invaluable assistance in the darkroom. Thea Hocker in Community Relations added her special advice and good humor. Carol Kalbaugh, at the Center for Research and Graduate Studies, helped greatly by transcribing my tapes of interviews, and Ruth Runion of the Heindel Library came to the rescue more than once with books I needed.

Many gracious neighbors and correspondents across New York State provided invaluable information. I am grateful to Marjorie Crawford of New Berlin, Milo Kouf of Newfield, Atwood Manley and David Murray of Canton, Frank McBride and H. Preston White of Hornell, Ralph Fudge of Elmira, Fred Palmer of Alfred Station, Ross Bartlett, Leslie O'Malley, and Larry Harrington of Cortland, Milo and Ruth Stewart of Cooperstown, Norman Carlson of Jamestown, Daniel Franklin Ward of Seneca Falls, Dick Case of Syracuse, and John Raitt of Delhi. I also thank various state and local historical organizations that are so effective in documenting local culture. I received welcome aid from the Chemung Historical Society, Cortland County Historical Society, Delaware Historical Association, Madison County Historical Society, Museums at Stony Brook, and the New York State Historical Association.

Many colleagues working in this field were extremely generous with their time and knowledge. For their aid, I extend thanks to William K. McNeil of the Ozark Folk Center, Joe Hickerson and Gerald Parsons of the Archive of Folk Culture in the Library of Congress, Paul Wells of the Center for Popular Music, John Hasse and Scott Hambly of the Smithsonian Institution, Bob Pinson, Patty Hall, William Ivey, and Kyle Young of the Country Music Foundation, Rebecca Ziegler and Norm Cohen of the John Edwards Memorial Foundation, Leah S. Burt of the Edison Archives at the Edison National Historic Site in West Orange, New Jersey, Dew Shonsey and Robert Sieber of the Archive of New York State Folklife, Alan Jabbour of the American Folklife Center, David Winslow of the State University of New York at Oswego, Robert Bethke of the University of Delaware, Tony Russell of *Old Time Music Magazine,* Roy Horton of Peer-Southern Organization, John Braunlein of the Rockwood Museum, Wilmington, Delaware, Bruce Buckley of Cooperstown, New York, Joe Bussard of Frederick, Maryland, Bob Kinney of Springfield, Missouri, John W. Rumble of Nashville, Tennessee, Mark Downing of Tulsa, Oklahoma, Louis C. Jones of the New York State Historical Association, Frank Gillis of the Archives of Traditional Music, and the late Richard M. Dorson of Indiana University.

Most of all, to the old-time musicians and their families who have become part of my life, I extend my gratitude for letting me tell their stories and share their songs.

Middletown, Pennsylvania   SJB
Spring 1987

Old-Time Music Makers of New York State

Strike Up a Familiar Strain

THE NEW YORK THRUWAY was taking me quickly across the Empire State. Speeding along its concrete swath, I barely noticed the many villages in the distance dotting the green countryside. I veered off long enough to hear sounds from some of those villages that my radio didn't play. Rather than taking the main road into Cooperstown, a mecca for baseball fans, I turned sharply onto a quiet hill road. There the farm land and forest sprawled oblivious to the concrete spaces further away. A one-room schoolhouse sat at the top of the hill. Signs dropped away as I drove further. Turning again, the road thinned out with dirt, and I heard the sound of a fiddle getting closer. I wasn't given a house number to find the place I was looking for. I was told to simply ask for Ken Kane's place up on the hill. I found it all right, and when I entered his parlor, he waved me a toothless grin and put his fiddle to his chin.

"Here's one we all play," he said. "This'll get you going," he beamed.

It got me going into a world of music and its people, a land and its lore. Its story hadn't been told, and with the help of Ken Kane and others like him, I began to figure out how it went so I could report it here. It is a story of a music overshadowed by its country cousin in the South, but one that has a rich legacy of its own. It is a story of a music that has been a significant part of the cultural history of a region and its people.

I was in Central New York State, or what New York City people simply call "Upstate." It has not received the folk cultural appreciation reserved for old New England and the romantic Southeast, yet with its notable cultural history and its distinctive mix of eastern settlers on what was once America's western frontier, Upstate has much tradition to claim. The region lies across the Thruway at Utica and Syracuse and above Route 17 at Binghamton and the Pennsylvania border. The Genesee River is a natural western border. It cuts a line from Allegany County, three counties in from Lake Erie, north to Rochester and Lake On-

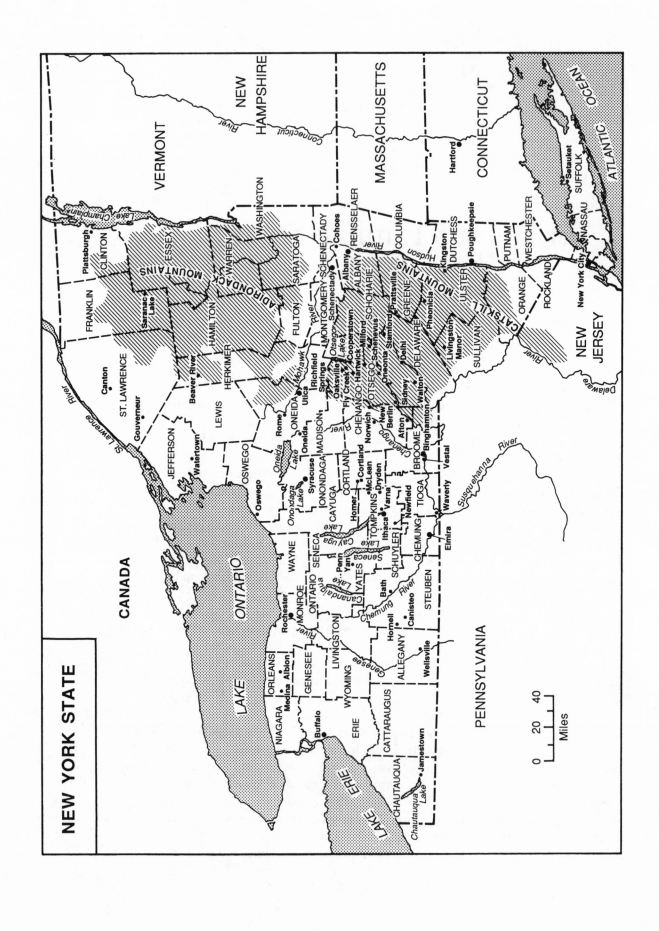

tario. To the east, the Catskill Mountains and the Adirondacks wall in the region. To the southeast, the Susquehanna River, flowing from Otsego Lake at Cooperstown, forms a ribbon at the foot of the Catskills. Within these borders is a heart-shaped interior marked by the Chemung River running through Elmira and Corning to the west and the Chenango River running into Madison County to the east. Pouring into this heart are the Finger Lakes, which contribute to the region's unparalleled beauty. Rolling hills and plush valleys, many giving life to dense forests, fill in the scene; rugged dairy farms and various kinds of mills sprawl over the landscape. The interior of the heart forms a distinctive natural region called the "Appalachian Upland" by geographers. Working east from the western border of the state, you move across the Cattaraugus and Allegheny Hills, Finger Lake Hills, Susquehanna Hills, Helderberg Hills, Delaware Hills, and Catskill Mountains, before dipping suddenly into the Hudson and Mohawk River Lowlands. Adding to its sense of isolation, the region lies in what meteorologists call the "snow belt." Forecasters usually predict between 60 and 200 inches of snow every winter. Ringing the region to the north are the metropolitan industrial centers of Syracuse, Utica, and Rochester, and to the south is the auto crossroads and high-tech center of Binghamton. Above the cities on the northern rim of the region, the landscape drastically transforms into the level plains of the Erie-Ontario Lowland. With the rising influence of the cities in the region, the area is no longer dominated by the farm economy, but it still retains the splendor noted by James Fenimore Cooper when he wrote, "The mountains are generally arable to the tops, although instances are not wanting where the sides are jutted with rocks that aid greatly in giving to the country that romantic and picturesque character which it so eminently possesses."[1]

The roots of old-time music in central New York State rest in the traditional dance tunes and unaccompanied ballads brought to the area in the late eighteenth and early nineteenth century by settlers of Anglo-Celtic descent migrating from eastern New England. The British had heavily promoted the area to New England settlers to block the spread of Dutch and German settlement that had dominated upstate New York. Boasted George Bickham in a tract published in 1747, "The air of New York differs not greatly from that of New England behind which it in a great measure lies:—But ye Capital is in a more temperate Climate than Boston. As to the Soil, it is so fertile, that one Bushel of English Wheat is said to have produce a hundred."

By 1800 the western part of the state remained scarcely populated. It ranked with the most rural regions of the thirteen original colonies. Chiefly responsible for the exodus from New England and Long Island farms to Central New York State was the opening of the Erie Canal in 1825. The building of the canal also brought a fresh wave of Irish, English, and Scottish workers to the region. The result, as historian Ulysses Prentiss Hedrick notes, was that "the rural population of New York is overwhelmingly British—English, Scotch, Irish—disciples of Tusser, Markham, Hartlib, Tull, Young, and Cobbett. And so the people, language, modes of life, methods of tillage, crops, animals and domestic practices are chiefly those that came from the British Isles."[2]

In one respect the New Englanders who moved to New York outdid their British cousins. During the late eighteenth century, country dancing to the accompaniment of fiddle and fife had become fashionable in New England centers such as Hartford and Boston. Among the favorite dances were jigs, reels, contra dances, cotillions (forerunner of the square dance), quadrilles, minuets, and hornpipes. "In the regions of fashion," a follower of Boston society commented, "dancing still continues the rage. Private balls are numerous, and little cotillon (sic) parties occur every week. The dancing disease having gradually ascended till it reached the middle-aged, now begins to descend on the other side of the hill, and attacks the old." The Boston *Times* for March 12, 1847, commended the fashion as "a very pleasant thing, for it gives a circulation to the blood and a flow to the spirits. . . . Were people to dance a little more in this world the cares of life would not weigh so heavy on them."

In backcountry New England, the fondness for dancing and folk fiddle tunes had long been traditional at weddings, seasonal festivals, and parties. And a less sedate version of country dancing and fiddling was commonly reported at taverns and inns. Urban advisers tried to add refinement to the rustic folk dances with publications such as the *Guide to Politeness or a System of Directions for the Acquirement of Ease and Elegance of Manners, Together with a Variety of Approved Sets of Cotillions and Contra Dances* (1810) by Boston dancing instructor Francis D. Nichols. Other guides to the traditional music to be played at dances gave the old British Isles tunes an American twist. In 1807, *A Selection of Cotillions & Country-Dances* offered the "Federal Cotillion" and "College Hornpipe" along with "Money Musk." The same year, *Collection of the Most Celebrated Figures of Cotillions and Contra Dances* included "Humors of Boston," "Jefferson and Liberty," "American Fair," "Democratic Rage," and "Independence." "Despite Puritan and prig," historian Arthur Cole reports, "the dance, old-style and new, plain and fancy, went on merrily to new heights of popularity. Balls and dancing parties of every type became a measure of the prosperity of the eighteen-fifties, that new age of gilt and glitter that dazzled the nation." A New England native visiting England during the 1860s quipped, "When Englishmen have dinners, Americans have balls. Englishmen support their charities by eating, Americans by dancing."[3]

Moving west to New York State, settlers took up small farms in the valleys and established a village life reminiscent of New England life. A settlement pattern took shape in Central New York State that lasted into the twentieth century. Towns grew along a line in the lowlands around the canal, but below them in the hills developed a rural economy covering the extent of the wide Appalachian Upland. In this region, settlers took up relatively small farms of less than 200 acres and established crossroads villages for the services of the blacksmith, general store, and church. Among the chief products of the farms were milk and cheese, hops, apples, corn, buckwheat, and potatoes. The farm family and village community became the wellspring of tradition. Farm families in a community, often formed naturally by one of New York's many valleys, depended on one another for information and entertainment. Farmers relied on family labor and the extended family unit became a small tight-knit community in itself. Indeed, the strength of the extended family on these New York farms created a cheap labor supply that formed a hedge against adopting mechanized farming techniques that appeared on the market in the mid-nineteenth century.

But with stiffer competition from the western states and the combination of higher demand and higher prices for foodstuffs after the Civil War, more mechanization took hold and more farms were established in upstate New York. Joining the old New England settlers in the valleys were new farmers from northern Pennsylvania. After the Civil War, agriculture dominated 75 percent of the state's acreage. More than 226,000 farms dotted the landscape. But the agricultural depression of 1873–79 signalled the wane of agrarian dominance. In 1875, the number of farms had reached their peak in New York as elsewhere on the Eastern Seaboard.

Improvements in farm machinery and transportation lowered foodstuff prices but they also increased the cost of starting and maintaining a farm. Another agricultural depression from 1893 to 1897 convinced many farmers to make the trek to the towns for industrial work. The towns grew in population. The towns also grew in importance as they provided centers for new services like the telephone, automobile, and railroad. Another agricultural depression beginning in the 1920s marked a cultural and economic turning point for the farm family bound to the land and tradition. After more than a century of cultural continuity, the change appeared to come suddenly, transforming both the people and the landscape.

In the older way of life, fiddle music was more than entertainment. It was part of the round of life. Scottish bookseller Richard Weston travelled through Central New York in the 1830s and noticed that music was a regular part of communal work shared by Central New York farm families. About a quilting bee he wrote, "The quilt was finished in about three hours, and taken down, hands washed, the frame put away, and the room swept. A fiddler, the same at whose house I had been at the raising (saw-mill), was engaged, and he could play well."[4] Indeed, Weston recognized in the tunes something of his own Scottish tradition. As he continued west toward the Great Lakes, he observed that the same old tunes were used. This music, he wrote, was "traditionary" for Americans. Again, music and dance was the reward for pitching in for work—raisings and bees that brought scattered farmers and their families together. Recalling his youth in the early nineteenth century, an old country physician gives an account similar to Weston's:

> After the "raising" was completed the young men would repair to the house in the dusk of the evening. If the quilt was done it would be taken out of the frames; if not it would be wound up—that is lifted to the ceiling or loft, and then securely tied overhead. If there was a bed in the "big room" it would be taken down and removed. The fiddler would get busy while everybody ate a hasty supper. The evening meal was enjoyed most by the old folks, for the younger ones would be so elated with the prospect of what was to come that they could not eat. The fiddlers would take their places in the corner and begin to tune up. Four young men would seek partners and take their places. Then the fiddlers would strike up a familiar strain and the dancing would begin.[5]

The custom of having fiddle music at such work gatherings continued in the York State countryside into the early twentieth century. A York State resident who testifies to the role of music in the rural round of work is William Dingler. His father had passed his fiddle to his son along with the work on their Ithaca farm. He described the early twentieth-century work party this way:

It was a community affair, you know. It would pass from mouth to mouth. They had meetings up here in the country where the farmers help each other. They'd gather hay, harvesting corn—they'd have parties in that. Harvesting other grains, they'd have gatherings. If a man wanted to fill his silo with corn, there'd be five, six, half-a-dozen different farmers come help bring the corn in, put it in the cutter, it was a day's work. They'd talk to each other, then they'd go home and figure out a night to have a party—they were sociable in that manner. They usually set up in the front of the house—dining room and parlor about winter time. They usually had just a violin or possibly a piano or accordion. The fiddler usually done the prompting. There were usually just one or two sets in one room. They had usually a midnight snack—pretty good feed. It was mostly standard dances. There was also clogs—we played clogs for a schottische type dance. Once in a while you'd get a Virginia Reel. I'd play "Turkey in the Straw," "Devil's Dream," "Oh, Those Golden Slippers," "Money Musk"—all those.

The "traditionary" fiddle music was also a regular part of house-warmings held at mock serenades for brides and grooms. Long before there was the idea of a family reception and a honeymoon for the couple, the tradition in the villages was to initiate the couple by a loud display at their residence. Lest the couple feel too independent, the family and neighbors reminded them of their participation in the community. In Central New York State these affairs were known as "hornings" or "horning bees"; in the Catskills, they were known as "skimmertons" or "skimiltons." Further south, they were called "shivarees."[6]

Music served to bring farm families together, too, during the lonely winter months. Dances celebrated the harvest and provided activity during the more idle months that followed. Families often held house dances, also called "kitchen hops" and "junkets." Each family in the community would take their turn at hosting the event. The New England houses that the area had inherited usually included a large parlor and kitchen addition which would be cleared for the event. The dances would include play-party games, sets and quadrilles, reels, schottisches, and waltzes. Atwood Manley from Canton, New York, recalled the dances during his boyhood in the dawn of the twentieth century: "They held 'hoe downs' in farmhouse kitchens, district school houses, rural town halls, away back when and before Teddy Roosevelt led the Rough Riders up the slopes of the San Juan Hills. I was taught the College Lancers, and the quadrills (sic) same time I was being taught the waltz, two-step, and gavotte. Virginia Reel! My, my how old John Bird could swing the gals during those square dance sessions up in Miner Hall just before pre–World War I days."[7]

Religious and seasonal festivals provided other occasions for traditional music in New York. The *Long Islander* for January 23, 1852, for instance, carried the following account of a winter frolic.

A party of ten sleighs, containing a choice lot of the beaux and belles of our village, made a snow excursion to Hempstead, on Wednesday, and partook of the hospitality and good cheer of mine host, of Hewlett's Hotel. They returned just as the evening shades prevailed, and made their head quarters at Scudder's, and repairing to the Ball Room, where

The day after a Christmas country dance, Hastings, New York. Photo by
P. D. Edick, 1863 (courtesy David Winslow)

To the tones of the enchanting fiddle,
'Twas all hands 'round—forward three—
Cross over—down the middle.

The supper provided and other entertainments passed away the evening
pleasantly until

The sweet short hour 'ayont the twal,
Just past the Winter night's noon.

A Christmas photograph from the snowy upper reaches of Central New York and
dated 1863 has these remarks inscribed on the back by the photographer: "This
picture was taken by P. D. Edick the morning after Christmas. The Parte's [sic]
and rigs drove from Hastings that was at the dance at the two hotels. In Hastings
stoped [sic] here and took Breckfast [sic] at the Tallaats Hotel as you see on their
way home from Union, Pulaski and the surrounding teritory [sic] North from
here. These days the people are always united to band together to go to all dances
and other interesting doings."[8]

Old-time string band from Otsego County, New York. Photo by P. Telfer, c. 1900 (New York State Historical Association)

One such interesting doing was photographed around 1900 by Putt Telfer in Otsego County. Telfer had left his farm to become a professional photographer in town, but he returned to the countryside often to record its get-togethers. One of the special occasions that he recorded was the rousing music of a six-piece country dance band drawn from musicians in the valley. In the days when the solo fiddler held sway at dances, the combination of two fiddles, guitar, banjo, bass viol (sometimes called a "bull fiddle" by locals), and flute (called a "fife" by locals) was indeed a treat.

Pictorial evidence of traditional fiddling and dancing from the second quarter of the nineteenth century is provided by the paintings of William Sidney Mount. Born in 1807 on a farm in Setauket, Long Island, New York, Mount became well known as a painter of rural scenes from downstate New York. Many of the neighbors that he depicted made up the stock that made the trek up the Hudson River to settle Central New York State. Beginning with "Rustic Dance After a Sleigh Ride," in 1830, and continuing with paintings such as "Dancing on the Barn Floor" in 1831, "Dance of the Haymakers (Music is Contagious)" and "The Power of Music" in 1845, Mount depicted fiddling and dance as basic to rural everyday life.

"Dance of the Haymakers" by William Sidney Mount, 1845 (Museums at Stony Brook)

In addition to painting folk musicians, he transcribed many of their tunes. Indeed, his interest was fed by his own abilities as a "country style fiddler," as his biographer Alfred Frankenstein called him. Mount described himself as "not being fashionable enough to run away from the scenes of his childhood." Mount's paintings were popular with New York City patrons for their nostalgic treatments of what already seemed like a passing scene, but for Mount they were also tributes to some of his favorite local fiddlers. The "Haymakers" painting, for example, depicts the real-life fiddler Shepard Smith Jones. Mount inscribed a lithograph of the painting to Jones with a transcription of a "Shep Jones Hornpipe." Mount early in his life also had a folk source for his fiddling in Anthony Hannibal Clapp, a black who lived from 1749 to 1816, who impressed Mount with his playing of jigs and hornpipes. In Mount's field collection of music from the area is evidence of the vitality of the folk fiddle-tune tradition in New York and the variety of country dances prevalent including reels, lanciers, quadrilles, jigs, and hornpipes.[9]

1. Haste to the Wedding

Milo Kouf, 1977

*Variation—Measures 1 and 3

**Variation—Measure 13

The influence of dances and tunes carried from the Northeast into the frontier often had a Yorker stamp on it. Writing in *Farm Life in Central Ohio Sixty Years Ago* (1892), Martin Welker wrote, "The dance was a favorite amusement and was indulged in by young and old. The fiddler of the occasion was the center of attraction of the evening. He regulated and called the dances and was commander in chief. The 'French Four,' 'Money Musk,' 'Virginia Reel,' 'the Jig,' and the 'hoe-down' were the principal figures danced. . . . 'Devil's Dream' and 'Fisher's Hornpipe' were the favorite tunes on the fiddle."[10] Complete with embellishments to bring out the emphasis placed by the fiddler in his calls, novelist Hamlin Garland gives an excellent account of the old dance music from New York State while recalling his boyhood from the 1870s.

At this dance I heard, for the first time, the local professional fiddler, old Daddy Fairbanks. . . . His queer "Calls" and his "York State" accent filled us all with delight. "*Ally* man left," "Chassay *by* your pardners," "Dozy-*do*" were some of the phrases he used as he played *Honest John* and *Haste to the Wedding*. At times he sang his calls in a high nasal chant, "*First* lady lead to the *right,* deedle, deedle dum-dum—*gent* foller after—dally-deedle-do-do *three* hands round"—and everybody laughed with frank enjoyment of his words and actions.[11]

To show an example of a popular British melody entering American folk tradition, Garland's reference to "Haste to the Wedding" can be further explored. William Chappell included the tune in his collection of English airs in 1840. He traced the tune back to 1767 when it was used in a pantomime to a song beginning "Come Haste to the Wedding." Musicians used it to accompany morris dances (a men's ceremonial dance) and other folk dances in the British Isles. In America, the tune often became a breakdown and was used in the countryside to accompany sets and reels.

But while many of the tunes used in America owed to British sources, American musicians did put their stylistic stamp on them. American performances tended to take away the ornamentation common to the British originals. Americans also regularized the beat and gave the music a bounciness instead of the droning quality of many British tunes. In the numerous repetitions of the tune with perhaps slight variations around the melody in each strain, the fiddler drew praise for his precision and consistency. The style lent itself to the demands of the old country dances through a long winter's night and to duets with a fife or another fiddle. And while repetition and refinement rather than improvisation and elaboration became watchwords of the Anglo-American aesthetic, musicians also picked up new tunes and retitled old ones, many of which actually took a poke at the British. A prominent example is the ballad "Hull's Victory" honoring the sea victory in 1812 off the coast of Nova Scotia of American Captain Isaac Hull in his ship *Constitution* over British Captain R. Dacres in the *Guerrière*. Although the ballad (to a tune resembling an old English drinking song) had a moderately successful life in oral tradition, it was as a dance tune that "Hull's Victory" got the most play among traditional fiddlers well into the twentieth century.[12]

As many of the dance tunes came from British sources, so too did old British ballads thrive anew on the American soil. Ballads commonly collected in America such as "Butcher's Boy," "Little Mo-Hee," and "In the Garden" drew from older British tradition. British folksong collector Cecil Sharp drew attention in the early twentieth century for his harvest of English and Scottish ballads in the southern Appalachians, and he exclaimed that the American hillfolk had perpetuated old British tunes and songs longer than the British themselves.

Meanwhile another folksong collector by the name of Emelyn Gardner had quietly scoured the Schoharie Hills of upstate New York. Sharp's collection overshadowed Gardner's and while Sharp's collection led the way for other collectors, it gave a false impression that British ballads in America persisted exclusively among the southern Appalachian folk. Searching the backroads of Vermont, Maine, and New Hampshire, Helen Hartness Flanders and Phillips Barry countered with a trove of collected British ballads from New England. Their evidence suggested that a vibrant folk tradition from the British Isles migrated across New England into country New York.[13]

Native ballads that sprang up on America's shores also spread to recount memorable events and to make moral statements. Among them are widely circulated songs in New York State such as "Murder in Cohoes," "Springfield Mountain," and "Mary Wyatt." "Mary Wyatt" typifies the genre. Using a formulaic rhyme and meter, the ballad describes the murder in Berlin, New York, during 1845 of Mary Ann Wyatt Green by her bridegroom of a week, the well-to-do Henry G. Green. The following verses from a long ballad text, for example, come from the field collection of Helen Hartness Flanders.

> Come, listen to my tragedy
> Good people young and old,
> An awful story you shall hear
> 'Twill make your blood run cold;
> Concerning a fair damsal—
> Mary Wyatt was her name—
> She was poisoned by her husband
> And he hung for the same
>
> Mary Wyatt, she was beautiful
> Not of a high degree.
> And Henry Green was wealthy
> As you may plainly see.
> He said, "My dearest Mary,
> If you'll become my wife
> I will guard you and protect you
> Through all this gloom of life."
>
> Believing what he said was true,
> She then became his wife.
> But little did she think, poor girl,
> That he would end her life.
> O, little did she think, poor child,
> And little did she explain
> That he would end her precious life.

In "The Murder in Cohoes," not far from the scene of "Mary Wyatt," according to a nineteenth-century broadside taken from the singing of "Miss B. L. Ryan of Albany, N.Y.," the theme shifts to the repentance of the murderer.

> Young people all, both great and small, come listen to
>   my news,
> It is a song I'm going to sing of the murder in Cohoes:
> When Catherine Dunsbach, the victim, was slain in her
>   house, you all know;
> And Latrimouille he murdered her, and soon to the
>   gallows he'll go.

> For three long months he laid in Jail, and no one could
>   he see,
> Except his father and his mother, and a Priest from
>   Albany.
> He chewed and smoked the whole day long, and at
>   night
>   fall on his knees,
> And beg the Lord to pardon him for all his wicked
>   deeds.[14]

These songs developed outside of the dance tradition. They were more common in family, rather than community settings. In addition to such songs sung around the home, occupational songs were a strong component of the Yorker's old-time repertoire. Especially remembered are songs dealing with canal building, lumbering, hop picking, and farming. Common songs are "Jam on Gerry's Rock" about lumbering or "E-R-I-E" about the canal.[15] Although generally outside the dance tradition, these songs were familiar to the fiddlers and when called upon to perform for minstrel and vaudeville shows, and later phonograph records and radio shows, the dance fiddlers often adapted the old songs and ballads to their performances or brought in friends to sing.

In addition to the influence of songs and tunes drawn from folk tradition, there were other more popular sources for music that became part of the country dance repertoire. The marches and waltzes of brass bands that developed in many towns and military units entered the repertoire of more than one fiddle and fife player and were passed on into oral tradition. During the nineteenth century, the theater stage was a primary source of popular entertainment. The New York stage featured two important comic American types: the blackface minstrel and the rustic Yankee. Many of the rollicking tunes from these shows entered popular tradition. A common example is minstrel-fiddler Dan Emmett's popularization of "Old Zip Coon," a song set to the folk tune of "Turkey in the Straw." From their base in New York City, minstrel shows travelled a circuit up to Albany and across to Syracuse, Rochester, and Buffalo. The shows continued to hit the smaller towns in upstate New York into the early twentieth century. Moreover, many of the minstrel show songs appealed to the rural reaches of New York because they were set to music in the Anglo-American tradition. Renowned writer Harold Frederic in *The Deserter and Other Stories* (1898) attested to the close relationship of old-time music to the minstrel stage. Born and reared in Utica, New York, Frederic used the rural Central New York region around the city, "away back in New York State," for his stories. Set during the Civil War, the story "A Day in the Wilderness" introduces Lafe Hornbeck. "All the Hornbecks since any one could remember had been musicians," Frederic wrote, "playing the fiddle or whatever else you liked at country dances, and some of them even journeying to distant parts as members of circus or minstrel bands."

Much of the minstrel stage humor came from witnessing familiar tunes to whites being delivered in a crude black or rustic dialect. The result of the adaptation of the folk tunes to songs, however, was that the tunes commonly enjoyed a second life in American oral tradition, often with new titles. "Sich a Getting Up Stairs" was related to an English morris dance tune, "My Long Tail Blue" followed a Scottish folk song, and "Jim Crow" resembled an Irish folk tune and an English stage song. Late into the nineteenth century, minstrel-styled songs like "Golden Slippers" and "Climbing Up the Golden Stairs" were adapted to country dances. Often, their strains were combined with other prevalent folk tunes to form medleys with several parts. And neither were these songs necessarily reminiscent of the plantation South. Micah Hawkins's hit blackface song of 1815, "The Siege of Plattsburgh" or "Backside Albany," was set in upstate New York and accompanied by a common Irish melody, "Boyne Water."[16]

Especially significant to the spread of country dance tunes was the wave of itinerant dance masters during the nineteenth century. In the transition from a pioneer to an agrarian economy, dance masters arose to give formal instruction in the prevalent country dances, especially to the young. The arrival of a dancing master in Hartford, Connecticut, from New York in the spring of 1787, for example, reportedly gave impetus to dancing there. Recruiting ninety pupils for up to three lessons a week, he taught them "four different kinds of minuets; also Cotillions, minuet Cotillions, Country-dances and the Hornpipe." The dances that were practiced had a remarkable longevity; similar tunes and dances continued to be taught to the end of the nineteenth century. In many places, churches and social advisers gave up the Puritan objections of a previous age and encouraged the movement to take up country dances because they provided "innocent recreations" that suggested the wholesomeness of rural life.

The dance masters usually played the fiddle or were assisted by a fiddler. The masters learned the old tunes from British Isles musical tradition and adapted new ones to dances. They travelled the towns in an area and formed dance and fiddle classes. While the dancing masters kept up the circulation of the country dances through the nineteenth century, they often corresponded with musicians back home to find new tunes and dances. William Sidney Mount, for example, sent his dancing master brother Robert (who had left the saturated market of downstate New York for Georgia) a version of the tune "Rustic Reel," along with a description of a dance which William described as "a fashionable dance in N.Y." To this day, the tune is collected from old-time fiddlers, often with the revealing title "O Dear Mother My Toes Are Sore."[17]

Often the countryside relied on dance leaders who were far less formal than the dancing masters. In rural Central New York State, where dances were the mainstays of social life, the dance leaders were often farmers or village merchants who were called upon to provide the music for dances. The fiddler would develop "calls" that would lead the dancers into their sets. The familiarity of the tunes helped to signal the dances. Younger dancers would follow the older dancers as they were cued by the calls. In rural stretches, the mid-nineteenth-century dances such as lanciers, quadrilles, and reels persisted well into the twentieth century through this process well after they had lost their favor in the towns. The continued reliance on the community dances for social entertainment helped to preserve the old folk tunes in the repertoire of local musicians and dance leaders. But the "old-time" repertoire common to country fiddlers in the early twentieth century became much more than an array of folk tunes. It took in many sources that had been in vogue in the countryside among earlier generations.

Description of "Rustic Reel" in a letter sent by William Sidney Mount to Robert Nelson Mount, 30 January 1839 (Museums at Stony Brook)

Today, little hard evidence survives of the nineteenth-century dance leaders in Central New York State. We do not have the advantage of recordings and clippings that preserved later traditions. It may indeed be testimony to the frequency of dances and the common knowledge of fiddlers that newspapers rarely noted the events and their musical leaders. The remarks made by the *Long Island Star* in its review of a local picnic in 1868 is revealing in this regard: "The music was furnished by Mr. Benj. Brewster, and anyone that ever heard *him fiddle* and *call off* knows he understands his 'bizz' and don't need any newspaper comment" (emphasis in original). Yet clues to at least one influential fiddler come from a reflective newspaper account of Delaware County that was sparked by the old-time-music revival of the 1920s. On January 22, 1926, an anonymous writer for the *Andes Recorder* observed close parallels between radio broadcasts of old-time music coming into the area and the music of Alva Belcher, a black fiddler from Delhi, New York, who was active through the nineteenth century. Entitled "When Violin was a 'Fiddle': Days of Yore When Alva Belcher was Famous Recalled," the article read:

> The revival of interest in the country square dances that flourished in a former generation and which is being so widely heralded and popularized by Henry Ford's program of broadcasting the old music, recalls some of the old time fiddlers who were famous in Delaware County in the eighties and nineties.
>
> Prominent among these melody makers was Alvah Belcher, the colored Delhi fiddler, with his noted band. Belcher's band was an attraction that was sure to draw a crowd. Doubtless many of our readers will remember his deep baritone voice, as he called the changes, "swing your partners," "alamand left," and "balance al."

In 1948, folk music collector Sam Eskin recorded a version of "Belcher's Reel" from Wordell Martin from Prattsville, Greene County. Martin told Eskin that it was a common dance tune in the area. The tune is a variant of "Mason's Apron," a catchy reel commonly traced back to Ireland, and collected in America from Pennsylvania to Canada. Passed into tradition, Belcher's name might have been attached to the tune because of the difficulty of its execution. In imitation of Belcher, Martin plays the many quick notes of the tune without slurs, a technique that requires fast separate bows across the strings. Belcher was still remembered in 1977 when John E. Raitt recounted a fire in 1866 which included the Belcher grocery store in Delhi. Reporting for the *Delaware Republican-Express,* Raitt wrote, "Alva Belcher, besides selling groceries, peanuts, and candy was famous as about the best black violinist in the area." At a time when local musicians rarely gained wide renown, Belcher was a name called for in villages from the Catskills well into Central New York. Belcher had formed a string band that included white players, and his style incorporated the Anglo-Celtic influence on the area. Indeed, Raitt reflected, Belcher's tunes and phrasings passed into the oral tradition beyond the county's borders.

Attaching a fiddler's name to a tune and having it persist in oral tradition more than a half of a century later, as "Belcher's Reel" did, is indeed a sign of the considerable respect given to a musician. Belcher's obituary further testifies to his renown. It appeared in the *Delaware Gazette* on January 10, 1900:

2. Belcher's Reel

Wordell Martin, 1948

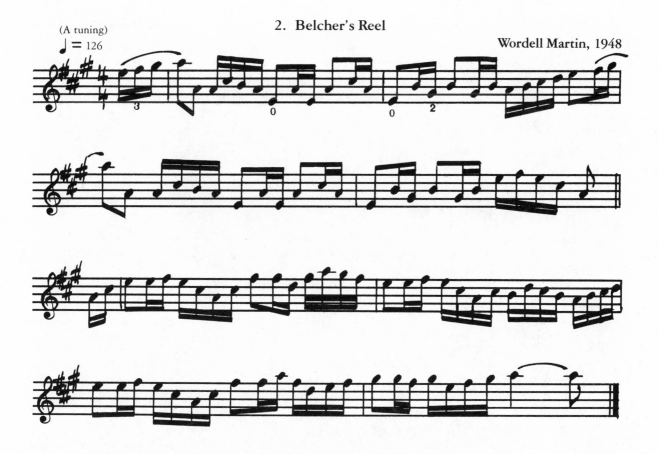

ALVA BELCHER died at his home in Kingston, New York, last Saturday aged 81 years. He was long a resident of this village, where he kept a grocery, but his chief business and life work was furnishing music to hops, parties, and other entertainment. He organized the famous Belcher Band, and probably supplied the music to more entertainments and parties than any other person in this vicinity. He had a loud and distinct voice and his services were solicited far and near. He was always pleasant and had a good word for all. A few years ago he married a wife in Kingston, and went there to reside. He leaves a widow, his third wife, to mourn his loss. He had no children. Burial at Kingston.

The *Gazette* was printed on Wednesdays, so that it could be presumed that Belcher's death occurred on Saturday, January 6, 1900 and his date of birth is 1819. It is unclear whether he was born into slavery since a gradual emancipation law was passed in New York in 1799 abolishing all slavery by 1827. Belcher must have performed right up to the time of his death as another entry in the *Delaware Gazette* of January 11, 1899, states that "Belcher was in Delhi, Monday. He was heard to sing out 'honors all.' " A portrait, possibly showing Belcher's visage and fiddle and dating from the late nineteenth century, is in the collection of the New York State Historical Association. Holding the fiddle cocked under his chin and gripping the bow loosely a couple of inches in from the end, Belcher strikes a commanding pose.

"Negro Violinist" (New York State Historical Association)

John McDermott, c. 1940 (Cortland County Historical Society)

The events of February 6, 1866, also put Belcher in the news. A spectacular fire engulfed his store and his home as well as several other buildings on Main Street. Belcher rebuilt his store and sold it in 1879. Then in his sixties, Belcher devoted his time solely to performing music. By most accounts, Belcher performed mostly fiddle tunes from the Anglo-American experience to accompany country dances. Toward the end of his career, he played with a band which had besides Belcher's fiddle a tenor banjo, guitar, and sometimes a piano or accordion.[18]

While Belcher's legacy lives in an occasional tune in his honor, another nineteenth-century performer left a recording legacy. He too left an indelible imprint on the old-time music of the region, but his mark is on the other side of the region, to the northwest around Cortland, New York. His name was John McDermott and he called himself not just the fiddling champion of New York, but the "World's Champion Fiddler." In his playing, he continued a tradition inherited from a local nineteenth-century performer, Bill Daniels. By no means a commercial hillbilly recording star, though he did record for Brunswick in 1926, McDermott does have a long performance history stretching from the late nineteenth century up into the 1940s.

Born in the rural village of McLean, New York, Tompkins County, on April 2, 1869, John McDermott was the son of Irish immigrants. John and his brother Jim learned to play music early in their lives. John was exclusively a fiddler and vocalist, while Jim played the piano, four-string banjo, and harmonica.

3. Happy Bill Daniels' Quadrille

John McDermott, 1926

segue to B or C

segue to A

segue to A

segue to B

segue to A

Turkey in the Straw

John was greatly influenced by "Happy" Bill Daniels, an older fiddler from nearby Varna, New York, who had lived for many years in Cortland. Daniels was known for being generous with his musical knowledge, especially with younger musicians. McDermott's repertoire drew greatly from Daniels' tunes and among McDermott's first recordings is a " 'Happy' Bill Daniels Quadrille."

Daniels' reputation as a fiddler is still remembered by older musicians, and by most accounts it spread through at least ten counties. Daniels was born in rural Vestal, Broome County, in 1853 and was already playing professionally by 1872. When he died on November 26, 1923, his obituary in the *Cortland Standard* testified to his renown: " 'Happy Bill' Daniels was a unique, happy character, the product of a day that is past. For fifty years he traveled the roads of central New York and few were the towns in Cortland, Tompkins, Madison, Onondaga, Broome, Tioga, Southern Cayuga, Chemung, Watkins or Seneca counties where his fiddle had not been heard. For years no big dance was complete without him and the remarkable feature is that during all these years he never missed an appointment of his own volition. . . . The popular violinist, or fiddler as he would say, loved music and time and again played at gatherings only through pure love of playing. . . . He was loved by many and he had the respect of all the thousands who knew him."

John McDermott moved to the town of Cortland from the countryside just prior to 1894 to work as a wire weaver in the T. H. Wickwire factory, the first major industrial site in the county. McDermott found an active musical life in Cortland. The town took pride in several brass bands like the "Citizens Band," with which McDermott apparently had a connection in 1912. His extensive repertoire of old-time country dance tunes and his ability on fiddle drew attention from his fellow band musicians. A musician from this era who remembers McDermott well is Larry Harrington. Though McDermott probably had already been performing publicly for some time, Harrington first became associated with McDermott in 1919 when he accompanied him to square dances and shows at Oddfellows halls, Grange halls, rural town halls, and schools.

I ran into Harrington in his office at the *Cortland Democrat* and I found McDermott still fresh in his mind. "Did John tell you where he learned his tunes?" I asked.

"Everybody had the same tunes," he replied. "They were common among musicians in this area. John, of course, played by ear. He didn't improvise at all and he remembered all his tunes—he had instant recall. He played things like 'Devil's Dream,' 'Turkey in the Straw,' 'Money Musk,' 'Irish Washerwoman,' 'Tips from the Bough'—a quadrille, 'Chicken Reel,' 'Lancers,' 'Soldier's Joy.' Now I heard of a 'Happy' Bill Daniels who seemed to have had quite a reputation with that kind of thing too—before my time, though."

"What kind of style did John have?"

Harrington was sure of his answer. "He had a rhythmic sound playing short, clean notes. He had the bow quite a ways up and held his fiddle under chin."

"Were there other bands of this type?"

The names came readily to Harrington. "Harry Westphal—he was a lot smoother. Not to take anything away from John. He was a good fiddler when it came to waltzes and things like that you couldn't tell what he was playing because he put so much accent on the rhythm. There's a fella who played, Lou Christman. He was a barn builder by occupation. We're talking about now the late teens, early twenties."

McDermott's emphasis on rhythm and clean notes is a carryover from the nineteenth-century dance-calling tradition. It was essential to the accuracy of the dancers. But as McDermott's sound was put on stage more in the 1920s and as he was accompanied with professional musicians, his style appeared antiquated, or less urbane to the likes of Harrington. But it was this sound that appealed to many rural migrants to the industrializing towns. It was the combination of his traditional repertoire and his rhythmic technique suited to dancing that qualified him and others at that time to the label of "old-time" fiddler. Adding a band to fill out his sound, McDermott played with Harry French, a pianist born in the 1870s, Don Kane, a banjoist who was born around 1900, Bert Boice, a drummer who was born in the 1870s, and Floyd Stanton, born in 1890, a pianist who played with John on his 1926 Brunswick recordings.

A perennial victor at New York State fiddle contests, McDermott was a regularly featured star at the annual State Fair in Syracuse, New York. On July 10, 1927, the *New York Times* took notice in an article, "Old Time Fiddlers to Compete at Fair." "John McDermott of Cortland," the article read, "well known throughout the state as an old-time fiddler with his playing of 'Money Musk' and 'Fiddler in the Straw' will be one of the judges." McDermott's duties were substantial, because he had to choose between at least twenty-one fiddlers from "all sections of the state." Indeed, the list would probably grow, organizers thought, and they contemplated restricting contestants to those over the age of sixty. Setting the backdrop for the contest was a log cabin. "The old log cabin," the article explained, "was taken to the fair last year and was representative of the agricultural home of 100 years ago. . . . The log cabin last year was the centre of interest and the johnny-cake that was baked there was in strong demand. . . . It has been suggested that only contestants of sixty years or older be eligible for the competition, but this will be determined later. . . . A large entry list is desired and the keen competition, when the old-time masters of the violin engage in the battle of the bows, is expected to furnish an entertainment which will again make the old log cabin the centre of attraction."

McDermott also helped his reputation with several radio broadcasts from Syracuse, some as early as 1924. The broadcasts seemed to have had some impact judging from clippings in 1924 from the Cortland papers. One piece was headlined "The Veteran Fiddler: Engagements Pile Up and Attest His Popularity." In the words of the anonymous reporter, "John A. McDermott of this city went on the air for the second time last evening at the Hotel Onondaga in Syracuse, broadcasting from Station WFBL another one of his popular oldtime fiddling programs. The local fiddler goes to Binghamton this evening for two engagements. He is scheduled to appear at the Binghamton theatre at 3 o'clock, heading a Keith vaudeville bill with one of his old time fiddling contests. Immediately after the theatre performance, he goes to the Masonic Temple to entertain at the sixth annual dinner of the Broome County Sportsmen's Association and the Ladies Auxiliary. Mr. McDermott has just closed an engagement to fiddle at Poughkeepsie on the afternoon of June 29 in connection with the state convention of the Exchange Club."

Gaining renown as New York's champion fiddler, McDermott went on to claim the title of "World's Champion Fiddler." Larry Harrington recalls McDermott's claim to the title and reveals something of the star's personality:

> He was the undisputed world's champion fiddler because he issued a challenge; his challenge was accepted and a contest was held "far and squar"—at the State Theater in Cortland. John won. Sometime later he issued another challenge and nobody took him up on it. In John's eyes that made him the world's champion fiddler and if you could have looked him in the eye and disputed his claim you are a braver man than I am.

As Larry Harrington talked more of John McDermott, his words conveyed both mirth and great respect. Harrington conjured up an image of McDermott as a kind of medieval knight engaging in public contests. For the right to title, John proudly brandished his fiddle like a lance. With his fiddle in hand and an audience in tow, John was larger than life. In the 1920s, McDermott's musical entertainment harked back to a kind of rural golden age. Maybe there was something of an anachronism in John McDermott, but there was also something timeless in his appeal. More than providing entertainment, McDermott also had honor to uphold—the pride of a Yorker old-time music lineage, the dignity of his rural tradition, and the personal glory that comes from accomplishment.

While the yarns about McDermott's antics are still being spun by Cortland old-timers, the press coverage of McDermott's notoriety during the 1920s was no less colorful or widespread. The *Syracuse Herald* for March 10, 1926, carried a picture of McDermott cutting a Yankee Jonathan figure in knee-boots and an old-fashioned suit above a headline that read "Cortland Fiddler Ready to Meet World With Bow." The paper even took a swipe at McDermott's rural roots by referring to his first name as "Jawn," a common dialect pronunciation in the Yorker countryside. Here's what the article said:

John McDermott, veteran Cortland fiddler, has moved into the spotlight again. This time "Jawn" goes his previous challenge one better and announces that he is now ready to fiddle against the world. . . . Nero fiddled during the burning of Rome, but he had little on the local fiddler who modestly claims that he is in a class by himself when it comes to doing unusual stunts while swinging the bow. "Jawn" can call off the dances, converse and fiddle at the same time. McDermott in his younger days acquired the reputation of being one of the foremost fiddlers of the early school of musicians and the president of the Cortland County Sportsmen's Association, Inc., has not permitted the years to stiffen his fingers and joints which are so essential to the execution of the bow. He has kept in the harness even in face of the present day jazz craze and still possesses the ability to remind the public that it was in the days of his youth that real music was written . . . His friends predict a belated career and that in the very near future his name and photographs will blaze in the lights of Broadway.

His name may not have shone along Broadway, but he earned enough of a reputation to be invited to record his old-time fiddle tunes for Brunswick, a major recording company of the period. Larry Harrington recalls the events this way: "John, through his stature as world's champion fiddler, signed a contract with the Brunswick Record Company. Later he told us how he locked himself alone in his hotel room in New York City and practiced for three whole days before the recording was made. 'I am the only man in the world who can see in my head every move the dancers make. When I recorded I could see everyone of 'em so my calls on the records came out just where they should.' " McDermott recorded two of his sides in New York City on December 30, 1926, accompanied by Floyd Stanton on piano. Listed on the label as a "Pioneer Fiddler and Caller," McDermott recorded "Happy Bill Daniels Quadrille" on two sides. McDermott also recorded "Virginia Reel Medley" on two sides. His Virginia Reel includes two traditional fiddle tunes, "Miss McLeod's Reel" and "The Girl I Left Behind Me," a hymn tune which usually goes by the name "Jesus Loves the Little Children," and a tricky violin shuffle.

As was often the custom, the title that McDermott chose for the medley refers to the dance rather than the tunes used. In the medley McDermott shows his range of tradition and simultaneously the sources that gave life to his performance of old-time music. His fiddling bounces out a sure but light beat. Like most other New York and New England folk fiddlers McDermott emphasizes a rapid succession of notes coming from single melodic strings. A listener can easily sing out a deedle-ee-deedle-ee in imitation of the tune. McDermott uses a variety of bowing strokes to punch out an uncluttered and unhurried melody. McDermott's emphasis on rhythm is distinctive as is his Irish-sounding shuffle that shows off his dexterity on the bow. A sacred tune and the shuffle join "Miss McLeod's Reel." Rounding out the medley is "The Girl I Left Behind Me," a traditional melody documented back to the British Isles in the eighteenth century, which in America was used both as a dance and song tune.[19]

It may seem strange to combine sacred and secular tunes in a dance medley but in old-time music they often drew from a similar nineteenth-century tradi-

4. Virginia Reel Medley

Miss McLeod's Reel

John McDermott, 1926

segue

Jesus Loves the Little Children

segue

McDermott's Shuffle

segue

The Girl I Left Behind Me

fine

tion. As musicologist William Mahar notes, "Most of the songs and hymns of the 19th Century share the same melodic vocabulary, the identical verse and chorus pattern, and belong to the Anglo-American musical tradition. Because of those similarities and because both forms of music seem to evoke powerful feelings, soldiers and civilians mixed sacred and secular music in their private informal music-making activities."[20] Although the country dances were secular events and the tunes were known almost exclusively by secular names, it was not unusual to quote a strain from a sacred piece, especially to signal a march step such as "Shall We Gather by the River" or "The Old Churchyard." To this day, sacred and secular forms regularly mix in country-music performances. There is a basis musically in the nineteenth-century, and there is also a cultural connection to the communal rural value placed on a strong spiritual tie.

Around the time that McDermott recorded the sides for Brunswick, he purchased the Leland Hotel on Watson Street in Cortland and ran McDermott's Restaurant. According to the *Cortland Standard,* he added to his busy schedule by touring and promoting his records. The paper reported that "Mr. McDermott toured the country in the 1930s as an old-time fiddler. He entertained area groups many times and recorded several tunes."

Although he devoted himself more to his business, McDermott's music could still be heard. During the 1940s, the Cortland papers would regular carry the line "John McDermott entertained with old-time fiddling." There were, for example, the annual picnics of the Lake Como cottages and nearby farmers and the annual reunions of the McDermott-McGuire clan at the Homer Water Works. On July 22, 1949, the *Syracuse Herald* carried a large photograph of the aged McDermott entertaining an audience at the village green in Homer. During the intermission of the Homer Band's performance, the paper reported, "John McDermott, old time fiddler entertained with numbers which were favorites of long ago. The audience showed their enthusiasm for John's type of entertainment." Having reached his eighties, McDermott made headlines again when he was pictured in the *Cortland Standard* with his 210-year-old fiddle. The headline, "Champion Cortland Fiddler Values Violin at $10,000," had the double message of promoting McDermott and of stating that the worn instruments and music belonging to the likes of country fiddlers like McDermott did indeed have value.

Contributing to McDermott's popularity was his active role in twenty-four local and statewide organizations. Most of his affiliations were with conservation groups, another nod toward the preservation of the passing landscape and way of life. Ross Bartlett, an old friend of McDermott, recalls that McDermott frequently distributed tree seedlings when he performed with his fiddle at schools. McDermott's obituary notes his contribution to conservation by stating that he "caused the planting of 4,600,000 trees by talking to students in schools through the state."[21] Much of his conservation work was as president of the Cortland County Sportsmen's Association, a post he held for twenty-two straight terms beginning in 1919. According to the *Syracuse Herald* for March 20, 1940, McDermott as president of the state Moose organization was "Cortland's most active emissary of good will." "He spoke and played his old-time fiddle last night at an open meeting of the Ithaca Moose Club," the paper reported, "where he was head-lined in 10 acts of vaudeville." In addition to his many organizational meetings, the paper observed, "Mr. McDermott speaks and fiddles at Grange and school meetings and elsewhere, so he frequently has barely enough time to hang up his hat as he comes in and goes out of Cortland."

McDermott's exuberant public presence also led him into politics. He was an alderman in Cortland from 1906 to 1910 and acting mayor for two years. But according to his sister-in-law Catherine McDermott, as John grew older he gradually devoted more and more time to the Leland Hotel and less to public performances, musical and political. John A. McDermott, a shaping figure in New York State's old-time music, died at the age of eighty-seven in Cortland on June 23, 1957. The *Cortland Standard* carried a headline, calling him the "Well Known Conservationist and Old Time Fiddler." Spanning two centuries, his legacy lives in Central New York State. The Trailblazers, a band formed in Cortland by Milt Faulkner and his wife prior to World War II, owed much to McDermott's inspiration, and from them Dick Thompson, leader of an Otsego County country group still active today, learned his old-time dance repertoire.

Although McDermott's performances are well remembered by old-timers in the state, in the history of the Yorker old-time music tradition, it is somehow fitting that McDermott made his mark on commercial recordings. He symbolized many of the transitions that the region and the country were making from a rural to a cosmopolitan nation. His career also manifested some of the ironies of old-time music in the twentieth century. He was a dapper performer and astute politician often putting on bumpkin airs. Further, his rural legacy meant for live performance in commune with neighbors was preserved by the very machine that changed the ways that music was heard and appreciated.

To view the transitions and ironies of old-time music from the nineteenth to the twentieth century, the legacy of New York's old-time music that McDermott preserved on record and the country life that it celebrated has to be placed in the broader context of an American revolution in recording and broadcasting. Popular music of the late nineteenth century was the music of the theaters and parlors, born of the cities. Commercial recording in the late nineteenth century and early twentieth century poked fun at the countryside left behind by urban progress. "Rube sketches" were among the first forms of comedy applied to records. As early as 1898, Billy Golden recorded a sketch, "Turkey in de Straw" (Edison Standard Size Cylinder 4011). In 1899, this issue was remade as a duet with Arthur Collins. There were three more releases of "Turkey in the Straw" on Edison Records before 1920. Another traditional piece, "The Arkansas Traveller" was also released by Edison at least three times before 1920. It appeared twice as a comedy sketch and once as a fiddle tune (Appendix—Table 1).[22]

The performers of these early sketches and tunes were cosmopolitan musicians aping the rural styles. But rather unexpectedly, a pair of authentic rural performers recorded traditional fiddle tunes for Victor in June of 1922. The pair was made up of the elderly Henry Gilliland from Oklahoma (born around 1848) and the younger Eck Robertson from Texas (born 1887). After attending a Confederate Soldiers' Reunion in Virginia, the duo decided to make a trek north to convince a company to record them. Perhaps taken by their charm or rather gall, Victor recorded six of their tunes including "Arkansaw Traveler," "Sallie Goodin," and "Ragtime Annie." It wasn't until April 1923, however, that the company released them. Although the records didn't enjoy success, they suggested to Victor the potential of a market for old-time music.

In April 1924, Victor released a catalogue supplement *Old Time Fiddlin'* *Tunes,* which described the records by Robertson and Gilliland this way:

> When we first saw these two artists, it was at our own Victor door, in the garb of Western plainsmen. They told us they could play the fiddle, and asked a hearing. As we knew several thousands persons who could play the fiddle, more or less, we were not especially impressed, but we asked them to begin. After the second number or so, we engaged them to make records of old American country dances. These are two of the best-known of all (Arkansaw Traveler and Sallie Goodin). They are played in the traditional fashion of the American country fiddler, without accompaniment. You will notice their fine, instinctive timing, and, if you are a musician, the difference in the quality of their tone from that of the concert violinist. Both these things are characteristic.

In its recording of the duo, Victor recognized not a southern style but a rural style that had once crossed the country.

Although Robertson and Gilliland's records came early, the real spark to the recording of rural talent came after the commercial success of Georgian Fiddlin' John Carson's "The Little Old Log Cabin in the Lane." The tune he chose was a piece penned by the popular composer Will S. Hays in 1871. Of significance is that the song was performed in old-time style and that its content again touched on the nostalgia for a passing way of life. Record executives were surprised by the demand for more of the Georgian's records. Distributed out of an Atlanta furniture store, the records were quickly snapped up by rural buyers. The company responded by leaping into the southern market. Besides his songs to fiddle accompaniment, Carson had a repertoire of old country dances. Indeed, there was enough of a similarity in traditions between Carson and fiddlers in points west that in 1919 Eck Robertson on behalf of the western fiddlers had challenged Carson and the Georgian fiddlers to a contest. Once realizing a rural market, however, the record companies didn't take unnecessary risks. They flocked to the established market centers of the Southeast to record authentic rural musicians performing the old dances and songs.

Even before the boom in southern hillbilly recording had taken place in the mid-1920s, northern musicians were putting old-time tunes on discs for a rural market. An especially strong tendency in these records was an appeal to the substantial Scottish and Irish population in the Northeast that also found favor in the musical aesthetic of the Yankee countryside. One of the most prolific recording stars in this vein was John J. Kimmel, an accomplished accordion player for Edison and Victor (Appendix—Table 2). Born in Brooklyn on December 13, 1866, Kimmel was a professional musician for most of his life except for a period of tavern keeping. His first recording was "Bedelia" for the Zon-o-phone company, followed soon after by "Irish Jigs and Reels Medley" in 1903. At his first session for Edison on May 8, 1906, he recorded "Medley of Reels" (Edison Standard Cylinder 9389) which was released in November 1906. Other traditional pieces followed, including "Medley of Straight Jigs" (Edison Standard Cylinder

9665) in October 1907 and "Medley of Irish Jigs" (Edison Standard Cylinder 9881) in July 1908. On May 27, 1910, Kimmel had another session for Edison which produced a popular cylinder recording of "Medley of Irish Reels" (Standard Cylinder 10284). The catalogue described it as "an accordion solo with piano accompaniment introducing a number of well-known popular Irish airs that are as infectious as they are melodious."

Kimmel was presented as an ethnic performer, but in the reaches of New York State, Kimmel's records were popular because of their similarity to the old-time tunes familiar in the area. This realization might have prompted the copy for Edison's *Along Broadway* in February 1920 to change the pitch from aiming at immigrants to the rural Yankee market. It bragged that Kimmel's "rhythm is so compelling that you feel like shouting 'swing your partner.' " Although the fiddle was still king in the countryside, Kimmel's records were known to influence the adaptation of the accordion to square-dance bands. Kimmel died where he was born, in Brooklyn in 1942.[23]

Edison's interest in old-time music prompted him to record the performance of traditional dance tunes on fiddle by professional musicians. Harold Veo recorded "Irish Washerwoman Medley" in 1918 (Edison Diamond Disc 50500). This tune included "Come Under My Pladdie," "Larry O'Gaff," and "Paddy Whack." Veo also issued "Reilly's Reel" in 1919 which included "Fairy Dance Reel," "Miss McCloud's Reel," "Pig Town Reel," and "Reilly's Reel." A similar artist was Joseph Samuels who recorded prolifically for Pathe and Banner after working for Edison. He recorded tunes for the rural market such as "Devil's Dream Medley," which included "Arkansas Traveller," "Chicken Reel," "Devil's Dream," "Fairy Dance," "Half Penny," and "Old Zip Coon" (Appendix—Table 3).

Yet these versions drew mixed reactions. The magazine *Outlook* gave this review on May 25, 1927: "It ought to be said here that those who have heard loose-arm fiddling on only the phonograph have not heard it at all. Such fiddlers and such fiddle tunes as have been recorded, unless quite recently, are not those most typical but those that have the jazz quality, foreign from real loose-arm fiddling, most highly developed." At least some calls for authenticity on fiddling records could be heard, and in response Edison officials put on disc some of the state fiddling champions who were already turning up on newsreels.

Edison officials sought to understand the rural market. Even after the popularity of Edison cylinders had declined because of the advancement of discs, the rural audience still bought what Edison executives referred to as "cracker barrel" perennials. The *Edison Phonograph Monthly* for February 1910 told dealers, "While . . . the Grand Opera lovers are saving up to buy more Records, the good old 'ragtime-coon songs-Sousa-Herbert-monologues-sentimental ballads' crowd will still be on the job buying Phonographs of the other styles, and Standard and Amberol Records, until there's frost on the sun." While recording companies pushed new sounds of jazz and classical music on disc to an urban market, the records of the sentimental ballads and fiddle tunes became mainstays of the rural parlor. Indeed, the popular influence of the commercially recorded ballads and sketches melded well with the fiddle repertoire to create the foundation of the old-time music repertoire.

John Baltzell out of Ohio came forward at Edison to lend authenticity to

5. Money Musk

John Baltzell, 1923

its recordings of old-time music. Born in Knox County, Ohio, in 1860, to parents from Pennsylvania, he was living in Mount Vernon, Ohio, when he recorded for Edison, and he broadcast regularly in Columbus, Cincinnati, and Cleveland. Baltzell was not a professional musician; he worked as a boilermaker in the railroad yards after leaving the farm. He learned to play fiddle by ear from farm neighbors, and he never learned to read music. He carried the nineteenth-century traditions of the solo country fiddler who played schottisches, hornpipes, and quadrilles into his dance and contest fiddling for hometown crowds of industrializing Mount Vernon in the 1920s. In the wake of Henry Ford's promotion of old-time music, Baltzell's musical career benefited from victory in the Ohio,

6. Durang's Hornpipe

(D tuning)
$\quad$ = 126

John Baltzell, 1923

Indiana, and Kentucky state fiddling championships. He also capitalized on his association with the renowned fiddler and minstrel song composer Dan Emmett who came from Baltzell's home town. Beginning his recording career in September 1923, he continued issuing sides until 1928 (Appendix — Table 4). His style on the recordings shows a strong resemblance to John McDermott's "pioneer" fiddling. Like McDermott, Baltzell put on disc old dance tunes such as "Durang's Hornpipe," "Sailor's Hornpipe," "The Girl I Left Behind Me," and "Money Musk" and also like McDermott, he doffed his cap to a mentor; for Baltzell the appreciation went to Dan Emmett with a recording of "Emmett Quadrille." Edison listed him on their label as a "Champion Old-Time Fiddler." In late March of 1927 he recorded for the Plaza group, which was the parent company for a number of labels including Broadway, Regal, and Paramount. These recordings spread Baltzell's fame; they were the most widely distributed fiddle records of 1927.[24]

Still another popular northern old-time musician on commercial records was Jasper "Jep" Bisbee, a fiddler from Paris, Michigan, with New England roots. Bisbee owed his notoriety to the endorsement of Henry Ford. Henry Ford had gone public with his sponsorship of old-time dances at his historic Wayside Inn in South Sudbury, Massachusetts, beginning in 1923, and soon after vowed to lead a crusade to bring country dancing and fiddling back into popularity. Seeking an authentic old-time star, Henry Ford discovered Bisbee, by then an octogenarian, at a Michigan dance in 1923. Excited by Bisbee's antique styles

7. Bisbee's Waltz

Henry Ford's Old-Fashioned Dance Orchestra, c. 1926

and his ability to play a variety of dance music including schottisches, reels, quadrilles, waltzes, minuets, and varsoviennes, Ford arranged a fiddling contest with Michigan fiddlers to highlight Bisbee's talent. Rather than a liability, Bisbee's age was an asset because he reached well back into the pre-industrial nineteenth century, an era that Ford romantically envisioned as his pioneer youth. With a good deal of hoopla, Ford crowned Bisbee as the "King of Old-Time Fiddlers." Ford then arranged to have Bisbee record for Edison (Appendix—Table 5). But after 1925 Bisbee's star fell as Ford looked further east for the old-time fiddling sound.[25]

Ford endorsed a host of old-time fiddlers, but it was Alanson Mellen Dunham, better known as "Mellie" Dunham, from Norway, Maine, who after 1925 became the best-known country fiddler in the nation. To the industrialist Ford, old-time music was a wholesome American form that helped to retain the basic values familiar in his rural youth. He promoted tours and recordings of Dunham and "Ford's Old Fashioned Dance Orchestra" across the country. Ford dealers joined in by sponsoring local fiddle contests whose winners went on to compete in regional competitions, with a national championship in Dearborn, Michigan. Ford arranged for nationwide broadcasts of old-time music to coincide with the unveiling of his cars during 1926 and 1927. Ford's weekly newspaper, the *Dearborn Independent*, had set the tone for the promotion by declaring in 1925:

> One of the astonishing features of the autumn and early winter has been the wide-spread revival of the old American dances. After long neglect they are now discovered to be the very thing that a jaded generation has been looking for. The old music, the neighborly mingling of people in the square dances, the "rollicking reels and joyous jigs, together with the vocal harmony of the calls, are all found to impart a pleasure which the more sophisticated of the manufactured dances and the synthetic music of Tin Pan Alley (N.Y.) can not give.[26]

An irony exists in Ford's promotion of old-time music. As the *Literary Digest* observed, Ford went about reviving old-time music in the methodical fashion he made cars. To be sure, some of his philosophy of making cars came from his farm-rooted belief of keeping things simple and of working with an organized consistency, although the methods of mass production that resulted helped changed the culture that farmers had once led. Ford's promotion of old-time music was intended to affirm the preservation of virtuous rural values in an industrializing and urbanizing nation. Ford's promotion was his response to the changing face of American music which reflected rapid changes in the society. Whereas the old fashioned country dances had persisted in popularity for a century and more, the life of "modern" music was short-lived and urbane. Change and novelty were catchwords of the industry. The music was more arranged, manufactured, and marketed than the music that Ford admired. Ford even accused the modern music of sharing the disreputable attributes of grimy cities. He railed against "foreign" influences, probably a reference to the post–World War I crazes for Hawaiian instrumentals, East European polka music, and black blues and jazz, that in Ford's eyes were less preferable for a popular American music than the blueblooded Anglo-Celtic connections of the old fashioned dance tunes with the first Puritan settlements.

Ford said that he heard in the old fiddle tunes "the large-hearted, social and wholesome way of those whose characters and traditions shaped the nation. Though the dance has somewhat departed from our practice these recent years, it can not be said to have departed from our art, literature and music. It was never completely absent from our national thought of merriment and play. Its return argues a better balancing of life in other respects as well."

Ford's campaign attracted the attention of national media until the end of the 1920s. In February 1926, *Radio Digest* announced, "Old Style Dances Win Favor: Grandad Fiddlers All the Rage as Colleges Join Movement to Displace Jazz. 'Everybody's Doing It.' " The *New York Times* spread the news of challenges to Mellie Dunham's crown from figures such as Bisbee, Baltzell, a Tennessee fiddler named Bunt Stephens, and even president Calvin Coolidge's eighty-one-year-old uncle (by marriage) John Wilder from Vermont. The press carried accounts of their favorite tunes. Although spread between Maine and Michigan, the players all knew "Money Musk," "Sailor's Hornpipe," "Haste to the Wedding," "Mrs. McCloud's Reel," and "Soldier's Joy" (Appendix—Table 6). When Maine's Mellie Dunham played for one of Ford's dancing parties on December 11, 1925, reporters took note that Dunham played the also familiar "Pop Goes the Weasel," "Weevily Wheat," "Speed the Plough," "Fisher's Hornpipe," and "Old Zip Coon" (Appendix—Table 7).[27] From his vantage in Michigan, the sound that Ford chose for the old-time music orchestras (actually they were small string bands) followed the path of migration from New England across New York to the upper Midwest.

Ford especially celebrated Mellie Dunham as much for his image as for his music. Coming from Maine, Dunham's locale raised images of the first settlements of the nation in the Puritan New England tradition. His crusty face, wrinkled skin, shock of white hair, short stature, full flowing mustache, and austere clothing lent an air of country charm. He was described looking like "an aged turtle trying to retire for the night." Thrust into the limelight, the Dunhams were happily not, the *Literary Digest* reported, influenced "by their glimpse of Fifth Avenue and Broadway." The Boston *Herald* reported that they were "real," and "their manners are naive, straightforward and honest. Their minds are those of kindly, sequestered country folk somewhat past their prime, and their clothes are just their 'Sunday suits,' not costumes devised to attract attention." Dunham was not a professional; he farmed and made snowshoes. He used his fiddle playing for community events. He learned to play by ear from local sources. Dunham told the *Literary Digest,* "I don't pretend to be a musician. I'm just a fiddler. Everything I play, I've learned by hearin' others."

Dunham was seventy-two when he came to Dearborn to meet Ford in 1925. His response to Ford's invitation delighted the industrial mogul: "I'll come as soon as I can. I live on a farm, and you know we farmers must get ready for winter." Dunham also expressed disdain for "modern dances," especially jazz. Dunham told an interviewer, "It has no rhythm and melody to my way of thinking. Perhaps they're all right, but I don't think much of these modern dances. This jazzing is not so good for young people. It lets 'em loaf too much." The New York *Evening World* published a cartoon of Dunham with the caption, "Like the Pied Piper of Hamelin." It showed Dunham along Broadway fiddling. He was followed by crowds of sophisticates coming out of jazz clubs.[28] Captured in this conflict of musical preferences was a larger cultural conflict between an urban society that had come to dominate the nation that had once held more closely the values and appearances of an agrarian society.

Dunham's recollection of old-time dances reminded Ford and others of rural experience from New England to New York to Michigan. The *Literary Digest* paraphrased Dunham's account:

> In the era of "kitchen whangs," parties began at eight o'clock, after supper. . . . In the winter they would come across the snowy roads in their sleds, while in the summer they would jolt over the ruts in carts or come on horseback. "Break-downs" were always held in the ample, immaculate kitchens, where New England hospitality was freely dispensed. Dancing continued until ten or thereabout; then followed an intermission. Couples had time to flirt. Supper was served—pie (in season), doughnuts, baked beans and many other delectable dishes—and the fiddler was given a chance to rest. After that they returned to their rollicking jolly dances, and more often than not the sun was peeping over the hilltops when the merrymaking came to an end. "Nowadays they stop at twelve and one o'clock."[29]

The reporter for the *Literary Digest* noted that his last remark was said "in a tone of pity." He commented, "The tunes that live in fiddles like Mr. Dunham's are fast dying out. Here and there they have been captured and put down so that they may live for future generations. Their origin is, more often than not, entirely unknown to the men who have played them countless times; like Mellie, they have heard them on other fiddles and repeated them on their own." But the notoriety given to Dunham in the press and on recordings helped to encourage many of his contemporaries to perform anew or for their sons to take it up. Fiddle contests abounded and the new medium of radio gave them chances to play. Although Ford's promotion only lasted a few years, it had a lasting effect. It had the message that music didn't have to be new to be popular. Ford showed that the old-time music and its memories held a deeper meaning in the roots of the American soil.

The rapid rise of radio technology helped to keep old-time entertainment in rural parlors after the craze for Ford's campaign died down. One reporter commented in 1928 that "the boom might not have got very far, and certainly it

8. Hull's Victory

Mellie Dunham, 1926

could not have made such stupendous progress, but for the intervention of radio, which has enabled millions of people to discover for themselves what the old-time fiddling was like." Radio, stations like Chicago's WLS realized, was "as important a part of the farm as the plow, silo, or cream separator. The farmer was truly one of radio's favorite children." *Better Homes and Gardens* reflected in 1931

WHAM out of Rochester, New York, appealed to the rural market with "two beloved 'old-timers' Hank and Herb," c. 1930s

that "some of the ways in which the radio is influencing us could not possibly have been predicted by even the shrewdest of projects. One of them is the revival of interest in the American folk song. . . . Turn the dial this way or that, before long you are perfectly sure to hear some songs that are as wholly and originally American as cornbread. They are usually presented along with other songs, but it is safe to say that no program of oldtime tunes is without a sprinkle of genuine folk music."

The *New York Times* reported in 1926 that one in every five families in the United States had a radio, more per capita than any other nation in the world. By 1922, New York State already had twenty-eight broadcasting stations, third in the nation behind California and Ohio, and closely followed by its neighbor Pennsylvania. The many independent stations at the time relied on live broadcasts to fill their time. Local entertainment came on the air to appeal to the small-town markets. Fiddlers, whose clear sounds could be easily picked up by early microphones, and whose names were familiar to small-town residents, were frequent choices for radio programmers. Indeed, it was this kind of format that immediately preceded live shows like the Grand Ole Opry. New York State had its share of such programming well before the Opry went on the air. Residents could tune into WFBL out of Syracuse where John McDermott could be heard and WIBX out of Utica where A. E. and William Bowen's Old-Time Orchestra was a regular.[30]

Yet the recordings and radio broadcasts of old-time music that emerged in the South were given credit in the popular press for the rise of hillbilly and later country music. How do we explain the southern mystique and where do we place New York's role in the development of the commercial music that grew out of old-time music? In his "Introduction to the Study of Hillbilly Music," folklorist and music historian D. K. Wilgus states "that hillbilly music is a phenomenon solely of the South in general and of the Southern Appalachians in particular is a myth in the best sense of the word."[31] Despite Wilgus's disclaimer, the myth of southern origin is a persistent theme in the literature of old-time music repeated by various historians, most notably the premier chronicler of country music and proud Texan Bill C. Malone.

Malone flatly states in his pivotal book *Country Music, U.S.A.* that "although British ballads and folksongs were perpetuated in all areas of early America, only in the South did they contribute to the creation of a lasting regional music. . . . Commercial country music developed out of folk culture of the rural South." Malone explained this development by citing several historical conditions prevalent in the South:

   1. a rural agricultural population composed of white Protestant Anglo-Celtic inhabitants,
   2. a basic isolation because of rough topography, deficient education, widespread poverty, and poor communication,
   3. a commitment to and preservation of traditional cultural values summarized as a basic conservatism, and
   4. a socioeconomic system resting on a base of slavery.[32]

Malone is correct about finding historical conditions that helped to perpetuate a rurally based music that later developed into country music. But he is wrong in claiming that these conditions and the old-time music associated with them are unique to the South. Just look at Otsego County in New York State as an example of trends throughout the region. It is the kind of place that raises a pastoral image that helped foster the legend of baseball's rustic beginnings

Otsego County landscape seen from Fly Creek Hill (Rt. 28 North), January 1987 (Simon Bronner)

around Cooperstown, the county's best known attraction. The county contained 48,967 residents in a 1,024 square mile area in 1870. This figure decreased in 1910 to 47,216. By 1960 the population had increased slightly to 51,942, but in contrast the population for the rest of the state and the rest of the country doubled in population. The majority of townships in the county contained less than forty persons per square mile. According to the United States Census, 68.9 percent of the area was considered rural in 1960, although the state's rural population has steadily shrunk after comprising almost half the state in 1870. The county is aging. Most of the residents under 25 leave for the cities, and the percentage of residents over 60 has climbed apace. Since the 1960s, the county has led the state in percentage of the population over 55 and its neighboring counties closely challenge Otsego for the lead.

Farming is the dominant occupation in Otsego County. A monument to its agricultural heritage, and a bookend to the Baseball Museum's pastoral mythology in Cooperstown, is the Farmers' Museum. Established after World War II when changes in the society made the demise of rural hegemony apparent, the Farmers' Museum preserves the old prosperity and joy of the traditional farm and crossroads life that marked upstate New York. Still, farming dominates the landscape. Agriculture continued to employ the largest percentage of the civilian labor force in the decades after World War II, and the farms were still family-run.

General Store, Fly Creek, New York, 1987 (Simon Bronner)

Although they now share the difficulties plaguing farmers across the country, farmers in Otsego County have managed to hang on by taking other jobs and raising a variety of crops and stock. Still, the county ranked forty-fourth among the fifty-seven counties in the state in median income. Weighing on the minds of farmers who have inherited their land and occupation from their fathers and grandfathers is the memory of nineteenth-century affluence. The turn-of-the-century years were hopeful times as dairying and hop growing had brought in profits that had been given up when the earlier cash crop, wheat, had moved west. When folklorist Henry Glassie came to Otsego County in 1964, he found "no topic of conversation in the taprooms and parlors of today is more popular than the happiness of the hop picking era."[33] Songs such as "Never Mortgage the Farm" and "Stay on the Farm, Boys" were sung by elders. Sons struggle today in the midst of talk of past happiness. Many farms lay abandoned or half-abandoned with no takers.

The county, like the region, has the profile of a rooted, agrarian, and white population. The ethnic composition of Otsego County is predominantly of Anglo-Celtic stock. The area is almost racially homogeneous. Only 0.4 percent of the total population is non-white. In addition, 87 percent of the population is native born and of native parentage. Residents are not as mobile as city dwellers; 56.2 percent of the residents in Otsego County had the same house in 1970 as they did in 1965. Of the 40 percent who moved to a different house in the United

One-room school that was active before World War II, Toddsville, Otsego
County, New York, 1975 (Simon Bronner)

States, 18.4 percent stayed in the county and 16.3 percent stayed in the state.

Until highways and snowmobiles came to the region, residents felt isolated in the county. Harsh winters, flood waters, and rolling hills contributed to
the sense of isolation. Until the 1950s, the one-room schoolhouse was still a common sight in the county. The region is under-educated. Out of a total enrollment
of 14,398 students in Otsego County in 1960, only 21 percent were in high
school. Many had quit to go to their farms or to find jobs elsewhere.

While it is true that the socio-economic system of Central New York did
not rest "on a base of human slavery," there certainly was the reverse of this coin
of conservatism present: "commitment to and preservation of traditional cultural values." And although blacks were not prevalent in the region, residents
attended the many minstrel shows that came through the fairs of the area and the
county's musicians were well aware of black performers such as Alva Belcher. To
be sure, Yankee tunes rarely display a bluesy quality sometimes found in southern fiddling, but at the same time the northern sound showcases the heavy British Isles influence that informed the fiddling tradition of the South. Indeed, despite the stereotype of southern antiquity, the Yankee legacy on the whole is
probably closer to the older British styles.

In addition to this attachment to the British and New England inheritance, more evidence of the persistence of tradition in the region is found in the

Hartwick Grange Hall, Otsego County, New York, 1975 (Simon Bronner)

Archive of New York State Folklife in the New York State Historical Association's headquarters at Cooperstown. It contains a strikingly continuous and widespread record of traditional practices handed down through generations. Old crafts, songs, and tales recalled by residents in the 1960s and 1970s support the earlier evidence of a commitment to tradition in Central New York found by folklorists Louis C. Jones and Harold W. Thompson.[34] Herbert Hume, a caller from Edmeston, New York, recognized the conservatism of the residents when he told me, "If you try something new on these people, they won't do it! They go for the tried and true, what their parents knew." The attitude may well hark back to James Fenimore Cooper's observation of Hume's ancestors: "The expedients of the pioneers who first broke ground in the settlement of this country are succeeded by the permanent improvements of the yeoman, who intends to leave his remains to molder under the sod which he tills, or, perhaps, of the son, who, born in the land, piously wishes to linger around the grave of his father." This is a place, Cooper wrote, where "the whole district is hourly exhibiting how much can be done, in even a rugged country, and with a severe climate, under the dominion of mild laws, and where every man feels a direct interest in the prosperity of a commonwealth of which he knows himself to form a part."[35]

The conditions that nurtured an old-time music in the countryside after it had gone out of fashion in the cities were present in parts of the North as well as of the South. Those conditions also were responsible for an acceptance of a commercial hillbilly, and later, country music in the rural and town markets. While the reins of American culture had passed from the country to the city after the massive urbanization of the late nineteenth century, the countryside tried to buy back its cultural claim with the development of "rural entertainment."

The split in American musical culture that emerged during the twentieth century was more between the forward-moving city and old-fashioned country, translated into a conflict of high and low, popular and vernacular levels, than between the North and South. A new standard-bearing popular music stressing novelty and individuality flexed its urban muscles across the nation while a vernacular music favored by country folk hung on to an old communal aesthetic in the face of dwindling rural influence. Stereotypes of isolated Appalachian folk helped to exaggerate this more national split. The preference for a southern myth fitted well into a romantic image of the primitive Southeast and a contrasting progressive image for the Northeast.

A story told to me by a Nebraska couple living in Cooperstown, New York, illustrates the image of New York. They amusingly described informing their rural neighbors about moving to upstate New York. The reply came back, "Can you get used to living in skyscrapers?"

The image of the Northeast in the American consciousness is one of a megalopolis where industry, intellectualism, and technology run rampant. Country music scholarship displays similar biases. In their study of country music "notables," Richard Petersen and Russell Davis contrasted the South which "has been, and still is the cradle of country music," with the "long-term urban and industrial Northeast—New England, New York, New Jersey, and Pennsylvania."[36] The South, despite the fact of its substantial industrialization, continues to stereotypically connote the old rural way of life. In movies, recordings, and novels, the South encapsulates the primitive folk poetry of the American soil. Northern folklorists and recording executives alike were lured southward to capture the primitive specimens of the pioneer music, although they could have found similar strains in their backyards. The results of such attitudes are that the Northeast remains inadequately represented in folklore and folk music collections and dismissed as a producer of rural music in country music histories. A history of a national music has been put forward on incomplete evidence. It has been shaped to a peculiarly southern romanticism.

Part of that romanticism is the enriching diffusion of a somehow fuller southern culture to other parts of the country. Originally, folklorist Archie Green defined early country music as the combination of Appalachian folksong and commercial influences. Later commentators discussed country music origin in the Southeast. Bill Malone expanded country music's breeding ground to the South in general.[37]

Regionalism is tossed about loosely. With the inclusion of western swing in the history of country music, the South was expanded to include Texas, Oklahoma, and other points west. Country music became popular in the North, he surmised ethnocentrically, because southerners came there. This migration thesis is a contrived means of expanding the concept of southern regionalism to wherever southerners are located. Wasn't there anybody already in those places outside the South who accounted for the performance of old-time music? Were they immaterial? The answer is no, and an approach that recognizes the cultural processes that are and aren't shared in different locales is one that can reveal the complexity of American musical culture.

As folklorist Roderick Roberts comments, "A more plausible reading of the facts might be that in all those areas of the country where conditions of isolation from mainstream culture prevailed, the imported musical aesthetic was transmuted by the particular alien influence that it encountered in such a way that a number of distinctive regional musical traditions evolved, and when by historical accident, one of these traditions was commercially recorded and distributed, it struck a responsive chord in all those regions because of its underlying structure, which was the old imported Anglo-Celtic one shared by all those regional musical traditions. Thus, tradition-oriented people outside the South bought commercially recorded Southern music because it was the closest available approximation to their musical aesthetic."[38]

Probably the most significant reason for the southern emphasis is the historical accident of old-time musical recording settling in the South after a period of both northern and southern participation in the commercialization of old-time fiddling. With help from shrewd southern record distributors, recording companies concentrated their efforts on the southeastern market. Although northern areas continued to perform old-time and later hillbilly music, residents in these areas seemed less willing to purchase records than they were to listen to radio and attend local performances.

The attention to radio and local performances in the North tended to perpetuate older styles suitable for dances. The emphasis in the North on performance, notably at dances and theater shows, rather than on the creative medium of recordings, helped to shape many of the differences between later southern and northern commercial styles. The spate of recording activity in the South influenced southern musicians to heighten the listening appeal of their tunes by speeding them up and adding flashy phrases and bowing techniques. They also picked up songs that they could perform for shows and they developed a star system that drew attention to the creative performer rather than to the old familiar tunes or to the old dance tradition. In the North where old-time musicians continued to play dances and answered to communal pressure, the tradition remained attached longer to the old norms of danceable tempos, clearly pronounced strains, and repetitive playing. The emphasis of the repertoire remained on the dance tunes, and the old-time styles persisted through the hillbilly period.

A headline in *Newsweek* on August 11, 1952, expressed the situation that emerged from commercial promotion: "Country Music is Big Business and Nashville is its Detroit." An industry had built up around both cities, and often obscured because of the association in the popular mind were the cultural sources of developments in other places.[39] The location of the industry in Nashville fostered an ethnocentric history, at the expense of considering the wider cultural process that allowed rural music to become a nationwide phenomenon.

This is not to doubt the large shadow cast by the South over country music. Rather, the argument is that the prevalent picture of the commercialization of southern old-time music and its development into country music is too narrow. To begin with, the influence is not all in one direction emanating from the South, as the host of Canadian stars such as Don Messer and Wilf Carter will attest. Second, rather than being imported into northern areas, a brand of country music took hold in New York State from the mix of commercial and home-grown traditions. And third, that the commercially recorded output from New York State is not as large as southern centers should not demean the cultural importance of the music that was produced there. Indeed, there are many musicians from New York State who should be honored for their ability as well as for their contribution to a regional heritage. But as the thrust of this book is a cultural study rather than an aesthetic critique, I have stressed what could be learned from the experience of old-time musicians in New York State. It is the performance of the music and the character of the communities in which it is performed that are at the heart of the formation of my cultural history.

We can benefit from the fullness of a cultural history (or as some would call it, an ethnohistory) provided by the story of old-time music in New York State and other places outside of the commercial centers. It is a human history centering on grassroots reactions to the conditions that set music in motion. We can ask then about the meaning that regional performances of old-time music had for farmers and townsfolk. We can ask then about the transition of the sounds of the pioneer fiddle in the nineteenth century to the revival of old-time music in the 1920s, to its conversion into hillbilly music in the 1930s, and to its persistence amidst modern country styles of the present. And we can ask about how that transition fitted with the cultural transition from a rural to industrial economy occurring in various American regions. These are not changes wrought solely by the signal of a Nashville radio station or the introduction of southern hillbilly records. They are changes that force a recognition of cultural sources in the experience of various rural locales, for it is those common experiences that allowed a music of an old heritage like country music to be accepted and to spread.

To be sure, the placement of the Grand Ole Opry radio show in Nashville helped promote the area as the home of country music and the show featured southerners as the first hillbilly "stars." Radio station WSM, which broadcast the show, had a national hookup after 1939 that reached well beyond southern borders. Movies such as *Grand Ol' Opry* (1940) and a profusion of fanzines were based in Nashville. The effects of such promotion parallel New Orleans's connection with the birth of jazz, or even Cooperstown's tie to the creation of baseball. There is a basis in fact for such cases, but the conclusions derived from the promoted images are overstated and simplistic. For example, there is the story of the origin of Nashville as a home for country music deriving from the original broadcasts of southern fiddler Uncle Jimmy Thompson on WSM in 1925. Even earlier, however, John McDermott, a genuine old-time music star, had broadcasted in upstate New York and national celebrity Mellie Dunham of Maine brought attention to rural music with his radio appearances and a triumphant tour on the Keith-Albee vaudeville circuit from New England across to the Midwest. Hearing of the acclaim that followed later for Jimmy Thompson's fiddling, Dunham challenged Thompson to a fiddle contest.[40]

The basis of the challenge in 1925 was a similarity of traditions and not a radical difference between northern and southern conditions. Their plain melodic playing was related and a check of Dunham's limited folio of tunes and the incomplete list of Thompson's repertoire compiled by his niece reveals that the two had at least 16 tunes in common.[41] The fiddlers shared the common font of British Isles tradition that spread across the Eastern Seaboard and persisted in its rural stretches, and they shared common playing techniques that were influenced by playing for rural dances.

The similarity was still apparent at the end of the decade when the Atlanta *Journal* carried the news of old-time fiddling from Missouri and New England side by side for its Georgia readers. "When the folks who attend the barn dances at Bloomfield, Conn., 'swing their partners,' " one article read, "they gyrate through the old-time steps at the direction of Sammy Spring, fiddler and prompter of an old-fashioned orchestra. So popular is Sammy and his group that WTIC, Hartford, has wired the hall in which the dances are held and broadcasts his music every Thursday evening." The other piece told the story of radio manager Jack Heinz of WOS in Jefferson City, Missouri. "Heinz looked with disfavor at first on old fiddlin' programs. 'I refused to put the old fiddlers on the air,' he says. 'But soon I found the lively jingle of *Turkey in the Straw* and its companion tunes had a permanent place in the hearts of radio fans in Missouri and neighboring states.' " The piece ends on a reflective note that associates old-time music with the national pioneer experience: "America has emerged from the pioneer era but we treasure our antique furniture and build museums for relics of the past. It is probably this instinct that causes us to preserve our traditional music and arts, and builds the popularity of the old-time fiddlers' lively scrapings."[42]

Certainly there were regional preferences for different tunes and instrumental styles. For example, quadrilles and jigs in 6/8 time favored in New England and New York arise less frequently in the southern Appalachians, and northern musicians usually prefer the more Anglo-sounding picked 4-string banjo over the black-inspired frailed 5-string variety clung to by southerners.

Some differences owe to distinctive paths of migration from different ports of entry on the Eastern Seaboard. Cultural ideas often entered the ports of Boston, New York, Philadelphia, Baltimore, and Charleston and fanned out into the backcountry as settlers moved, thus forming what we think of as regions of the United States. Yet the British-influenced oral and musical features of American culture responded far less to the regional landscape than material features such as architecture. Houses stood still in place and showed features such as chimney placement and elevation off the ground that adapted to local climate and terrain, but settlers from different parts of the British Isles mixed and then moved socially and geographically more than they had in the Old World. The movement had a leveling effect on linguistic and musical differences. Another leveler was the scattering of small towns across the expanse of the nation. The American settlement pattern stunted the growth of the kind of class-related linguistic differences that characterized the central metropolitan center of Old World London. Foreign travellers and American chroniclers noticed the remarkable linguistic uniformity of the United States. The Reverend Jonathan Boucher at the end of the eighteenth century wrote that it is "extraordinary that, in North America, there prevails not only, I believe, the purest Pronunciation of the English Tongue that is anywhere to be met with, but a perfect Uniformity." John Pickering pointed out after compiling a vocabulary of Americanisms (1816) the "greater uniformity of dialect throughout the United States . . . than is to be found throughout England." The reason, as Scottish immigrant John Witherspoon noted in 1781, was "that being much more unsettled, and moving frequently from place to place, they are not so liable to local peculiarities either in accent or phraseology. There is a greater difference in dialect between one county and another in Britain, than there is between one state and another in America." New Yorker Robert Mount found musical differences leveled as well. During 1839 he wrote his brother about his exchange of tunes with a fiddler in Georgia. He delighted in the fact that so far away from home, their fiddles conversed in the same tongue.[43]

The legacy of the pioneer fiddlers reveals more continuity than discontinuity. After folklorist Samuel Bayard traced the circulation of 651 old-time fiddle and fife tunes that he collected in Pennsylvania between 1928 and 1963, for instance, he concluded that the community of Pennsylvania tradition extends to "eastern North America as a whole," and he made his point by printing versions of his tunes from other collections, thus "concretely showing that some pieces were likely to turn up anywhere in the area."[44] Comparing early recording artists John Baltzell from Ohio to Virginia's Emmett Lundy (like Baltzell, born in the 1860s) and Tennessee's Allen Sisson (born in 1874), music historian Howard Sacks again finds remarkable similarities. Like the playing of John McDermott, the styles of these fiddlers use a short, heavy bow stroke to increase volume and accent the beat, they emphasize the rhythm by playing each note, and they work around the basic melody, or put another way, they avoid slurring. Sacks concludes that "regional styles themselves may have been preceded by a more homogeneous fiddling, born of similar roots and parallel experiences on the frontier."[45]

Corroborating the argument for a later regionalization of American music from a national base rather than the other way around is musicologist William Mahar's study of Civil War music. According to Mahar, despite the Confederacy's hope that secession provided a golden opportunity for their musicians and composers to create a distinctly southern style, no unique style developed. The war showed that "Americans shared the same musical traditions, loved the same types of songs, and encouraged the migration of hit songs back and forth across the lines."[46]

A romanticism for the imagined purity and antiquity of the South led to the popular assumption that *old-time* traditions must therefore be southern. A revealing commentary on this misconception was made in the popular magazine *Outlook* on May 25, 1927. Commenting on the rage for old-time fiddling, the anonymous reporter wrote:

> Reference has been made to loose-arm fiddlers below Mason and Dixon's line. There may be those who will think this unnecessary, believing that all such fiddlers are below that line. It is not so. The loose-arm fiddler has flourished, and doubtless still does to an extent, in every section of this country. The same fiddle tunes are known, frequently by the same name, from the Gulf to the Lakes. Not long ago, a group of persons were listening to some fiddle pieces played on a phonograph. One, on the record entitled "Ragtime Annie," awoke old memories in the mind of a Tennessean well along in years. He recognized it, resented the new name, but could not recall the old one. A young woman from up-State New York promptly announced, "It's 'Money Musk.'" And so it was.

Reflecting on the romanticism for old things southern, the writer fell back on the contrast between a primitive South and a progressive North: "If the South has more gatherings of these fiddlers and, to employ a New England phrase, sets more store by them, it is simply that the South clings more tenaciously to tradition, is less afraid of being old-fashioned." My purpose is to re-examine such assumptions by looking at themes in the old-time music of New York and the ways that they combined with the state's rural preference for country music.

As a romantic celebration of a way of life that no longer stood as the bellwether for the nation, country music incorporated the styles and values of old-time music. One frequent manifestation of that celebration in the popular revival of old-time music was the donning of a hillbilly image. Indeed, for many recording and radio people old-time music became better known as "hillbilly" music. Another kind of manifestation was an emphasis on family and communal bonds that were forged from farm life. For performers of old-time music in the first half of the twentieth century, the hillbilly image satirized a previous generation but also allied them to it. The emphasis on family in a performing medium like music brought forth for questioning the role of tradition in a changing culture. The next chapters discuss these themes through the experiences of old-time musicians and their communities in New York State.

2

It Just Leaned Naturally Toward a Farmer or Hillbilly Image

FLOYD WOODHULL slid back in his chair and looked away. His accordion sat at his feet while pictures on a nearby table spread eighty years of memories before him. The view of Elmira, New York, from his window was packed thick with houses, but he recalled when farmland lay preciously close. He talked of days before World War II when Elmira first began to bustle. Everyone, it seemed, knew his name, because Saturday nights at the "Old Barn" belonged to his band. Woodhull's group, "Woodhull's Old Tyme Masters," was the king of the barn dance in New York State. And competition was stiff. Many four-or-five instrument bands had replaced the aging old-time solo fiddlers during the 1930s. The bands still played the old favorites, but they added new combinations of instruments and a slicker sound. Their leaders were often the sons of the old-time fiddlers and while they retained features of the past rural tradition, they often put into their bands signs of a new age. More than playing for farmhouse dances as their fathers had done, the sons performed on show stages and filled dance halls.

Floyd's band was a family band. It included at one time his father and two brothers. His father had taught the old tunes to his sons and reminded them of how it was to play dances in the country. But at the "Old Barn" (a skating rink converted into a dance hall holding as many as 700 persons) and in dance halls across the state, the band took on a stage presence unknown in the "kitchen whangs." Band members wore fake beards and wore rustic clothing.

Floyd leaned forward in his chair and answered my questions on the new look. "Why did you wear the fake beards?" I asked.

"Well, that was part of the deal, dressing up."

"Did most bands dress up then?"

"Yes they did. Everybody did."

Floyd Woodhull at home in Elmira, New York, 1976 (Simon Bronner)

"Is this a hillbilly image?"

"That's what it is. Not country and western," Floyd emphasized, "but *hillbilly.*"

I sought more information about the band, but the hillbilly image still ran through Floyd's mind. "What was your father's name?" I asked.

"Fred." Floyd replied. "We all had trade names in the band: his name was Pop, mine was Ezra, and my brother Herbert was Zeke, and my brother John was Josh."

9. Irish Washerwoman

Floyd Woodhull, 1976

"Were those again for the hillbilly image?"

"Yes."

"When was that popular?"

"I can't really tell you how far back but from the farm dances in the houses, it just leaned naturally toward a farmer or hillbilly image." He punctuated the words and let them linger.

After a pause, I followed up his answer by asking "Was it a southern hillbilly?"

"Oh no, no, no," Floyd exclaimed. "Of course I have the utmost respect for the South, don't get me wrong, but I think it was a hillbilly, the hills of this area and that was the image." Floyd hung on the "this" and "that" and continued. "It was a farmer's image or a hillbilly image but not a hillbilly like you connect with moonshiners like you say Tennessee or something like that. It's not that type."

"They would know it was a sort of dressing up but they still enjoyed it?"

"Oh yeah," he nodded. "That was half the deal."

The hillbilly look was a kind of dialect joke made visual. The popularity of the dialect joke seems to be a twentieth-century phenomenon, born of the tide of second-generation children poking fun at the broken English and bumpkin ways of their parents in the cosmopolitan setting of America. Through humor the teller

10. Sailor's Hornpipe

♩ = 116

Floyd Woodhull, 1976

remarks on how far he's come. But while separating himself from the backward sounding immigrant, the teller also connects himself to an ethnic tradition. The satirical humor encases a certain pride. It is a humor that grows from cultural transition. Folklorist Richard Dorson found a trove of such jokes in the Upper Peninsula of Michigan, where immigrants from Finland, French Canada, and Cornwall descended in the late nineteenth century to work in the mines and woods. In this country, the tellers are sons who have turned away from the mines and woods. They are "men of business" who recall the struggle of their parents in a new environment and the decline of the mining and forestry industries in that part of the country. Dorson reported that the stories gravitate to stock comedy characters—the Finnish Eino and Weino, the Cornish Jan and Bill, the Swedish Ole and Yon. For Dorson, the jokes are "irresistibly funny to any American-educated listener." "The humor of ignorant speech," he found, "converges on humor of situation; while the brief anecdotes may deal solely with language misuse, the lengthy narratives which burgeon forth in the genre confront the immigrant with strange and baffling American mores."[1]

The rural inhabitant, frequently turned into a rural migrant, also found himself an immigrant in the twentieth century. Once considered the backbone of the country, the ideal citizen in Jeffersonian democracy, he now was considered behind the time, on the fringe of the urban civilizing process. He spoke a different language, cherished a different music, and defended an antiquated tradition.

The fake beards, colorful clothing, and rustic backgrounds that appeared on Woodhull's stages drew smiles from his audiences. The humor came from memories of ways that not long ago were part of everyday life, but now seemed strangely out of place. Many in the audience had become men of business, but they found that they still valued the inheritance from the countryside.

The characters on stage seemed like stock comedy characters—the country bumpkin known in Yankee yarns. From the stage to the minstrel show to oral tradition, Yankee Jonathan was a rustic on his own turf up against a city slicker or adrift away from the homestead in town. Take one of the better known Yankee Jonathan musical comedies, *Saw Mill, Or, A Yankee Trick* (1824). The playbill announced above the title, "The Dresses Characteristic of the Country." Set in "A mountainous country through which runs the Grand Western (Erie) Canal," the scene showed "an old fashion'd House, on the right part of the Garden, Barn, with outbuildings, the whole representing an established Farm, in the Western part of the State of New York." The story revolved around the attempts of two rustics, Ezekiel Amos and Zebedee Freelove, to outwit British aristocrats out of some land. Included in the music of the play was a "Scotch Air" and a dance to a lively fiddle tune. The composer Micah Hawkins probably had access to some authentic New York sources, for he was the uncle of William Sidney Mount.

The rustic Yankee on stage also took the colorful form of Calvin Cartwheel, Jedidiah Homebred, Deuteronomy Dutiful, Zachariah Dicerwell, Solon Shingle, Horsebean Hemlock, Elam W. Pancake, Ichabod Inkling, Moderation Easterbrook, Podijah B. Peazley, Zephaniah Makepeace, and Jonathan Ploughboy. Despite the name changes, the characters shared a lanky homespun look and a linsey-woolsey talk that came from the country around New York and New England. It was a character who in a stage play would tell a British captor, "I'm jest as meek and gentle as 16 lambs' tails, if you use me right—but if you don't, I can be jest as kantankerous as Aunt Patience's old brindle cow, and from *horns to tail*, she is the crookedest varmint on this universal hemisphere." Or it is the Yankee character described in the New York *Spirit of the Times* for December 23, 1843. The scene is a traveller of some sophistication making his way across the hills of New England. When asked whether the distance to the next house is three and a half miles, Yankee Jonathan replies, "Yes, sir; 'twas a spell ago, and I don't believe it's grow'd much shorter since." The dialogue is of course reminiscent of the "Arkansas Traveller," but its characterization is decidedly Yankee. As the paper comments, "There, reader—there is a Jonathan for you of the first water. You don't find his equal every place."

Although apparently backward in this humor, the Yankee draws admiration for his vigor, his innocence, homespun wisdom, and most of all his good heart. Adding to his charm, of course, is his everpresent music. In most plays, Jonathan breaks into the tune of "Yankee Doodle," another British Isles melody given an American twist, "Irish Washerwoman," or some rustic hornpipe. Little Yankee Hill brought the house down during the 1830s and 1840s with his folksy rendition of "Corn Cobs Twist Your Hair" sung to the tune of Yankee Doodle. Even after the clamor for Yankee Jonathan had died down in the cities after the Civil War, a long string of Yankee local-color productions still drew audiences throughout the many backcountry towns. Resting, according to historian and folklorist Richard Dorson, "on certain invariables: the husking-bee and quilt-

Sketch of a nineteenth-century Yankee theater character attributed to William Sidney Mount (Museums at Stony Brook)

ing-party atmosphere of a rural setting," the local-color productions revealed the aged Yankee at home on his farm rather than as a young whippersnapper adrift in the city. In this bucolic image is "a sentiment of nostalgia for a bygone day, and a sustained implication of the open-hearted virtues of the simple country folk."[2]

An example of this bucolic image applied to the old-time musician comes from *Musical America* on October 26, 1912. Usually devoted to formally trained musicians, the magazine gave notice of fiddler "Bub" Cone of Tylerville, Connecticut (a village of one hundred or so sitting along the Connecticut River near the Long Island Sound), who without the benefit of reading music played "old-time airs and jigs, keeping time with his foot as he plays, also whistling the air." An illustrator by the name of Margery Stocking, vacationing near the town took notice of Bub and sent sketches to the magazine. The editor wrote, "In one of her first letters were embodied a series of water-color sketches representing the types of villagers out in Connecticut—every one of them worthy of a frame of pure gold. One of these types, an old violinist with white hair and a red nose, nonchalantly sitting on a chair and resting a bandaged foot on another chair, particularly attracted my attention, especially when I read the vivid description of the subject of this sketch." In her description Stocking adds a touch of Yankee country humor as well as urban snobbism:

> I neglected to say that the "artist" made a very pleasing appearance in an old blue outing shirt, dark spotted trousers, white socks and tin ties, not to mention the red bandanna handkerchief with which he mopped the perspiration from his noble head.
>
> "Bub" told me before hand that Addie Matson (his accompanist) could play an accompaniment to *anything*. So I saw, but—the only trouble was that the said accompaniment was always the same.
>
> But no matter, "Bub" *can* play jigs.
>
> During his "recital" our artist kept time with his head, feet and mouth, while "Addie" bobbed up and down on the organ stool.
>
> "Bub" confided to me on the quiet that when he didn't have any rosin for his bow he "jist tuck a hunk o' pork fat."
>
> On the way home my small brother declared, "I tell you, if Bub should play in New York, at the grand opera, he'd bring down the public."

The Yankee hillbilly character was an equally homebred character in New York State. But in the early twentieth century the hillbilly image had a meaning that went beyond its surface comic effect. It telescoped the rapid transition from the homey kitchen whang to the commercial hall. It conveyed the equally rapid cultural change from village life to a new cosmopolitan standard. Although some people connect hillbilly simply to the stubbornly independent character and scraggly appearance of a "billy-goat," in "hillbilly" there is also an emphasis on communal virtues going back to ancestral Scottish tradition. Living in the hills of Scotland, "hillmen" or "hillfolk" also characterized a tight-knit band of conservative "covenanters" who vowed to maintain the evangelical movement in Scotland against changes wrought by the British King. The *Oxford English Dictionary* notes that "billy" or "billie" stems from a dialect term in Scotland and the northern British Isles for "fellow, companion, comrade, mate." Although a direct connection between the Scottish and American forms is hard to prove, certainly there are ample examples of other Scottish influences on rural American dialect, not to mention balladry and music. In both American and Scottish versions of "hillfolk" and "billy" are references to an isolated location, to a close, sometimes exclusive, relation among those in the group, and a conservative, old-fashioned attitude. But while the hillfolk hung on to a fierce spirit of independence, a rural heart of gold, and a home sweet home, in a nation like America where novelty became the keyword of an urbanizing and progressive country, the rural label frequently appeared condescending, if not contemptuous.

Were these people who were closer to the land and closer to each other more virtuous or more ridiculous? The extreme isolation, poverty, and roughcast behavior of the literary hillbilly exaggerated the general predicament of rural America. Further adding hyperbole to the image was the stage and literary appearance of self-reliant hill-folk intimately bound by an extended-family covenant. They talked in an ancient dialect and they were callously oblivious to the cosmopolitan world. They wore tattered garments and lay surrounded by primitive, or rather pre-industrial, conditions. "Hillbilly" in America became both a term of derision and endearment that expressed some of the ambivalence found in the industrial era's second-generation.

The first appearance of the term *hillbilly* in print has been traced to the *New York Journal* for April 23, 1900. On that date the paper reported that "a Hill-Billie is a free and untrammelled white citizen of Alabama, who lives in the hills." Even earlier, it had become a slang term comparable to the farmer "hayseed" for a poor white mountaineer. But "hillbilly" did not get attached to a kind of music until the 1920s, when radio stations and recording companies picked up and popularized the phrase.

The old-time fiddlers who came into the studios and participated in local contests did not perform as "hillbillies." They did not wear costumes or have a comic bumpkin act to present. Most record companies listed their fiddlers' records under "Old Time Tunes." Plunging into the competition, Columbia records plugged its recordings of Georgia old-time performers by exclaiming in the *Talking Machine World* for May 1924, "No Southerner can hear them and go away without them. And it will take a pretty hard-shelled Yankee to leave them." In June the company announced that "the fiddle and guitar craze is sweeping northward." Okeh retaliated by declaring that "the craze for this 'Hill Country Music' has spread to thousands of communities north, east, west, as well as in the south and the fame of these artists is ever increasing." In November, Victor plugged its own old-time line by giving a visual reference: "The old-time fiddler has come into his own again with the music loving public and this fact is reflected in the demand for records of the music of the old fiddlers. The Victor Talking Machine Company has taken cognizance of public interest to issue an attractive four-page folder for dealer distribution with a cover design showing the fiddler presiding over the old-time barn dance, and a caption of 'Olde Time Fiddlin' Tunes.' "[3]

"Hillbilly" was used in July 1924 when Tennessean Uncle Dave Macon recorded "Hill Billie Blues," which was released at the end of the year. Opening with "I am a billy and I live in the hills," the song was an adaptation of an old blues song, "Hesitation Blues." Macon commonly brought comic effects into his performances. He wore an old hat and did routines from his medicine-show days. He proudly displayed his backcountry manners on stage, often with colorful effect. One report described him this way: "He wore a high wing collar, a bright red tie, a coat, long sideburns, gold teeth and a sensational goatee . . . He did wonderful things on a variety of banjos, and he sang in a voice you could hear a mile up the road on quiet nights."[4] Macon's influence was to add a strong vocal tradition to commercial old-time music. At a time when the music was dominated by fiddlers, he became the Grand Ole Opry's first singing star. Yet his "Hill Billie Blues" did not usher in the crowd of hillbilly images and groups into commercial old-time music. That was left to the intervention of a recording executive working with a group of musicians from North Carolina and Virginia.

On January 15, 1925, Ralph Peer of Okeh records supervised a recording session of an old-time quartet led by Al Hopkins in New York City. Folklorist Archie Green reports what happened: "At the end of the last number, Peer asked for the group's name. Al was unprepared. They had no name and he searched for words. 'We're nothing but a bunch of hillbillies from North Carolina and Virginia. Call us anything.' Peer, responding at once to the humorous image, turned to his secretary and told her to list the Hill Billies on her ledger slips for the six selections."[5] A month later, Okeh put out a supplement to their catalogue announcing a new release, "Silly Bill" and "Old Time Cinda," by "The Hill Billies." The April catalogue described their music this way: "Hear, folks, the music of the Hill Billies! These rollicking melodies will quicken the memory of the tunes of yesterday. The heart beats time to them while the feet move with the desire to cut a lively shine. These here mountaineers sure have a way of fetching music out of the banjo, fiddle, and guitar that surprises listeners, old and young, into feeling skittish. Theirs is a spirited entertainment and one you will warm to."

Some members of the group had misgivings about the name. A. E. Alderman from the band was worried that his family would be critical of the name. As Alderman told Archie Green, "Hillbilly was not only a funny word; it was a fighting word." To be sure, Alderman had been reared in an isolated Virginia log cabin, but his family was hardly backward. His father was a self-educated surveyor and civil engineer, and a justice of the peace. Alderman respected the favorable opinion of "Pop" Stoneman, a friend of the group who had recording experience. After breaking into laughter upon hearing the name given to the group, Stoneman assured Alderman and the group, "Well, boys, you have come up with a good one. Nobody could beat it."

The name stuck and when they were pictured in the *Radio Digest* for March 6, 1926, they donned hillbilly outfits. Working out of radio station WRC in Washington, D.C., they added humorous skits to their live show of ballads and breakdown instrumentals. They took their show on the road, touring Tennessee, Ohio, Pennsylvania, and New York. After early doubts, the Hill Billies proudly defended their name. Early in 1925, for example, a group broadcasting out of Atlanta was known as George Daniell's Hill Billies, and on an early tour the Hill Billies found themselves playing across the street from the Ozark Hill Billies. It is unclear how many of these groups actually took their name from Alderman's group, but the band tried anyway to legally protect the name of the group from others who wanted to use it for themselves. Yet they couldn't stop the cascade of new groups brandishing "hillbillies" in their names.[6]

The Hill Billies were successful and Ralph Peer along with other executives talked more of the genre they recorded as hillbilly music. In November 1925, the sales director for Edison cylinders told a reporter for the *Talking Machine World* that the rural demand "is largely for Blues, Coon songs, and Hilly-Billy numbers." In its issue for December 29, 1926, *Variety* responded with a column on " 'Hill-Billy' Music" on the trade paper's front page. Music editor Abel Green wrote that "This particular branch of pop-song music is worthy of treatment on its own, being peculiar unto itself." While he recognized the distinctiveness of the rural sound, he invoked the southern myth to describe it: "The 'hillbilly' is a North Carolina or Tennessee and adjacent mountaineer type of illiterate white whose creed and allegiance are to the Bible, the chautauqua, and the phonograph."

In 1929, Sears and Roebuck used "hillbilly" as a tag for records in its catalogue, followed the next year by Montgomery Ward. In 1933, Okeh switched from the label of "Old Time Tunes" to "Hill Billy." After 1935 Decca used the heading of "Hill Billy Records" to cover subdivisions of "Old Time Singing," "String Bands," "Sacred," "Fiddlin'," and "Old Time Dance." The hillbilly image had replaced the older pioneer image used for the music. The new image gave a more southern look to the commercial music, even though the old-time music catalogue represented a national cross section.

The 1930s and 1940s became the "hillbilly" period in commercial folk music. But whereas the old-time music had close connections to nineteenth-century folk traditions, hillbilly music was, in the words of one reporter, "a conscious, calculated form of commercial expression." On the hillbilly image, he commented, "Although, for the purpose of atmosphere, the performers wear blue jeans, checked shirts and gingham frocks, they live with all the conveniences of modern life."[7] And neither was the music appealing narrowly to a rural market. Pointing to the music's attraction to rural migrants and their sons and daughters in the cities, *Good Housekeeping* reported that hillbilly music was especially popular in "the big towns—in Cleveland, St. Louis, Baltimore, Philadelphia, Cincinnati, San Francisco, and even conservative Boston . . . Small groups performing such music are traveling to America's small towns, playing jamborees. Mountain music has left the mountains and gone down to the plains."[8]

The magazine noted two divisions to the music: the country-styled song and the square dance. The square dance carried over from the old-time recordings. According to the magazine, "In pioneer days it was accompanied by a fiddle only, held against the chest, not under the chin. Nowadays the orchestration is more elaborate, but the dance itself remains simple. It has recently become a favorite with young people who dance; but it's also a favorite with young people who merely listen."

In 1943, *Time* magazine declared that "the dominant popular music of the U.S. today is hillbilly." Sales for the music accounted for 40 percent of all single popular music records. In 1949, *Newsweek* observed that New York and Pennsylvania residents rivalled the South for buying the most hillbilly records.[9]

Confirmation of the hillbilly wave came from the *Saturday Evening Post* on February 12, 1944. The national magazine headlined a feature story with the announcement, "Hillbilly Boom." The story documented the growth of the hillbilly music audience estimated at 25 million, the record-setting sales of songs such as "Pistol Packin' Mama" by Al Dexter which had sold more than 1,600,000 copies, and the spread of hillbilly radio programming including three shows picked up by a major network, NBC, for national hookup. "Almost as remarkable," the article continued, "are the grosses amassed by hillbilly units which play one-night stands all over the country in county auditoriums, schools, barns, and theaters. Obscure performers playing in hamlets like Reeds Ferry, New Hampshire, will draw $5600 in a single night. On the road, hillbilly troupes will consistently outdraw legitimate Broadway plays, symphony concerts, sophisticated comedians and beautiful girls."

To find an explanation for its success, the reporter interviewed Art Satherley, a Columbia record scout: "He says that the explanation of the hillbilly phenomenon is quite simple. He explains that most Americans either live on farms today or came from farms, and that the strains of a hoedown fiddle or a cowboy plaint are their own native folk music and the one they will always respond to, no matter how far they have gone from the farm." Satherley went on to recognize the strength of the music in its sincerity, its foundation in real experience and local culture. The article reported that "the qualities Satherley says must always be present in fine hillbilly music are simplicity of language, an emotional depth in the music, sincerity in the rendition, and an indigenous genuineness of dialect and twang. 'I would never think of hiring a Mississippi boy to play in a Texas band,' he says. 'Any Texan would know right off it was wrong.' "[10] Satherley spent most of his time looking for music in the South, although the pattern that emerged from old-time music had occurred further north.

The story of the "Hill Billies" and the influence of recording executives are usually credited with the rise of a hillbilly genre that followed old-time music and the rage for the hillbilly image. The new genre featured more bands singing ballads and topical and novelty songs, and performing old-time dance tunes and comic sketches. With the rise of the new genre, recording executives turned from the old-fashioned dance recordings of northern as well as southern artists to developing the southern pool of performing groups and their large market in the South. The commercialization of old-time music had in trying to open rural markets across the country ironically contributed to the regionalization of the music. Yet that's only part of the story. For the chronicle of the "Hill Billies" neglects the working in of hillbilly themes at the grass roots level. Performers such as the Woodhulls had not heard of the "Hill Billies," but with the changing conditions of the countryside and the revival of old-time music taking its course, they incorporated the hillbilly image into their act. Their audiences in New York State found it easy to identify with the dialect joke they visually presented.

Floyd's father Fred was an old-time fiddler from the village of Penn Yan, New York. Born in 1874, he left this western agricultural outpost of the Finger Lakes to find opportunities in the growing city of Elmira. Elmira had been incorporated as a city in 1864 and by 1870 had a population of 16,000. By 1920, its population had tripled. Lying at the intersection of the Erie, Lackawanna, Lehigh Valley, and Pennsylvania railways, it grew as a railroad and manufacturing center. It produced many of the glass products for the profitable New York State dairy industry. An industrial belt emerged from Corning in the west to Binghamton in the east. Workers for the industries were drawn from the rural countryside with promises of more income. Fred Woodhull was one who came to Elmira in the early 1890s. He worked construction for a dollar a day, twelve hours a day. In between this rigorous schedule, he turned to his fiddle for solace.

Fred was soon joined by a guitarist who would later be his wife. In 1895, Elizabeth Blanche Schmidt came to Elmira from an isolated farm village named Snowshoe, Pennsylvania. It lay near Lock Haven, two counties down from the New York State line on the west branch of the Susquehanna River. Barn dances were the social events of the rural village and from them she learned how to strum a guitar behind a fiddler and to call square dances to tunes such as the "College Lancers," "McCloud's Reel," and "Soldier's Joy." Her piercing voice was a strong asset at a time before amplification. As her son recalled, "You could hear her a block away!" She was also a noted church and ballad singer. She could give a stirring version of "The Old Rugged Cross" and "In the Garden." Fred and Elizabeth teamed up to do house dances around Elmira to add to their incomes. They usually took in three dollars apiece in a night which was worth about three days work. Besides being an opportunity to make money, the house dances kept them in touch with the rural culture with which they felt comfortable. Fred and Elizabeth sought out more jobs playing music.

The couple had three boys and each of them took up an instrument. John was born in 1898; Herbert in 1902. In 1903 Floyd was born and his parents took him along as an infant to the house dances. He still remembers them:

> They would be in the winter because farmers, after they get their field work done, all they have is barn chores. They'd have them any night. It wouldn't have to be a weekend night. They have them on a Monday night or a Wednesday or a Tuesday. And they start at eight o'clock, take about an hour out for supper. Set all the furniture out in the yard—didn't make any difference whether it was snowing or not—and dance in two or three rooms. And the music would get in one corner out of the way or something. You didn't have to have a place to plug in because there were no mikes or anything. And, it was pretty near all square dance. Once in a while you'd play a waltz or something, but not very often. They were all local musicians on the house dances. There was no set fee. They'd take up a collection for the music. Everybody would put something in the hat. All the farmers' wives would bring salads, sandwiches and the lady of the house where they had the dance would make a hot pot of coffee. The first one I played she had a wash boiler, an old copper wash boiler on the kitchen stove full of coffee. I tell you, that was something.

Floyd had been learning piano to back up his father and mother, and in 1916, at the age of thirteen, he joined them when they played the house dances. That winter Elizabeth contracted asthma. She taught Floyd the calls that she knew so he could take over. Floyd recalls learning "all the shouting calls like Duck and Dive Six, Down the Center and Cut off Six, and jigs like the Irish

Woodhull's Old Tyme Masters, 1939. Left to right: Herb Woodhull, John Taggart, John Woodhull, Fred Woodhull, Floyd Woodhull (courtesy Floyd Woodhull)

Washerwoman, McCloud's Reel, Turkey in the Straw, Arkansas Traveler, Soldier's Joy—those were all jig tunes. Some places they call them the breakdown, but in this area we call them jigs—what we call the third number. Most square dances, you use three numbers and you use your first change or your second and then the third is generally a livelier tune, what they call a jig or a breakdown. That's when they want to cut loose, that third number."

Floyd also listened to other callers and introduced singing calls when amplification allowed him to cut down on the shouting calls. Floyd played piano and learned the old-time repertoire by ear from his father. To Floyd, his father's fiddling was "tremendous" and his main influence, but he fondly remembers the appearances of John McDermott in the area. Reflecting on the sound he learned, Floyd said, "I really think that most of the basic material that we use in New York State originally came from New England. I think this was the base from which it started. It was all based on the fiddle. The fiddle was the whole thing on a square dance." The rhythm was also important and Floyd's steady accompaniment put the Woodhulls in demand. Yet having a tuned piano with all the keys intact at the house wasn't always a sure thing. Floyd switched to the more reliable and portable accordion for his performances.

In these years after World War I, Floyd and his father occasionally expanded into a band. Floyd's brother Herb joined them on harmonica and Billy Held, a friend of Floyd's father, sat in on Hawaiian steel guitar. To preserve the family image, Held went by the name of "Uncle Billy." His Hawaiian sound adapted to square dance music was an innovation influenced by popular touring bands such as the Irene West Royal Hawaiians that appeared at theaters and chautauquas in the area.

With the revival of old-time dances sweeping the country in the 1920s, dance halls in the industrial towns began sponsoring dances with barn-dance entertainment. The Woodhulls played fewer house dances as rural entertainment moved into the cities. To play in the halls called for a bigger sound. The solo fiddler did not hold a crowd as well in the larger halls. Demand went out for bands with a bigger sound, so the Woodhulls adapted. The third Woodhull brother John was learning to play violin from his father. But when he expressed a desire to join the family at the dances, he was told to play guitar. To provide a strong accompaniment to the fiddle, Herb picked up the plectrum banjo. The plectrum banjo was not an innovation, however. It was present in square dance bands at least to the turn of the century, if not before. The player of the instrument could crisply pick out the traditional melodies as well as provide a bouncy rhythm. Old-time players of the instrument often credit the 4-string banjos they heard in vaudeville and minstrel shows touring the region for some of their inspiration. In addition, Floyd remembers that recordings by banjo virtuosos such as Harry Reser had helped to spread the instrument's popularity.

Indeed, it was in nearby Binghamton that virtuoso Roy Smeck—a popular vaudeville and recording star on banjo, mandolin, and uke—got his start. To round out the Woodhull band, John "Tiny" Taggart was added on bass. Rather than the improvisation and takeoff solos characteristic of jazz bands from the 1920s, the Woodhulls drew attention to their melodic precision and consistency. This was a band shaped out of the old-time Yankee mold. Their familiar melodies were sharply performed at easy danceable tempos. Further showing their musical accuracy, Floyd Woodhull's accordion and Fred Woodhull's violin would often sound out the melodies in unison or an octave apart.

In October 1928, the group took on a name: Woodhull's Old Tyme Masters (Appendix—Table 8). The name drew attention to the band's repertoire and its continuity with the past. But the band blended the old with the new. Fred was the old man of the group flanked by youngsters. They spanned the nineteenth-century solo fiddler to the house dance duo to the multi-instrumental group of the 1920s. Capitalizing on their rural house-dance experience, they began dressing up in old farmer's clothes when they appeared at the dance halls. Finding that the look was warmly greeted by rural migrants and their children, they added fake beards, large glasses, and floppy hats. They put out comical signs on their stands such as "We're Not Bughouse, We Just Look That Way" and "That Noise You Hear is the Orchestra." Herb occasionally blew into a jug and Fred played a novelty percussion instrument called a "boom-bah." Floyd added the sounds of bells on some numbers.

The Woodhulls were not alone in presenting the image around the area.

Jehile Kirkhuff, 1974 (Simon Bronner)

Rivalling the Woodhulls were the Hornellsville Hillbillies out of Hornell, New York, Ott's Woodchoppers (Kouf Family) from Ithaca, the North Country Hillbillies from Oneida, the Rusty Reubens out of Wellsville, Woody Kelly's Old Timers from Perry, the Trail Blazers from Cortland, Old Dan Sherman and his Family from Oneonta, and the Lone Pine Ramblers, the Bennett Family, and the Tune Twisters from Elmira. Tessie Sherman, whose father had organized his family into a touring band and operated a hillbilly music park, remembered the time as one in which "every band was hillbilly."

Following the prevailing format of featuring an older fiddler and a younger second fiddler, in 1926 Jehile Kirkhuff, a twenty-one-year-old champion fiddler from the Pennsylvania side of the New York border, toured the string of towns along New York State's southern tier with Charles Dyer, then 76, and a young pianist by the name of Emily Wailey. The format of an older and younger fiddler often gave the look of a family bond that was important to the rustic image, and it had the practical effect of allowing groups to play some newer pieces along with nineteenth-century standards. But beneath the surface, it also conveyed a strong note of continuity that fitted well with the theme of many hillbilly bands in an era of change.

11. Durang's Hornpipe

Jehile Kirkhuff, 1976

Repeat measure 1 and end same as A above.

Although eclipsed by the Old Tyme Masters, Ott's Woodchoppers showed many similarities to the Woodhull band. The group owed its inspiration to Willard Kouf, a traditional nineteenth-century fiddler from Schuylerville, New York, Saratoga County (near the Vermont border) who came west to Ithaca. In the years before World War I he brought up his four sons on old-time dance music. During those years Willard played house dances with his wife Alice. By the early 1920s, the boys began to play with their dad at house dances in the countryside. Milo, who was following in his dad's steps as a fiddler, recalled that "he and the boys played in one room while the partygoers danced next door. The caller stood at the doorway in between and shouted the steps."

In 1927, Milo got together with his brothers Zeke, Otto, and George, and formed Ott's Woodchoppers, a name taken from the family's past livelihood. The elder Willard was the centerpiece of the group until he died in 1933. William Dingler, a fiddler influenced by Fred Woodhull, replaced Willard in the group for a few years. He then left to organize his own sons into a hillbilly band.

Ott's Woodchoppers, Ithaca, New York, 1955. Left to right: Zeke Kouf, Otto Kouf, Milo Kouf, Kent Compton, Louis Mikula (courtesy Milo Kouf)

The Woodchoppers continued with the core of four Kouf brothers. Occasionally they added a bass player or harmonica player. The core of the group featured a fiddle, tenor banjo, guitar, and a "tub fiddle"—a homemade coffin-looking instrument with strings that produced a bass sound when plucked. Otto, George, and Milo dressed up in fake beards, oversized shoes, floppy hats, and old-fashioned clothes while Zeke on the "tub fiddle" appeared in blackface. Their specialties were the dance tunes such as "Haste to the Wedding," "Devil's Dream," "Sailor's Hornpipe," and "Lancashire Clog" that were learned from their father. But unlike their father who relied on word of mouth to get him hired for dances, the Woodchoppers capitalized on the medium of display advertising. They carried a log cabin behind their touring car at one point and made up cards that read "Ott's Woodchoppers; Dine and Dance with ITHACA's Happy-Go-Lucky H--L Raising Fun Loving HILLBILLY RUBES." Another card announced, "FOLLOW THE CROWD; Find Out Why 200 Couples Follow These Lovable Rubes." Looking back over the period, when I talked to him in 1978, Milo described the hillbilly image as "fun on a Saturday night." "Some of it seemed like a combination of the old minstrel shows and hillbilly house dances," he contin-

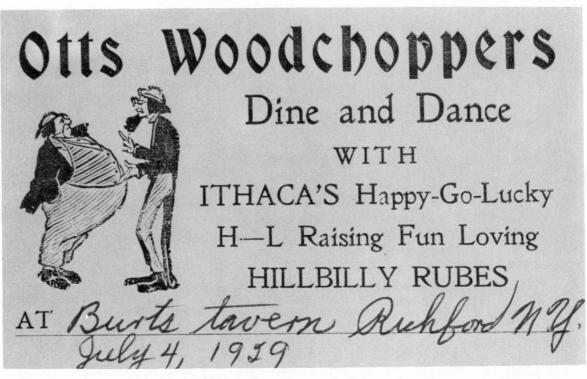

Advertising card for Ott's Woodchoppers, 1929 (courtesy Milo Kouf)

ued, "but the main thing was to have fun and poke fun at ourselves. The old familiar music lifted the spirits. Those weren't the best of times, you know." The group turned to performing music full-time and went on the road. Through the 1930s they crisscrossed the state several times playing dance halls, radio spots, lodge shows, and clubs.

Floyd Woodhull admitted that the bands freely borrowed from one another. He told me,

> Callers would come to where you are playing and if you had a new call, you'd see them with a pencil and paper. Nobody complained that they couldn't use it. It wasn't copyrighted. Everybody used whatever they wanted and everybody was delighted because another band would use a tune or call, pretty near the same thing, but he had a style, see. It's just like two singers that would sing the same song but it sounds differently. Not because of the quality of their voice but they have a different way of presenting it. We all shared the tradition from the area, but everybody had a style.

The bands and their old-time sound filled the airwaves. WESG (the call letters stand for the newspaper owners, the *Elmira Star Gazette*) was the prominent host to hillbilly entertainment in Elmira. The Old Tyme Masters, Ott's Woodchoppers, and the Tune Twisters all had half-hour spots on the radio station. They would play tunes and often give a humorous sketch followed by a plug

12. Soldier's Joy

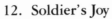

Woodhull's Old Tyme Masters, 1941

Soldier's Joy
(second version)

Floyd Woodhull, 1976

*Ornament in measure 2

for the band's appearances at dances in the area. The Woodhulls also played on WHCU out of Ithaca (the call letters stand for Home of Cornell University) where they had a regular Saturday noon-time slot for fifteen years and WELM out of Elmira where they hosted "The Woodhull Program" every Saturday in the early evening.

Unlike most bands whose members held other jobs, the Woodhulls took the chance on becoming full-time professional musicians. In the 1930s, the band played six nights a week. They played Grange halls, auditoriums, schools, and barn dances. They worked the string of towns stretching from Hornell to Oneonta. Their performances must have been memorable events judging from some of the oral histories collected in the 1970s well away from the Woodhull base in Elmira. The highlight of 1943, the *Historical Memories of Otsego County* (1976) reported for example, was "the old fashioned sleigh ride and Woodhull dance." "One Saturday night in January 1943, six sleigh loads of young and not so old people made a trip to Stephen's Hall at West Burlington to dance. It was a stormy night. There were about 140 who attended this dance. Earl White, who drove a bus to Sidney each day for all Scintilla workers, made the trip for us to Stephen's Hall for another 'Woodhull' dance. He came after us after bringing his workers home. These were some of the good times we had in Edmeston in 1943."[11] Apparently the dances of the Old Tyme Masters had entered the slang of the area as "Woodhull dances." Just that simple reference could draw imme-diate recognition from readers of the oral history. The assumption-making ref-erence to their dances even after thirty-three years shows that indeed the band had become a New York cultural institution. In the testimony is also the irony of culture in a changing region. While the towns often re-created the nineteenth-

Woodhull's Old Tyme Masters at the "Old Barn," Elmira Heights, New York, 1949. Left to right: John Taggart, Herb Woodhull, Carl Zagadusky, Eddie Pettingill, Floyd Woodhull (courtesy Floyd Woodhull)

century farm tradition of the Yankee sleigh ride and dance, many of those attending had broken with the older occupational culture.

The Woodhulls found plenty of work in the Central New York State area, although they would venture as far south as central Pennsylvania, west to the state line near Lake Erie, and east to Long Island. They didn't venture too far because every Saturday night they were expected back at home at the "Old Barn" in Elmira Heights where they put on their own dances. With 75 cents, a couple could get in and dance the entire night. At these events, the group would not be teaching the dances. The audience knew them from years of participation in the tradition. "Dancing with the Woodhull Boys, Loads of Fun Every Saturday Nite," the advertising flyer for the "Old Barn" read. Foregrounded by instruments, an old coal-oil lantern, and ceramic drinking jug, the "boys," by then into their thirties and forties, struck a mischievous pose in their old fashioned outfits.

The Woodhulls had the chance to showcase their talents before a national audience on several occasions. One was at the New York World's Fair in 1940. In 1939, the World's Fair in New York City had only moderate success with the theme of "The World of Tomorrow." While visitors marvelled at the wonders of

Woodhull's Old Tyme Masters with Vestal Dancers, Utica, New York,
1939 (courtesy Floyd Woodhull)

technology, poll takers reported, they felt disturbed by the futuristic theme cou-
pled with the winds of change threatened by the shadow of war in Europe. In
1940, organizers decided to switch to a nostalgic theme. They decided to make
the fair "a super country fair." Where the Soviet pavilion once stood, a bandstand
went up. Folk and hillbilly acts were the featured attractions.[12] The fair was perhaps influenced by a report in the *New York Times Magazine* entitled "The Country Dance Goes to Town." In the article which appeared on March 31, 1940, reporter Esther Grayson wrote,

> In trying to forget wars and rumors of wars, and all the other complica-
> tions of modern life, both youngsters and adults turned a few years ago
> from the tango and the fox trot to the shag and the truck, where speed
> and skill were the chief requisites. . . . The country dances have the same
> elements. They are built on a similar pattern. They, too, provide speed,
> change, hilarity, good fellowship; their music is fast and the steps are var-

Woodhull's Old Tyme Masters, 1941. Left to right: Herb Woodhull,
John Taggart, John Woodhull, Ransom Terwilliger, Floyd Woodhull
(courtesy Floyd Woodhull)

ied. And the calls that go with them leave plenty of room for wisecracks
and sly wit. There is sound reason for dragging the square and the country
dance out of the barn and the grange hall and giving them places of honor
on private and public dance floors.[13]

To her New York City audience, Grayson pointed out that "in the outlying counties of New York State enthusiastic square dance groups have perfected their routines and are in demand for exhibition work." Later in the spring, the World's
Fair sponsored a national square dance exhibition with the best bands from the
various states. After winning a state square dance competition in Utica in 1939,
the Woodhulls were selected to represent New York at the World's Fair. Another
opportunity in the 1940s to reach a wider audience came back in Elmira when
the band opened up a show for jazz bandleader Art Mooney at the Strand Theater.
Mooney had a hit performing songs like "I'm Looking Over a Four-Leaf Clover"
in a corny style reminiscent of the 1920s. The show at the Strand with Mooney
and the Woodhulls was carried on a national radio hookup.

13. Blackberry Quadrille

Woodhull's Old Tyme Masters, 1941

After their success at the New York World's Fair, listeners pressed the Woodhulls for recordings of their performances. But the elder Fred had had enough. Approaching seventy years of age and tired of the six-night-a-week regimen, Fred Woodhull stepped down from the band and let his sons take charge (Fred died in 1946). Ransom Terwilliger, a talented fiddler from Binghamton, stepped in. Floyd Woodhull made a wax-disc recording of two old-time tunes by the band at a radio station and sent it to Victor, the largest of the record companies working in the hillbilly field. Floyd tells what happens: "I got the address of Victor in New York and the next week I got a letter back with a contract. Now the reason for that was this: at the time they had been searching for a recording band for square dances because they hadn't found anything they liked." On July 14, 1941, the band went to New York City and recorded numbers mostly from Fred Woodhull's old-time repertoire. The band recorded "Blackberry Quadrille," "Soldier's Joy," "The Girl Behind Me," and "Captain Jinks." Yet the set of four 78 rpm records were not released until 1948. The records must have sold well. The company invited the band for another recording session in 1949 and reissued the records from the 1941 session on LP in 1952. On the second session, the band recorded the old-time standards of "Irish Washerwoman" and "Ann Green," but they also did a square-dance adaptation of a Tin-Pan-Alley song "Take Me Out to the Ballgame" and a song made famous by the hillbilly performer Haywire Mac, "The Bum Song." In 1950 the band was in the studio again, this time for the Folkraft label. They recorded the square-dance standards

14. Ann Green

"Promenade in the Moonlight" and "Forward All-Kick in the Middle" along with an old dance tune called "Last of the Lancers" and a World War I tune, "Hinky Dinky Parley Voo," as well as the popular "Wabash Cannonball" (Appendix—Table 9).

15. Campbells are Coming

Floyd Woodhull, 1976

But even as the Woodhull records flourished across the nation and especially in New York State, there were signs that the hillbilly boom was waning. The fiddle tunes that were the bread and butter of the hillbilly bands became less important to the radio-listening and record-buying public. More songs incorporating swing melodies and original words came into favor. Hank Williams and Eddy Arnold were two harbingers of the new "country and western" or "country-pop" sound. The hillbilly image gave way to a western image as stage bands like Bob Wills and his Texas Playboys drew attention for their swinging arrangements. In 1956 *Life* Magazine complained that "country music has lost much of the freshness of the old folk songs from which it stems."[14] The new musical style felt more like silk than sorghum. Youngsters removed from their parents' traditional rural roots were increasingly drawn to the urban beat of rock and roll rather than the country dances of their parents and grandparents.

Floyd Woodhull saw the influence of network radio and television entertainment in the early 1950s cutting into his audiences. The schools that the band used to play regularly in the 1940s restricted their dances to weekend nights.

16. Pop Goes the Weasel

Floyd Woodhull, 1976

Variation—Measures 7–8

Variation—Measures 11–12

Variation—Measures 15–16

John Woodhull left the band to go into business. The band sold the "Old Barn." Floyd Woodhull explains, "We had sold our property down here because when television got popular people started staying home. We lost half the crowd and I could see it was on the way out, as far as big dances were concerned. . . . We stuck

17. Captain Jinks

Floyd Woodhull, 1976

it out until '53 and it just kept falling apart.'' While the band had adapted earlier to new currents in the 1920s and 1930s, it could not make the adjustment to the tides that engulfed rural folk music in the 1950s. The band played their last dance in July 1953. John and Herb Woodhull hung up their instruments and rarely played again.

Label for first recording of Woodhull's Old Tyme Masters (Simon Bronner)

Despite the end of the Old Tyme Masters, Floyd did not abandon its music. He recorded two more albums for Folkraft. Given solo billing, Floyd was backed up by musicians brought in by the recording company from the New York City area. Although Floyd no longer played large dances with a band, he teamed up with a drummer and played small clubs and school programs through the fifties, sixties, and seventies. The audiences were smaller, but Floyd stayed loyal to

Cover of Woodhull's second set of recordings, 1949. Left to right: Carl Zagadusky, Eddie Pettingill, Herb Woodhull, Bob Regan, Floyd Woodhull (Simon Bronner)

the old-time music. Beyond those who grew up with the tunes that Floyd played, a new audience drew Floyd to folk festivals during the 1960s and 1970s. At festivals like the Natick Folk Festival in Massachusetts, he conducted workshops on old-time dancing and performed his tunes. He taught urban "folkies" who were taking up old-time New England dancing anew in the folk music revival of the 1960s. But the hillbilly boom was over. Floyd no longer dressed up as a bumpkin. He now played himself—the part of an old master.

Sam Rossi and Floyd Woodhull, 1962 (courtesy Floyd Woodhull)

In 1976 Floyd Woodhull first thought of retiring from music. "We quit at the time," Floyd recounts, "and in a couple of months we were so damn unhappy, we went back to playing. We just folded and in two months we were just going nuts." He went back to playing solo as "Uncle Woody," or "Woody Woodhull, The Old Time Master" and sometimes in a duo with drummer Sam Rossi. He performed at the Elmira Heights Senior Citizens Group dances and at special engagements. In 1977 came an especially happy moment when he teamed with the McNett family to form a six-piece old-time orchestra for the opening of Fraley's Park in Waverly, New York. "McNetts have four men (fiddle, guitar, banjo, and bass)," he wrote me, "and with Sam and I it made a 6 piece band and that was simply fantastic. The previous hall record was 50 sets. We had 60, approximately 700 people. It was a great dance, believe me." It brought back fond memories of the Old Tyme Masters' heyday, and he was called back to the park several times for encore performances. Later that winter, the New York State Country Music Association inducted Floyd Woodhull into its freshly minted Hall of Fame.[15]

Because music was no longer a full-time occupation, Floyd went into selling advertising products like calendars and pens. It put him on a familiar trail—

Lyle Miles, 1977 (Simon Bronner)

the open road. He especially worked the truck stops and country stores that used to be regular stops on his tours. Turning eighty in 1983, he finally quit performing in public. He wrote me just before Christmas to explain, "I have had to give up playing commercially. My wife is not too good and I feel guilty about coming in after a dance at 2 to 3 in the morning and having her worry. I guess after sixty years of playing and calling I'm entitled to a 'vacation.' But if I said I didn't miss it I'd be lying thru my teeth."

But Floyd Woodhull hasn't stopped playing and he hasn't stopped fondly remembering the days when the Woodhulls were New York's finest. Looking back from the years of memories captured in the photographs on the table nearby, he picked up the accordion. He played a series of tunes capped by a lively old fiddle tune called "The Campbells Are Coming."

"Were those popular?" I asked.

"Oh," he chimed, "they still are." After a pause, he said, "They are old timers all of them." The words hung in the air.

Lyle Miles is an old-timer who remembers the Woodhulls well. Born a year before Floyd, Miles played many of the same halls as the Old Tyme Masters. Like Floyd, he took in influences from local fiddlers and constructed a hillbilly band around the old-time sound. He recalls the favor for square dances and old-time bands that were the regular fare on Saturday nights in Central New York. His band, the Hornellsville Hillbillies, had a reputation that rivalled that of the Old Tyme Masters. The Old Tyme Masters were well known because of the steadiness of the "Old Barn" and their circuit through the rising cities of Central New York State. But in the smaller towns to the western border of the state, the Hillbillies held sway. Indeed, in 1986, when folklorist Roderick Roberts surveyed the folk music of Wyoming and Genesee counties (the counties midway between the Pennsylvania border and Lake Ontario at Albion), old-time fiddlers responded to his questions about influences on their style with the names of the Old Tyme Masters and the Hillbillies topping the list.[16] The Hillbillies were especially renowned through the many backcountry towns tucked between Lake Ontario, Lake Erie, and the Pennsylvania border.

Lyle Miles, fiddler and leader of the Hornellsville Hillbillies, was born on a farm in the tiny hamlet of Springwater, New York, Livingston County, on May 12, 1902. This farm had supported the family for two previous generations, but in 1905, Lyle's father made the trip to Hornellsville, as Hornell was known then, to seek better earnings. With a generous hand from the railroads, Hornellsville grew quickly. Farmers arriving in the city took up new jobs in textile, hosiery, and brick and tile factories. By 1915, the quaint-sounding name of the town, Hornellsville, belied the town's urban aspirations and it was changed to the more dignified Hornell.

Lyle Miles began to play the violin by the age of ten. He heard old-time fiddlers like Fred Woodhull at dances and he learned their tunes. The wide-eyed youngster sold packages of Bluing to obtain his first violin. Lyle looked back on what happened:

> When Wells Fargo Express called and said, "I have a package here," I run all the way there from the house that was probably a mile or better down to the central part of town and I picked up my violin. I know I couldn't wait till I got home to look at it. I opened it on the church lawn on the way home. I was just enthused about it and I think that's what all musicians have to be. I heard other people and I just seemed to have an urge for violin and that's the way I got it. I learned a lot from Leonard Hefter in Hornell at that time and he got me off on the right foot.

Better violins followed and as a teenager, Miles played house dances and sat in the violinist's chair at silent-movie theaters in Hornell. He developed a repertoire of the new Tin-Pan-Alley songs for the theaters as well as the old country dance tunes for the house dances. He left home to play vaudeville shows in Buffalo, but he returned unhappy with his experience. With talking pictures eliminating the theater bands and with vaudeville jobs in shorter supply, Miles stuck with old-time music. Minstrel shows that toured through Hornell piqued his interest in the old-time sound. He recalled what they were like:

> They were of the general old minstrel type. They have end men and one thing and another. This was in what they call the "oleo." They'd have some blackface and then they might have a dancing act, something else and we come up with this here hillbilly act. It was real natural for us. We used to play an old fiddle tune and used to sing. Used to have a fella down there, he sung in blackface of course, he used to do a little tune and he had a little dance that went with it.

Around 1920, he found two friends back home who also played old-time music and they formed a band. Ken Pierce played the piano and Lloyd Hegadorn brought in the plectrum banjo. Led by Lyle on fiddle, the band was known simply as the Lyle Miles Band. The band played for Grange halls and fire halls in the county. Fooling around with bucolic hats and props reminiscent of his minstrel show experience, he found that his audiences roared with approval. "Put you in character," Lyle reflected, "and make you look like Elmer from the sticks or something. It seemed to have a drawing power to play your jobs that way."

That band had moderate success but by 1927, its fabric had unravelled. Lloyd Hegadorn left to form his own group, Hegadorn's Banjo Band, and many of the smaller housedance jobs disappeared. Demand in the area seemed to favor a larger band with a bigger fiddle sound. The beginnings of the Hornellsville Hillbillies then took shape. Lyle Miles explains:

> The Hillbillies came about after the Elks Minstrel Show. Fella by the name of Fay McChesney and Archie Thorpe and myself. We would go hunting together at Beaver River, New York, and we took our instruments. We'd get to fooling around with that and we'd be sawing around with old-time tunes, one thing and another. . . . We always took music up there and we get out of the hotel about every night. We take the band down the hotel. It's way out the sticks out there. Anyway, we did the minstrel show at Hornell. The name we was announced at the show was the Hornellsville Hillbillies and we done something like forty different engagements after that because we had a couple of medleys that really went right down the road. Had the corn in them enough so that everybody seemed to enjoy it. . . . So these medleys we got them throwed together a nice shape and we really tore the house down. And then we did the show on the stage with the general make-up that we had and everything.

They were the "Hornellsville Hillbillies," the announcer emphasized, and the audience smiled immediately in recognition. For they harked back just a few years before to Hornellsville when it was barely paved. They looked like many from the surrounding hills who had entered Hornell to work a more industrial life. While McChesney was five years older than Miles, Thorpe was twenty years older than Miles and favored tunes like "Money Musk" and "Devil's Dream" that

18. Money Musk

(A tuning)
♩ = 116

Archie Thorpe, c. 1940

Miles considered of pioneer vintage. Originally from the farm country around Jamestown in western New York, he had come to Hornell to work in the steam-fitting and roofing industry. "He was really an old-time fiddler," Miles observed. "He'd get in the darndest keys you ever heard. But he had a good ear. He was full of rhythm and he had a kind of jerky sound that came from the hills." Also showing his nineteenth-century roots, Thorpe favored a pace slower than Miles's jazz-influenced reels to the old country dances like the quadrilles. But the two combined to form a tight working unit. Together they bridged the styles of the nineteenth and twentieth centuries.

The original Hornellsville Hillbillies, 1932. Left to right: Edwin Rio-pelli, Fay McChesney, Pete Madison, Joseph Solan, Archie Thorpe, Lyle Miles (courtesy Lyle Miles)

     The trio then played closer to home at Lake Demmon, New York. Every Saturday night, the large hall filled with dancers and listeners: the group attracted hundreds of people in an evening. Archie Thorpe was the lead fiddler with Lyle doing second-fiddle duties; Fay McChesney was a competent banjo and tenor guitar player and an especially good comic and showman. To round out the group, the trio added Joe Solan on piano and Pete Madison to sing and call dances. Edwin Riopelli was also added on tenor banjo to add a loud, piercing rhythm and to free McChesney for comic routines. Together, they put together medleys that featured "Irish Washerwoman," "Buffalo Gals," "Climbing Up the Golden Stairs," "Turkey in the Straw," and "Chicken Reel." Showing his versatility, Thorpe would also lead the group in a sparkling old-time quadrille like "D-A Quadrille" that would wind through different keys and tempos. Their audiences were often farmers but as the group played more cities in Central New York, they found many workers and youngsters for whom the farm was a fading memory.

     The group billed themselves as "A Modern Up-To-Date Old-Time Band." That billing translated into a band that spanned the nineteenth-century dance

19. Irish Washerwoman

Hornellsville Hillbillies, 1943

traditions and added some new songs as well as an elaborate instrumentation. The band was in short a hillbilly band. To highlight their hillbilly image, Joe Solan came up with a theme song that he adapted from a vaudeville "rube" act:

> When the sun rise in the morning,
> Down by the yellow corn,
> That's the time the boys take warning,
> Come Jenny blow your horn;
> Oh hey, go slow there,
> We're the boys from Big Creek;
> Hey go slow there,
> Yes we're coming home;
> Bum, bum, bum, bum.

After that introduction, the group went into their first dance tune "Black Cat."[17] To underscore its rural roots, the band invoked the village of "Big Creek," a tiny hamlet eight miles outside of Hornell. The song was unusual because the group all sang. The singing also led to a comic routine. When Miles sang the group donned ear-muffs. The theme song added "a rube effect," according to Miles, by using play-party references to "We're coming home, bum bum bum" and hillbilly commonplaces such as "Down by the yellow corn" and "When the sun rise in the morning." The song balanced with the group's closing number "Bye Bye

20. Buffalo Gals

Hornellsville Hillbillies, 1943

Blues," a popular song of the 1930s recorded by Cab Calloway and used as a signature piece by popular bandleader Bert Lown and his New York Biltmore Orchestra.[18]

While the Hornellsville Hillbillies incorporated some popular tunes like "Bye Bye Blues" into their repertoire, they found the demand for old-fashioned dances strong. Young and old would attend their dances. Rather than the format of concerts in which bands choose their program, the format of country dances called for the bands to serve the dancers. Members of the audience would regularly come up and demand an old number "from the hills" or a new number making the rounds. The old-time bands did not merely serve the old-timers, but rather they served the whole community. As the band tried to introduce more contemporary songs, they found themselves drawn back to the old-time repertoire by the audience. Lyle Miles tells a story to illustrate the negotiation between band and audience in performances:

> We were playing at the Warsaw Grange Hall and some folks come up. They wanted us to play a schottische. Now I knew an old schottische but I thought to myself, "When do I ever play a schottische?" But I finally said, "Yes, I'll play one." But I thought this is foolish. You may have one couple out there doing a schottische and the rest of them sitting on the sidelines, see. Well I got the biggest surprise of my life. I played the schottische and they all got up and did it. The whole floor was full of peo-

21. Chicken Reel

ple doing the schottische. That taught us a little something. So we begin
to promote the schottische and another tune what they called a varsovienne. I didn't know anything about the varsovienne until a fella by the
name of Chris Glady—he was an old gentleman—he come up and ask
us if we could do it. The only way I got it was he hummed to us. We took
off and after that we had that under our belt so we could do the varsovienne for about every dance we did. That varsovienne was a pretty dance
and so was the schottische. We played the Mountain Belle Schottische and
there were a number of other schottisches I had. That was with no amplification. It was with this caller who shouted through a megaphone.

It was a negotiation that operated in the culture as well: a longstanding agrarian
tradition stressing family and communal values met up against a city of strangers. Bands like the Hillbillies helped to infuse some of the old-home feeling to
the new environs, but they also reminded transplanted farm families of new
sounds and new patterns of life.

I sat down to talk to Lyle Miles about the band in 1977. He was back in
Springwater and was again organizing. He was about to open a supper club near
the marine sales business that he runs. The club was just a maze of boards and
tools then but already he could see it take shape, and he promised that it would
include old-time music. "It's just a part of the tradition of the area," he observed.
He recalled his career in old-time music and he brushed off his fingers to count

22. Black Cat

Hornellsville Hillbillies, 1943

♩ = 108

Hornellsville Hillbillies, 1934. Standing, left to right: Monte Williams, Fay McChesney, Bill Grover; sitting, left to right: Archie Thorpe, Lyle Miles, Joe Solan (courtesy Lyle Miles)

the places that he played. The pride that he showed was in his performances, not records. It was in the many names of dancers and fans that he still remembers. It was in the feeling of family he received from a lifetime of music. Central to that feeling was the fun that audience and performer alike had with the "Hillbillies" from Hornellsville.

I opened my questioning by asking "Why did they call you the Hillbillies?"

"Well, I tell you—it was through the make-up, the make-up of the band." He liked his pun. The checkered shirts, fake beards, and even some cosmetics that they applied certainly gave them a rustic look, but they also were sons of pioneers who still recalled a life in Central New York geared to nature rather than the factory.

Still, I asked Lyle to clarify this hillbilly image. "Was it a southern hillbilly?"

"No," he flatly answered.

"Did the audience associate your make-up as just a country bumpkin from this area?" I continued.

Hornellsville Hillbillies at Miller Grove, New York, 1936. Left to right:
George Regelsberger, Archie Thorpe, Lyle Miles, Fay McChesney, Ken
Pierce, Monte Williams (courtesy Lyle Miles)

"I'd think they'd have to if they saw the picture. I don't know where else."
The band pictures he laid out showed the homemade shovels carved with an axe,
the barn floor that dairy farmers would find familiar, and a pot-bellied stove that
was part of Yorker farmhomes.

After I looked at his pictures, I asked Lyle, "Whose idea was it to put on
the hats and the beard and the make-up?"

"You had to do it if you were going to put an act on the stage."

"Other bands would do it too, then?"

"Sure," Lyle exclaimed. "Floyd Woodhull was doing this. We all were, but
we quieted this down after a while."

"But your audiences associated these kinds of things like the hay and the
funny hats with this area?" I asked.

"Yes, and it also fit in terrifically with the music," Lyle concluded.

As with other bands, the Hornellsville Hillbillies depended on radio to
advertise their dances. The band broadcast over WLEA in Hornell and WMBO
in Auburn. To give a small-town feeling to the broadcasts, the band would issue
greetings, birthday announcements, personal dedications, and anniversary con-
gratulations to residents of the towns they would play. Although they used the

Hornellsville Hillbillies, 1941. Left to right: Claude Lewis, Archie Thorpe, Ed Ordway, Monte Williams, Cliff Dennis (courtesy Lyle Miles)

commercial medium of radio to span a wide area, they projected a feeling of being in a communal rural village among friends. Nonetheless, the new technology forced changes on the group. Monte Williams, for example, replaced the high-pitched caller Pete Madison because his smoother voice was better suited to radio and public address microphones. You can get a feel for a typical broadcast from the latter part of the era of New York hillbilly radio from these notes that Miles prepared for a WLEA show. The sheet is dated "Saturday 26, 1949" and reads:

> Theme—Black Cat
> Monte—Announcement
> Alabama Jubilee—For Mr. and Mrs. Green. regular listeners to our program down Canisteo way.
> The Waltz You Saved For Me—Here is a nice waltz for some folks over at Bath, N.Y. Mr. and Mrs. Van Vlake.
> Margie—Here is one for a little girl, two-year-old Margie Mix, and we will have Arlene, her mother, sing it for her.

Golden Slippers—this tune we dedicate to the lonely wives of the HORNELLSVILLE HILLBILLIES.

Monte—Last night, tonight Hapiland.

Climbing Up the Golden Stairs—for Dr. and Mrs. H. K. Hardy, Rushford, N.Y.

Cruising Down the River—We have a lot of requests to do this again so here it is, and Arlene give out with a little vocal.

12th St. Rag—for Mis Sindy Ordway, and Mr. and Mrs. Joe DuBoise from New Jersey, visiting at the Ordway Home RD #2 Hornell, N.Y.

Marching Thru Georgia—

By By Blues.

At their dances, the band would announce their upcoming radio broadcasts. This combination of radio and personal appearances promoted a following and offered an effective and intimate means of communication between the band and their regional audience. Word of the band spread further when they placed high in state square-dance-band contests in the 1930s. They were only bested by Woodhull's Old Tyme Masters. By 1937 the *Hornell Tribune* bragged of the Hillbillies, "The old-time orchestra has gained a state-wide reputation and are in great demand in this area."

In 1943, Fred Palmer, who ran a private studio in Alfred, New York, Allegany County, recorded the Hillbillies on several discs. The band was then composed of Archie Thorpe on first violin, Lyle Miles on second violin, Claude Lewis on bass, Ed Ordway on guitar, Cliff Dennis on piano, and Monte Williams on vocals. The band recorded "Money Musk," "Darling Nelly Gray," "Little Old Log Cabin in the Lane," "Hot Time in the Old Town Tonight," "Irish Washerwoman," "Black Cat" (which includes Chicken Reel), "Don't Sweetheart Me," "Bouquet Waltz," "Buffalo Gals," "When the Bloom is on the Sage," and "Girl I Left Behind Me." Copies of the discs were played on local juke boxes and given to musicians in the band. Plans for more commercial recordings were halted by the illness and later death of lead fiddler Archie Thorpe.

The deaths of old hands in the band and slipping demand for their old-time sound forced the demise of the Hillbillies in the 1950s. Miles explained, "One thing is we lost our members. Mr. Thorpe died, then Mr. Solan died— most of the ones I played with passed away. Rock and roll come in and kids get to doing different things. Of course amplification got to a point where the more amplifiers you could have the better, and we couldn't do that."

On October 11, 1955, in Medina, New York, up near Lake Ontario, the band played their last job. Miles turned more of his attention to his marine sales business and farm in Springwater. Still, Lyle hunted and played old-time music at Beaver River, where he was frequently joined by accordionist Woody Kelly. Around Hornell, Miles could be heard in a duo with Charlie Austin who used to accompany him on string and wash tub bass. After Austin's death in the 1970s, Lyle's fiddle became more idle, but he found that residents did not quickly forget his band. On December 3, 1978, the *Sunday Spectator* ran a story with the headline "Hillbilly Band Filled Area Dance Halls." The reporter, Robert F. Oakes, wrote, "Hornell area people won't soon forget the Hornellsville Hillbillies. They became a legend in country music in the area and they did their job well."

Doing their job well meant giving the people what they wanted. Their music and the dances they hosted became palliatives for a cultural change that seemed inevitable. Here were "orchestras" and "dance halls," as one might call them in popular cosmopolitan jazz centers, but upon closer examination, the sound and message were very different. They invoked the countryside and a life built on communal tradition. The hillbilly look with its nod to homespun pride, the square dance with its spirit of cooperation and innocence, and the tunes with their long backward glance at nineteenth-century life conveyed an identity shaped by the soil. But in its very setting, in the mockery being made of the bumpkins on stage, in its use merely as entertainment, the music looked ahead to a new role in a modern era. The audience in Central New York, and in Georgia, and in Tennessee, found in hillbilly music and its performance an expression of its ambivalence. As Archie Green explains, "Out of the long process of American urbanization-industrialization there has evolved a joint pattern of rejection as well as sentimentalization of rural mores. We flee the eroded land with its rotting cabin; at the same time we cover it in rose vines of memory. This national dualism created the need for a handle of laughter and ridicule to unite under one rubric the songs and culture of the yeoman and the varmint, the pioneer and the poor white."[19]

Another New York band branding the hillbilly name felt this dualism sharply. The North Country Hillbillies worked the area northeast of the terrain traversed by the Hornellsville Hillbillies. They were situated at the foothills of the Adirondacks around Oneida Lake. The prefix "North Country" is a local term for the region extending to Quebec, Canada, above Oneida Lake. The band was led by George Bourne of Oneida. Born in 1908, early in life Bourne started on piano, but he later moved over to the more portable accordion and played the old dance tunes that were in circulation. Looking to appeal to a local audience with old-time music, a radio promoter at WLBU in Canastota induced Bourne to broadcast over his station in 1927. He performed as "Radio's Ramblin' Hillbilly." The name, Bourne insisted, was drawn from the identity of old-time musicians in the area with the hills of the area. When he played at dances, he brought a group that he called the "Hill and Valley Boys." Without the reliance on recordings to announce their sound, Bourne, like other New York performers, depended on a series of simultaneous radio appearances. Through the 1930s Bourne appeared on WIBX in Utica, WSYR in Syracuse, and WSYB in Rutland, Vermont.[20]

Bourne formally organized the North Country Hillbillies in 1936. They, like the Old Tyme Masters, took on comical rustic names. George Bourne on accordion became Gib, the elderly fiddler Irving Flanders took the name Pappy, guitarist Eddie Kilson became Elmer, bass viol player Clyde Matthews was known as Hezzy. They worked comic routines in between their numbers and produced a stage show in addition to a dance repertoire. The band's antics became features of the radio barn dance on WIBX and theaters and Grange halls that they played in New York, Pennsylvania, Vermont, and New Hampshire. A program from their radio barn dance on WIBX reveals a combination of folk fiddle tunes and songs that characterized many of the hillbilly bands. On April 13, 1936, their program featured "Soldier's Joy," "Sucking Cider Through a Straw," "I Don't Work for a Living," "Cut Down the Old Pine Tree," "I'm Getting Ready

George "Gib" Bourne (courtesy John Braunlein)

for My Mother-in-Law," "Old Missouri Waltz," "Golden Slippers," "Red Wing," "Kicking Mule," "Little Brown Jug," and "Oh Susannah." At dances, they played more fiddle tunes. Some of their most commonly played ones were "Devil's Dream," "Soldier's Joy," "White Cockade," "Durang's Hornpipe," and "Irish Washerwoman."[21]

The Hillbillies were torn apart by World War II. Bourne as well as many others in the region went into industrial defense work. The industry in the region that had been quietly sprouting suddenly took on a new sense of urgency. With his group disbanded, Bourne set out on his own with his music. In a combina-

Clyde Matthews and Ray Allen of the North Country Hillbillies, c. 1940
(courtesy John Braunlein)

tion of the southern and northern highlands, Bourne toured in 1942 with the "Kentucky Mountain Boy," National Barn Dance star Bradley Kincaid, who had moved to New York with popular shows on WGY out of Schenectady, and WHAM from Rochester. Kincaid toured the state in a tent show that featured upstate New York performers as opening acts. To convince the New York audience that Kincaid's roots had genuinely spread to the Empire State, WHAM said of Kincaid, "Not content with the songs he learned as a boy, Bradley has been busy collecting songs of the hills and plains, as well as American Folk Tunes, for years. First he collected the songs that were right at hand. When the supply was exhausted there was only one place left in which to search them out, the mountain regions of our eastern seaboard."[22] And in New York, he found that his Kentucky songs were related to those already being performed by men like George Bourne who culled them from local tradition. But as in the western part of the state, changes in commercial music cut into Bourne's success. An agent offered him a contract to reconstruct the Hillbillies as the "Texas Rangers" which would play the cities. The Hillbillies did try a brief stint as the "Sons of the Prairie," but Bourne was left dissatisfied. After World War II he "headed back for the hills." He settled back into solo playing for WNBZ in Saranac Lake, a village nestled in the Adirondacks.

The country-bred generation growing up during World War II changed the hill-billy label. On the move and wanting to mix in, they didn't want to be portrayed as a people that time and society forgot. When the inside joke of the hillbilly image went public into mass culture, many younger country performers flinched. They became sensitive to playing up an image that cityfolk could laugh into a demeaning stereotype. The proud western pioneer gave them more of a sense of themselves. Like the cowboys and scouts of the West, they were adventurers establishing a new order based on down-home values. They too were uprooted and sought a feeling for home that would be appropriate to a new place. They accepted the virtue of a country raising but accepted the reality of an urbanizing and industrializing nation.

New audiences emerged. The trucker became the cowboy of the road, the factory worker thought of his old hillside home, the wholesome country boy contemplated his future under the city lights of a honky-tonk. The new audiences found less relief in the frivolity of the barn dance tunes; more and more, songs straightforwardly expressed their sentiments and their plaints. They respected the old tunes but sought to put into words their novel feelings. Their music was from the country moved to town; it came to be called "country and western" or just "country" music. In "country," many found a double meaning of a rural music and one that had spread across the country during the social jumble after World War II. Americans were on the move, and their popular music was changing. Like the crossing of town and state lines that Americans did so much of after the war, different kinds of music crossed too. The old categories of "race," "hill-billy," and "jazz" blended into new categories of rock, rockabilly, and country. Instead of the pioneer fiddlers who relied on the "old familiar tunes," the stars of the country and western period were singers who had songs composed for them. The commercial music heard on records superseded the familiar strains of the old-time musicians on radio. And the commercial music carried farther than ever before. The faces behind the recordings could be heard in concerts and shows, rather than in dances. Country singers "talked to" their audiences about situations and hopes as much as they played melodies for them.

But although the business of country music pushed old-time musicians aside after World War II, it did not force them into extinction. Many rural areas still kicked off a community festival with a square dance. And many families found the strength of the hearth through an old familiar tune. Or old friends felt like family through a tune that brought them together in a different day. In short, old-time music turned back to the communities and family settings from which it sprung. And its sounds and messages surfaced every so often within the contemporary currents of country music. These patterns hold in Central New York State, where, as the next chapter will show, old-time music came into focus as a tie that binds.

3

Brings You Back, Don't It?

THE YEAR 1974 was being hailed a pivotal year in country music circles. The audience for country music numbered more than it ever had, and as popularity soared, pundits noticed basic changes occurring to the once folksy music. Shedding its hillbilly image and recovered from the onslaught of rock and roll, a more "pop" sounding country music programming could be heard in almost every city of the United States. In their performances, new country musicians pushed electric instruments to the fore and pulled the fiddle to the rear. Approaching its golden anniversary, Nashville's Grand Ole Opry made the move from the homey Ryman Auditorium where it had been since 1941 to a glitzy new shrine in Opryland. While the music found more mass appeal, it also increasingly held up the nostalgic South as its scepter to invigorate it with downhome authenticity. The new stars of country music were no longer the fiddlers and bandleaders; they were singers and composers. Hardbitten country singer-composers Loretta Lynn and Merle Haggard graced the covers of *Time* and *Newsweek*. Nashville regulars Glenn Campbell and Johnny Cash had nationally televised variety shows. The songs of country music spread from speaking for the farmer to speaking for the common working man. In the midst of a stinging inflation, Merle Haggard's "Working Man's Blues" struck an oft-repeated theme through the 1970s. And in an acknowledgment of a national questioning of moral values, Jeanne Pruett's "Satin Sheets" rode the top of the charts. The backcountry innocence of old-time music seemed a thing of the past.

But while country music sounded more uptown in the 1970s, its rural old-time roots surfaced in a variety of settings. Many heard them in the growing cult of bluegrass festivals and their cousins, modern fiddling contests. Bluegrass music, while not an old-time style, attracted a number of old-time musical devotees, because bluegrass bands used traditional instrumentation and their repertoire commonly included many old-time tunes.[1] Many bluegrass festivals paid homage to the old-time masters by including them in a square-dance number on stage, but many more old-time performers stepped on the stages of summer folk festivals that brought college-educated youth in touch with a seemingly distant grassroots heritage. The movement came to a head with Bicentennial activities in 1976 when many communities sponsored fiddle contests or old-time music festivals to link them to the rough-hewn past. But putting the music in the artificial setting of festivals, while apparently emphasizing its significance, also underscored some of its weakening in the culture. Festivals implied that mass assembly and hoopla were necessary to boost the music. They intensified the listening experience rather than invigorating the music in daily life.

In Central New York State, a favor for square dance continued in the communities, but upstaters also sought out commercial stars at urban concerts. Several out-of-town country performers became regular sights. Doc Williams, originally from Pennsylvania and a star of the Wheeling Jamboree, and "the father of bluegrass" Bill Monroe frequently swung tours through the region. Other old stars like Kitty Wells and Jimmy Dickens were featured attractions at county fairs. At home, residents regularly tuned in to the popular television show *Hee Haw* to hear country music stars and to re-live old-time memories. A throwback to the hillbilly image, the show featured old-time performers like Grandpa Jones and traditional rural humorists like Archie Campbell set against a ramshackle-farm backdrop. As well as featuring Nashville artists, each show had the cast all joining in with their voices and acoustic instruments on an old folk song like "Buffalo Gals" amidst a barnyard scene. Residents recognized many of the tunes and scenes as their own, but they also became more aware of a difference between their musical heritage and the southern-styled entertainment they saw.

Perhaps that difference came out most in the square dance segments. Yorkers couldn't understand the apparent confusion of the southern clogging that they frequently saw on television. To their eyes, the feet of the dancers apparently floundered and fell in an irregular beat. To their ears, the fiddlers droned and wailed wildly. At their Yankee square dances, the dancing was crisp and ordered, the fiddling restrained and clean. Perhaps it was their New England Puritan background, some surmised, but they preferred the calmer tempos and organized stepping of the Yorker dances. The square dance supported many New York old-time performers who did not make the switch to country music during the 1970s. A reporter for the *Oneida Dispatch* listening to a southern barn dance show, while recognizing it as a relative of his rural music defended the old Yankee strains: "I am honestly tired of listening to the so-called radio hillbilly and cowboys bands that yodel and sing (mostly through their nose) about giving them their 'Boots and Saddles' . . . there is a wealth of early eastern ballads and folk tunes that have been sadly neglected . . . I decided to try to find some of the 'old timers' who remembered and could sing or play some of the old tunes once familiar in Madison County."[2] The square dances and the old-timers who tended to play them stayed in the community. The dances were most often held in the fire halls, schools, grange halls, and churches that still commanded the village crossroads.

The pop strains of country music moved into the more commercial clubs and bars. In rural Central New York, these establishments are often called "hotels," not because they have rooms to let, but because they are often leftovers from the small nineteenth-century inns and the days of Prohibition when the word "bar" was taboo. But even as the electric instruments of the country musicians work through "Have I Told You Lately that I Love You" and "Truck Driving Man," they typically still include a set or two of old-time Yankee squares. Often the source for the tunes and calls, as you discover after asking, is a father or uncle. The dances also open up the band to a feeling of the older communities. While members of the audience sit politely through the renditions of commercial country music, they feel free to chat with and make requests of the band during the old-time numbers. Speaking of this new mix, folklorist Henry Glassie observed that it shares much with the "old New York tradition" associated with nineteenth century life. He explains that "it has been inserted into the same slot in the culture: it functions in the same manner providing dance music for young people, entertainment for their elders, an aesthetic outlet for the manly male, and a means to local prestige. The old tradition, itself far removed—degenerated, advanced—from singing ancient ballads unaccompanied, is about dead, except insofar as it survives as strong influences in Country music. But, the tradition of playing and enjoying home-made music is most alive."[3]

At home is where old-time music is kept alive most. Despite the coming of highways, snowmobiles, and cable TV that broke up some of the feeling of isolation in the region, rural upstate residents still use the old music as their parents had, to break the boredom of the long winter nights and to bind youth and elders together in family. The strains of "Turkey in the Straw," "Darling Nelly Gray," and "Buffalo Gals" are commonly the first musical sounds that children hear. In many of the New England–styled houses that command the farms of upstate New York, the piano is still the centerpiece of the parlor and the fiddle a proud possession, much as they were at the turn of the century. Family members learn to play instruments and make music while the piano keeps the rhythm. Children might go on to appreciate records coming out of Nashville, but they start out on the old-time tunes and dances. Popular music increasingly sings of the American dream of success and the struggle of love and work in a modern society, but through their lives, old-time music plays out an American myth of the sanctity of the traditional home, family, and community in a changing culture. Popular country music may bring out the connection of a mass culture to their rural roots, but old-time music reminds them of local and familial experience.

While the year 1974 marked a time of change, it also was a year when I realized some of the persistent currents running through Central New York culture. I settled into an apartment above the Oaksville Hotel eight miles outside of Cooperstown. The "hotel" was actually a bar that had been around for several generations. It was an old frame structure barely reaching three stories high. A husband and wife team with family roots in the area ran the Oaksville hotel and lived above the taproom. Their clientele came from the surrounding villages. Talk inside the taproom went around from what the families in the community were doing, to hunting exploits and prizes at the "turkey shoots" behind the hotel, to changes in the region since their parents' and grandparents' days.

The village of Oaksville was a bend in the road with the hotel and a motorcycle shop guarding its sides. It sat below a patch of houses that residents refer to as "Cat Town." I received my mail down the road a few miles in Fly Creek,

23. Marching Through Georgia

Clyde McLean, 1976

24. Golden Slippers

♩ = 120

Clyde McLean, 1976

which gave the steep climb of Route 28 its local name of Fly Creek Hill. Fly Creek was a crossroads with its own "hotel," a hardware store, post office, and grocery. Surrounding the crossroads were dairy farms, some working and some abandoned. Going to "town" meant taking the trip to Cooperstown. Entertainment there consisted of several bars and one movie theater. Christmas shopping was done in the less-than-an-hour drive to Oneonta to the south or the hour-plus trip to Utica to the north.

Soon after I moved in, I was shaken by a thumping that ran through my apartment floor. I went down the stairs that led outside the building and I heard the sound of a fiddle cut through the crisp night air. Pushing past the couples holding up the doorway and the pool players hunched over in smoke-filled concentration, I found a crowd of dancers obeying the calls of a scraggly man with a harmonica (a "mouth organ," he called it) tucked in one hand. Behind him was a guitar, mandolin, and fiddle played by a group ranging from their forties to fifties. They had an old-time sound that the crowd understood well. Although the caller's voice was badly muffled by the ancient microphone, the dancers needed no clarification to go through their moves. As the band played "Marching Through Georgia," "Golden Slippers," and "Irish Washerwoman," the dancers stepped sharply. I turned toward a man who cradled a bottle of beer bearing an upstate New York label against his side, and asked him the identity of the band.

"They're the McLean family," he answered. "You got the three brothers, and Tad, he's a brother-in-law on fiddle."

"Have they been around long?" I asked.

Oaksville Hotel, 1974 (Simon Bronner)

"Sure, their farm's up on the Hartwick road. Been there a long time."

"I mean as a band."

"Oh, well, as a band maybe ten years, but as music making, a long time. Talk to Chub."

"Chub" was Clyde McLean, and seeing his girth gave away the source of his nickname. He was older than the others in the band and his cracked farmhand face and hands seem to add a few years to his visage. Dressed in a checkered flannel shirt and jeans, he seemed relaxed in this atmosphere. After the set, he worked through the crowd and made greetings to countless first names. I caught up with him on the front porch.

I asked him about the music he played.

He breathed into his hands and let out a soft chuckle. "Oh, it's nothing special. Just a family making music. We didn't have many records. We just used to have house dance parties and stuff like that. Dad and Mom played mouth organ a bunch—played all the old-fashioned stuff. We heard them play and decided maybe we ought to play too. Then barn dances come in, and here we are."

He paused. He silently contemplated his self-made evolutionary line from the house dance to the barn dance to the hotels, and then he continued, "This hotel stuff will go too like the rest of them. Most of them already are western or rock."

After his last words were uttered, Chub's eyes turned across the road to the motorcycle shop. But he seemed to see something else there in its place. "That was the place for this music," he said as he pointed with his chin, "Pop Weir's general store."

Chub smiled as he declared, "Pop Weir, he used to be awful good on violin. His son, Tad, pretty good on violin, he had one awful good violin . . . " As he spoke, someone else joined us and piped in, "He got a daughter real good there."

Chub answered, "Yeah, but her brother, one that got killed down in Syracuse, he was the one that could play the violin. *Man* how he could play that."

"He could really play the violin," the man echoed.

"And Ken Kane, and Herbie Hume, and Abe Hughes, they'd be there. Levant Rathbun come around too. I don't know as how Pop sold anything, but the place sounded good."

"Yeah, they could get right on it," the man agreed.

"What kind of fiddle tunes would they be playing?" I asked.

Without removing his gaze from the shop across the street, Chub answered, "Yeah, well yeah, they play a lot of the same ones. I mean they play a lot of the same ones we do. Like that 'Irish Wash Woman,' that's one they like to play on the fiddle. We'll play it for you on the mouth organ." And with that Chub turned back inside to play for the waiting crowd. He wouldn't get too many more chances to play there. Within two years, the hotel had closed down.

At least in one respect, time seemed to have stood still up Fly Creek Hill since 1965 when Henry Glassie reported his experience there. He wrote, "If you were to ask for makers of traditional music at the green lit country bar and pool hall in Phoenix Mills, New York, the filling station at Fly Creek, the hotel in Oaksville, or at the hardscrabble farms which circle Christian Hill, run up Rum Hill and perch on Bed Bug Hill, you would be directed to the Weirs. Those who do not know that he has recently died will tell you to 'look up Pop Weir'; those who do know will tell you that 'you should've heard the old man play the violin' but that all of his nine (or seven or twelve) sons are musicians and that the Weirs' home near Oaksville . . . would be about the only place in the area to hear 'good old fashioned music.' "[4]

While popular memory in the area still fondly recalls the days when Elial Glen "Pop" Weir ran a general store that promoted old-time fiddle music, it is not the only place to hear the old music. It is true that many of Weir's comrades are less visible, having relegated their music to private informal gatherings. But the Weirs' home is only one of many homes in the hills around Cooperstown to hear folk fiddle tunes, songs, and jests. As rooted as the residents in this region have been, music calls to mind the collective memory of prominent music-making families going back to the nineteenth century. They will tell you of the McLeans, the Weirs, the Hugheses. While residents point to the changing favor in the "towns" for "western" music and rock and roll, they still boast of a stronghold of Yankee old-time music stretching through the small crossroad villages of Delaware, Otsego, and Chenango counties in Central New York State. Pop

Elial "Pop" Weir, c. 1950s (courtesy Les Weir)

Weir's place begins my journey into Central New York State to view the region's changing old-time music traditions after World War II.

Pop Weir was born in 1890 in the "North Country" near Gouverneur, New York. Working in the lumber camps, he became adept at fiddling as well as lumbering. As his son Dorrance explains, "My father used to be a lumberjack and they take a fiddle into the camp with them. They would go in the fall and they stay there all winter. Out of sheer boredom they would play tunes and make up songs." Pop continued his playing at home as well. His wife accompanied him on piano, and the two of them played house dances. Seeking to leave the hard life of lumbering, Pop moved his family to Otsego County in the 1920s. At first he settled in Hubbell Hollow, an isolated spot about ten miles outside of Cooperstown. His son Dorrance described it as a dirt road, a place "where Christ kissed the hoot owl good bye." Life revolved around the home and the small community near Whig's Corners. At home, Pop's fiddle backed up songs that his children still remember. A reminder sung by Pop to young Dorrance stuck with the boy:

> You are young yet you know
> And perhaps you may grow
> But as yet you're a little too small
> You're a little too small my boy
> You never will answer at all
> You are young yet you know
> And perhaps you may grow
> But as yet you're a little too small

As if to emphasize the family connection, Dorrance tells me at one musical session, "My father used to sing that. Buster knows it too. I guess we all do." Pop's family swelled to twelve children. To house them all, he moved to a larger home in Oaksville. Music united the family at evening gatherings. Five of the children took up instruments and they all joined in the spirit of the occasion.

In addition to the various jobs he held around Cooperstown, Pop entertained at house dances. "He was pretty good," Dorrance declares, "People would come from miles around to hear my father fiddle. He fiddled clean, you know, it wasn't any of the slurry notes and all that." Pop preferred the plain bowing and old-fashioned slow tempos that he inherited from the nineteenth-century North Country dance tradition. Because he fiddled, some youngsters commonly asked him to play southern pieces like "Orange Blossom Special" that were coming over the radio, but Pop let his displeasure about the cluttered style and scurrying tempo of these pieces be known by calling them "God damned rebel tunes." He wasn't shy about letting his sons know that they were beginning to sound like the rebels either. If they hurried the tune, Pop would tap them with his fiddle bow. Judges at New York State old-time fiddling contests must have agreed with Pop's opinion, because he took first in two contests at Oneonta and Schenectady that he entered during the 1950s. The contests were broadcast widely over Central New York State and pictures of Pop with the news of his prize appeared in newspapers. Many wonder whether Pop could have gone further commercially with his music, but he turned down the opportunity, preferring to stay close to his family and community.

At his store in Oaksville, Pop would keep two or three fiddles on the wall. Other old-timers and some not-so-old timers would join Pop for mid-afternoon fiddling sessions. They would run through tunes such as "Rickett's Hornpipe," "Sailor's Hornpipe," "Money Musk," "Soldier's Joy," and "Opera Reel." Although not a native to Otsego County, Pop found kindred spirits in the area who shared a similar traditional repertoire and preference for plain bowing and easy tempos. Among the regulars were Herbert Hume from Edmeston, Abe Hughes of Milford, and Ken Kane of Hartwick. Les Weir remembered the sessions at the store this way: "Their fiddle music was old jigs and reels and Scottish tunes and

25. Soldier's Joy

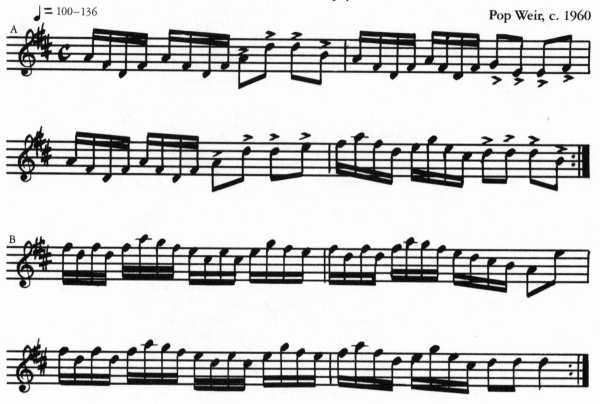

Irish tunes and some Irish ballads were popular." Pop was the acknowledged leader of the group. To this day, many fiddlers still refer to tunes as one of his. They would also ask him to lead the music at the barn and Grange dances that replaced the older house dances. Pop was regularly called to perform them until the end of his life in 1965.

Pop started Dorrance (nicknamed Haunch) out on tenor banjo in 1931. Soon, Don, Les (nicknamed Tad), and Violet (nicknamed Buster) took up the fiddle. Yet another Weir boy, Hy, picked up the mouth organ and joined his siblings in music. Early in their lives, Pop's children often carried their instruments to "parlor and play nights" at which rural youngsters sang the old songs and joined in play-party songs like "The Girl I Left Behind Me" and "Golden Slippers." Although the youngsters continued to dance to many of the old tunes, new songs brought by radio drew more attention in the parlors. Dorrance, for example, took in two new sources of songs that reached his radio set. One was the Grand Ole Opry from Nashville and the other was Don Messer's show from Ontario, Canada. In addition, Dorrance pulled in broadcasts of country music programming from New York. Schenectady's WGY and Utica's WRUN were among the more popular stations. Dorrance was the singer and guitarist of the Weir family, and he seemed to have inherited his father's leadership qualities. He can still be found making music at local gatherings. Having been relied on to accompany the fiddlers in the family, Dorrance snaps the bass strings of his guitar to create a commanding loud, rhythmic beat even when he plays alone. He calls

26. Rickett's Hornpipe

Pop Weir, c. 1960

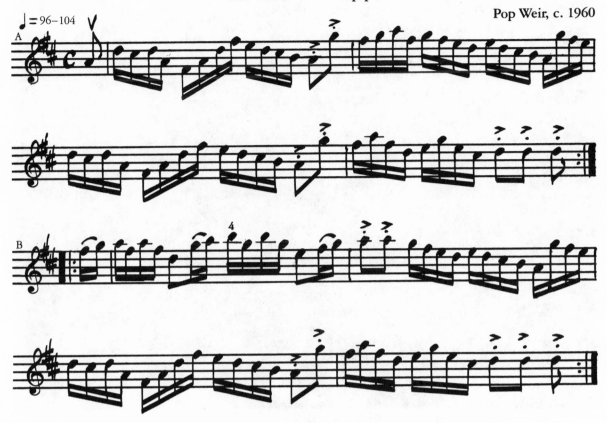

out a variety of songs ranging from old-time pieces learned from his father such as "Gold Top Walking Cane" to the old play-party and square dance tunes to country hits of recent vintage such as "Sunny Side of the Mountain."

Through the late 1950s and early 1960s, Don appeared likely to become the premier fiddler of the Weir clan, but an airplane accident prematurely ended his life. Many looked to Violet to carry the mantle, but attending to the rearing of eight children often kept her out of public view. She kept family tradition alive, however, by frequently hosting the family's music-making at her house, and on occasion, she would lead Les and Dorrance at a public appearance at the Farmers' Museum. Capable on accordion and piano in addition to mastering the fiddle, Violet became a craftsmanlike student of the music. She went beyond Pop's tutelage to take formal musical training and appreciate modern influences; "she had a real violin sound," Chub McLean liked to say. Playing in public far less than her brothers, Violet nonetheless drew attention from the area's residents, not only because she is Pop Weir's daughter, but also because in these parts (and most parts) an old-time fiddler who is a woman is a rarity. To Les, Violet is especially skilled in technique and knowledge. "She knew a song and knew exactly how it had to be played," he explained, "and that's the way she played it." In other words, influenced by her formal training her playing displayed less of the adornment and variation common to other local fiddlers.

Violet's house is now too small to host the whole Weir clan. Violet brought the family's music to a new generation of Weirs and at least two of her daughters

The Weir Family performing at the Farmer's Museum, Cooperstown, New York, 1973. Left to right: Les Weir, unidentified woman, Earl Pardini, Violet Weir Shallert, Dorrance Weir; the man standing below the stage on the left is caller Leonard McLean (courtesy Les Weir)

have picked up instruments. In 1984, the family, now numbering almost 150 relations directly from Pop and Ma Weir, held a reunion in a Fly Creek hall. With Violet's daughter offering a guitar backup, Violet and Les raised memories of Pop with renditions (done probably faster than Pop would have liked) of "St. Anne's Reel," "Raggedy Ann," "Wind that Shakes the Barley," and "Buffalo Gals."

Truest to the old-time fiddling of Pop is Les Weir, a talented carpenter by trade, who still lives in Oaksville. Les was born in 1932. He earned the name Tad (actually short for Tadpole) because he was too young to enter the military during World War II. Even today, Les's smile rounds out a cherubic face. Despite a noticeable paunch, his body has a muscular authority bred by hard manual labor. With his fiddle snuggled under his chin, however, his muscles seemed to relax. Les was the quiet accompanist in the family. He followed the lead of his father and brothers. Yet he was perhaps the most faithful follower of the old-time repertoire and style. With his fiddle down, he talks with a studied concentration. "I learned all my fiddle music from my dad," he explains. "He was born and brought up in the North Woods lumber camps. And he learned his fiddling

Les Weir at his home, Hartwick Township, New York, 1987 (Simon Bronner)

there up around Gouverneur where he was born. Well, it's come down through the family. I always like the music and I just picked up the fiddle and started practicing on it a little bit and playing along with Pop and my brothers. My dad used to play the house dances when I was kind of little. My mother played the piano and he played the fiddle and then my sister, she began to play and sometimes she would go and play the piano for them. I had learned to play the violin when the house dance were mostly past. I hated music in school. I liked the old-time dance tunes. I learned by ear. Besides Pop there was Jimmy Taylor, he used to live on the corner. He was an older man and he played the fiddle. Ken Kane has that old-time sound. He'll be here in a minute; he's up on Christian Hill. Course there weren't things going on when I was small that there are today and if there was a barn dance or husking bee why they had music. And it was furnished by the local talent. We played so much, but we never really had a band, as you know it now. We played with whoever was entertaining. It was a family thing, a community thing. We played at people's houses; we played at Grange halls; we played at barn dances. After the family went their ways, I played with the McLeans off and on for several years and some with Levant Rathbun."

Les looks expectedly at the door for Ken Kane to join him. While we wait, with his fiddle he recalls his father. "This is just a funny old song he used to sing and he could play the fiddle and sing. I can't say a word when I play. But he could play and call and sing." He plays a tune that he calls "Ebenezeer Fry." Then he puts his fiddle aside and sings:

> I own the old mill down there at Rubinville
> My name is Joshua Ebenezeer Fry
> I know a thing or two
> Yes you bet your neck I do
> You can't fool me because I'm too darn sly
> Well I swan, I must be jogging on
> Get up Napoleon it looks like rain
> I'll be switched the hay ain't pitched
> Call me when you're down by the farm again
> I went to town the other day
> For to sell a load of hay
> I met a man who said your barn's on fire
> But I had the barn key right along with me
> So I knew he was a fool or a god-darn liar
> Well I swan, I must be jogging on
> Get up Napoleon it looks like rain
> I'll be switched the hay ain't pitched
> Call me when you're down by the farm again
> My son Joshua went to the fair the other day
> He hitched his horse to the railroad fence
> Thought he tied him good and strong
> The darn train came along
> I ain't seen the horse or the wagon since
> Well I swan, I must be jogging on
> Get up Napoleon it looks like rain
> I'll be switched the hay ain't pitched
> Call me when you're down by the farm again.[5]

Les smiles as he finishes. The rural images appeal to him. He sits back and imagines his father at home singing it. Dorrance had sung it for me earlier, but his version varied from Les's. Unlike Les who performs it like a ballad set to a fiddle tune, Dorrance worked the piece into a snappy song:

> My son Joshua went down the other day
> Hitched his horse to the railroad fence
> Gosh darn train came along and it yanked him
> He ain't seen his horse or his wagon since
> Hey John I must be joggin' on
> Get up Napoleon, it looks like rain
> Hey John I must be joggin' on
> Get up Napoleon I got to be home

Les returns from his brief reflection. He perks up and tells me "There's one, it's a really old song, 'High Silk Hat and a Gold Top Walking Cane.' You

27. Get Up Napoleon (Ebenezer Fry)

Dorrance Weir, 1976

Get Up Napoleon (Ebenezer Fry)
(second version)

Les Weir, 1976

Variation—Measures 1–2

probably heard that; we used to sing that. Course, Dorrance and Hydie sing that all the time. Of course, I'm not a singer; I'm a fiddler."[6] With that announcement, Les plays a succession of tunes learned from his father and spread through the hills of Otsego County. Les reaches back with "Lamplighters Horn Pipe," "Rakes of Mallow," and "Miss McLeod's Reel." Recalling the dance that I witnessed at the Oaksville Hotel, he then plays "Golden Slippers" and "Red Wing."

Les pauses to tell me about Ken Kane. He calmly explains that Ken "is a real character; he really knows some old songs." "He used to play with my father." Les suggests that indeed, the elder Ken Kane is the heir to the musical

28. Lamplighter's Hornpipe

Les Weir, 1976

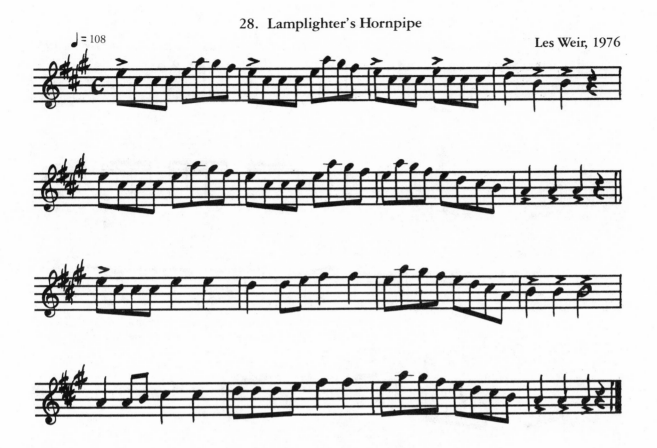

world that Pop built. Just then, Ken Kane walks in without knocking. Les stands and helps Ken with his instruments.

Ken makes his greetings in cackling tones. Dressed in overalls, Ken is a gaunt figure sporting a white goatee. Although not very tall, Ken conveys a farm-bred ruggedness. A matchstick twirls to the side of his mouth. Well-worn lines run through his face and hands. His woolly white hair and crinkly eyes give exuberance to each expression. Adding to his lively appearance is his zigzag profile formed by his jutting goatee, nose, and forehead. Ken takes his place on the couch next to Les and takes out his guitar. Without prompting, Ken responds quickly with proper chords to the tunes that Les plays.

After finishing "The Girl I Left Behind Me," I ask the two men where they heard the tune. Les credits his father. Ken explains that "an old man used to whistle that when I was a kid." "How about the other tunes?" I ask him. Ken replies, "My dad knew a lot of songs. My oldest brother Clarence was a fiddler and he played the notes and any song we thought we wanted to learn we asked him to play it and we just remembered it. Of course we never got it a hundred percent right. I suppose if so many notes didn't fit, we put in the ones we wanted."

With his last words, Ken snickers and shoots Les a glance. He then takes out a fiddle and leads Les through several duets. After finishing "Darling Nelly Gray," his eyes sparkle. I asked him when he first heard the tune. Ken cocks his

29. Rakes of Mallow

♩ = 108

Les Weir, 1976

head and exclaims, "I kicked three slats out of the cradle first time I heard that!"

Les lets a smile round his face. This fiddle music has been a great part of both their lives. Like Ken, Les remembers growing up on these tunes. Dorrance also remembers "Darling Nelly Gray" as the first tune played to him by his father. Pop Weir may have been a strong figure in the area's Grange Halls and barn dances, but the web of old-time music extended to many childhoods inside these Yankee homes. These men continued that tradition. Les talked of playing Pop's tunes for his young daughter. Ken Kane had taught his daughter to play the guitar and he even built her an instrument made from pieces of other guitars and decorated with red and green glass motorcycle reflectors. From his father, Ken's son knows the calls to the old country dances. At a gathering with Dorrance Weir in 1965 that Henry Glassie witnessed, the first songs that Ken Kane performed with his family present were ones learned from his father. He recalled the times that he used to go to Pop Weir's store to play with Pop. He greatly admired Pop's fiddling, especially of the jigs and reels that Pop loved to play, and he criticized Pop's sons for playing too fast.

More than ten years later, Ken Kane's daughter is married and lives only two miles away from the old homestead. Although she doesn't play regularly, she will accompany her father when he asks. Guests and family alike enter the same door

30. Miss McLeod's Reel

Les Weir, 1976

on the side of the house. There Ken's front room is in a constant state of disarray. Along with guns and electrical equipment it is filled with instruments that he likes to play for guests. A powerful furnace that Ken built now commands the front room and provides a hearth-like setting. Ken sits on a cot across from the furnace and plays while his older brother Leon leans back in a rocker to the right of the furnace. Ken prefers the sound of the old tunes on the fiddle but he also can play them on guitar, "button accordion," concertina, harmonica, piano, banjo, dobro, and "mouth organ."

Ken's grandfather Jim came to the Schoharie Hills of Central New York State during the 1840s from New England. Around 1898, Jim's son, Emery moved the next county over to Otsego to farm. Once there, Emery met and married Minnie Hitt of Cooperstown. The newlywed couple moved to the farm that Ken still operates in Hartwick township. Ken, one of eight children, was born in the house on April 29, 1914. In 1942 Ken was married and set up house with his bride in the old homestead. He reared five children there. The aged New-England-style farmhouse also housed Ken's brother Leon until his death in 1981. As Ken aged, he developed many manual skills from carpentry to stone masonry that families needed to run their farms. In his lifetime, Ken has been a wagon-maker, millwright, welder, electrician, and dairy farmer. Music was yet another skill, one used for enjoyment on a winter's night and to connect families to one another in a community. But there's more to it. These skills were part of a self-

Ken Kane at Fenimore House, New York State Historical Association, Cooperstown, 1975 (Simon Bronner)

reliant attitude that had developed among these rural folk. Rather than viewing home-made music as inferior, these people preferred the participation and self-satisfaction that home-made artifacts provided them. For Ken Kane, "That storebought stuff is just no good. So you'd go take a look at something and then go home and make it yourself the way you want to. Everybody does it that way here. I made everything I ever had from my whole life, whether it be a chair, a wagon or any damn thing." Even consumer articles like egg cartons and bleach bottles are saved and converted to new home-uses around Ken's place.

The entertainment in the community was also home-made. "When I was a small boy," Ken explains, "it was all house dances and it was fiddles, banjos,

31. Turkey in the Straw

Les Weir and Ken Kane, 1976

and guitar maybe. They mostly local people. There'd be thirty-five, forty people up here at a neighbor's house. There just be one fiddler who'd be called on the most. Some people who couldn't dance used to sing with the fiddler—used to be a heck of a lot of fun." Ken preferred to play music rather than dance. The rough and tumble world of farming produced more than its share of boyhood accidents. "Every time I broke some bones," Ken recalls, "I learned another instrument." Ken started out on the family organ and moved on to the portable accordion, harmonica, and concertina. Ken showed an alert ear. He had a knack for picking up tunes and reproducing them on various instruments. The more challenging fiddle came next. On each instrument he picked out the predominant melodies that were circulating through the hills. Ken would not hesitate to ask a hop-picker or farmhand to whistle an old tune so he could reproduce it. Another source of song for Ken were corn husking bees. "Eight or ten farm families would be there," he explained, "and they would join in on the singing. My dad knew a lot of songs he would lead. He would have that "Letter Edged in Black" and "Don't Go Tommy Don't Go." They'd hear my father sing it once and get right in with him. You know in those old barns, like where the huskings were, there's something about singing in an old wooden building like that; it's housed in there but still you could hear it outdoors too. I used to love to hear them sing."

Today Ken recalls his youth with fondness. "They were good times, not

32. Nellie Gray

Ken Kane, 1976

segue

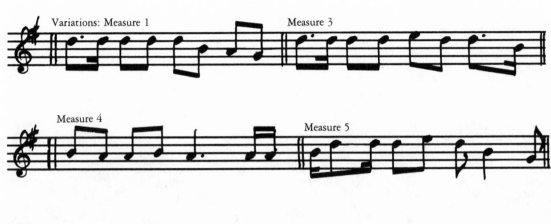

like now." What he means is that the farms in the countryside wove the social fabric of the area. He joined farmboys and girls in the small one-room schoolhouse at the top of the hill near his house. Entertainment and labor came from the cooperation of farmers. In the years after World War II, the county seat and tourist haven of Cooperstown had eclipsed the farm communities. With some resentment and an extra touch of rural pronunciation in his voice, he tells me, "I remember when Cooperstown was *nawthing*. Farmers out here ran everything. I've only been into town three times and each time I got bothered by the authorities. Back then you didn't have troopers bothering you; you ran your own business." The prosperity of the early twentieth century is a fading memory; most farmers are struggling to hang on. But in the 1920s the barns were full and the music seemed gay.

During the 1930s, according to Ken, larger Grange hall dances had replaced the neighborhood house dances. The difference between them and the house dances, he points out however, was that the Grange dances were about raising money. The house dances were about raising spirits. "It was just old country music," Ken tells of the Grange dances. "I would just go down here to the Grange hall, sit down on the bench and listen to them, come home and play it." At these Grange halls, Ken received his first public experiences. "Sometimes the fiddler wouldn't show and they'd ask a few of the Grangers who played to fill in. I'd do that once in a while, and later I got to playing them regular. We used to start out on a square dance with something easy like 'Red River Valley' or something like that. And then the second song we played would be 'Marching Through Georgia' and the third song we played, more or less, would always be a jig." As Ken Kane matured, he became a more versatile fiddler. He became a regular sight at Pop Weir's general store in Oaksville where the old man offered up jigs and hornpipes that Ken avidly followed.

While Ken was bringing home tunes in his head to re-play on his fiddle,

Kane Family farm, Hartwick Township, New York, 1976 (Simon Bronner)

in the parlor and in the fields Ken's father sang. Ken's parents had a parlor organ that would provide an evening's entertainment. Ken's father also carried a harmonica that he liked to play during a break from his chores. In addition to the songs that Emery wrote down from his memory of his father's singing, he collected broadsides containing the words to popular songs. Emery pasted the broadsides into a book which he passed on to Ken. Ken, however, always preferred learning by hearing rather than reading. To this day he remembers songs that were likely to be repeatedly performed around the house and fields. Taking up several instruments, Ken seemed more interested anyway in the music to the songs, and the broadsides did not contain music. That was provided by oral tradition.

The songs that Ken's father collected follow certain themes that characterize later country music. Many appear to be adaptations of old folk verses or ballad formulas. Others ring with the sentimentality of Victorian popular song. A batch of songs concern events of the day, especially those that occurred close by such as "The Johnstown Flood" (dated 1889, set in Pennsylvania) and "The Murder in Cohoes" (set near Albany, New York). Another set of songs show a sentimentality for things old and rustic. Emery saved the sheets for "Old Oaken Bucket," "Old Arm Chair," "Old Kitchen Floor," and "The Old Rustic Bridge

33. Pop Weir Tune

♩ = 120

Ken Kane, 1976

by the Mill" (dated 1881). These songs connected these old things with the virtue of the old homestead and the memory of dear old Mother. In addition to sentimentalizing about things old, many songs contemplated aging: "Poor Old Dad," "I Ain't as Young as I Used to Be," and "Will You Leave Me When I'm Old?" Related to this series of titles concerning the relations of parents to their children: "Little Footsteps" (dated 1868), "As I Sat Upon My Dear Old Mother's Knee" (1884), "Be Home Early To-night, My Dear Boy" and "Remember, You Have Children of Your Own." It is not surprising to find heart-wrenching love songs, except that they overwhelmingly concern aching separations and tragic deaths. Emery had "Good-Bye, My Lover, Good-Bye" (dated 1882), "Cast Aside," and "My Dream of Love is O'er." Death and tragedy are also strong themes in plaintive songs such as "Darling Nelly Gray," "Package of Old Letters" (dated 1870, also known as "Little Rosewood Casket"), "Fisherman and His Child" (dated 1878), and "Ship that Never Returned." Emery also collected homiletic songs like "Juice of the Forbidden Fruit" about lessons to be learned from the Garden of Eden story. Other songs appear to be of minstrel show or Yankee theater vintage. "In De Evening by De Moonlight" (dated 1880) appears to be a blackface number while "I'm A Man You Don't Meet Every Day" and "Duffy, The Swell" (dated 1884) are boastful Irish ditties. "Dorkins' Night" (dated 1877) tells the story of a popular comic actor who falls from grace because of drunkenness. Although these broadsides rarely mention a composer, they did use the names of stage performers as come-ons. "I Had But Fifty Cents," a fa-

Emery and Minnie Kane with family, c. 1920. Ken is at upper right
(courtesy Ken Kane)

vorite of Ken Kane's brother, had the line "As Sung by Frank Rothe, Banjoist"
beneath the title. The broadside "Old Kitchen Floor" bragged, "As Sung by Edward Burton" and "The Murder in Cohoes" came from the singing of "Miss B.
L. Ryan, of Albany, N.Y." As Ken and I flipped through the book of broadsides,
I asked him what kind of songs he picked up from his age-mates. He replied,
"about the same kind of stuff."

A few phonograph records made their way into Emery Kane's household.
"It was mostly old Edisons," Ken recalls. "There were some Irish accordion records and lots of comedy-type stuff like those Uncle Josh records. But we all got
a cheap radio and that pushed the phonograph back." Ken remembers listening
to the Grand Ole Opry and the Wheeling Jamboree on the radio. He liked the
material they played. The themes and instrumentation of their songs were similar to what he played. "But our fiddling used to be more precise," he objected;
"theirs went too fast and wasn't careful enough. Sounded slurred and some of the
beats were lost."

The various sources, printed, broadcasted, and orally circulated, are evident in Ken Kane's performing repertoire. In the list of songs are the old Yankee
dance tunes such as "Girl I Left Behind Me," "Turkey in the Straw," and "Irish
Washerwoman." Fiddle tunes of more recent nineteenth-century vintage are also

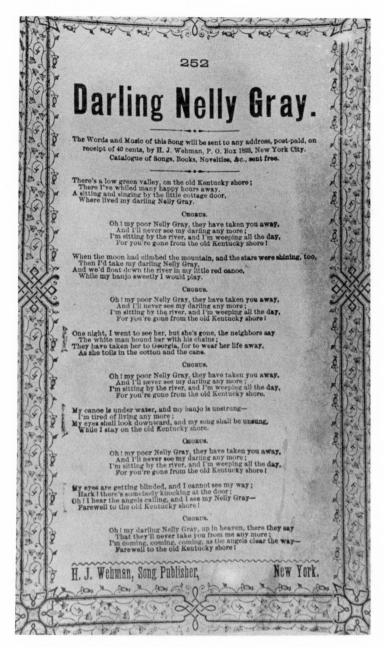

Broadside owned by Emery Kane (courtesy Ken Kane)

evident: "Marching Through Georgia," "Year of Jubelo," "Redwing," "Listen to the Mockingbird," "Little Brown Jug," and "Climbing Up the Golden Stairs." Many of Emery's sentimental favorites appear. Ken will play "Darling Nellie Gray," "Letter Edged in Black," "Ship That Never Returned," "I Had But Fifty Cents," "Old Grey Bonnet," and "Goodbye, My Lover, Goodbye." The minstrel show influence is detectable in Kane's performance of "Old Zip Coon" and "Old Black Joe." Several songs appear to come from older folk tradition: "Little Mo-Hee," "Rock All My Babies to Sleep," "Old Smokey," "Bury Me Beneath the

Willow," and "Buffalo Gals." The story-songs of prisoner life and train wrecks that were common in the early twentieth century round out Ken's repertoire. He sings "Twenty-One Years," "Ninety-Nine Years," "Prisoner's Song," "Wreck of the 97," and "Wreck of the No. 9." In addition, commercial influences are evident in his renditions of "Tennessee Waltz," "Please Release Me," and "Pistol Packin' Mama."

Like most of his friends, Ken doesn't compose songs, although he freely admits to "changing some around." A song, for example, that Ken's children ask for is "Rock All My Babies to Sleep." Ken's father sang it as a long heart-wrenching ballad of an errant mother, but Ken performs it with one or two verses and he inserts a yodel where his father used to sing "Hush a bye baby, thy mother will come by and by." Ken sings:

> My wife she run with a different kind,
> An' often goes out on a spree
> And she leaves me behind, the baby to mind,
> An' yodel um, a doodle um dee.
> Yodel-a-e-o, 'dl-a-e-o, 'dl-a-ee.
>
> She leaves me behind, the baby to mind
> The house in good order to keep
> An' while she does roam
> Far far from her home
> I rock her dear babies to sleep.[7]

Another favorite of Ken's from his father's day is "Letter Edged in Black." The title dates it from the Victorian era when mourners sent letters on black-edged stationery. Ken likes to play the song as an instrumental, but he will sing:

> Trembling hands I took that letter home dear
> Opened it and this is what it said,
> Come home my boy, your dear old father wants you
> Come home my boy, your dear old mother's dead.

From Emery's singing of the many mournful verses, Ken has preserved one, but he has changed some of the words. Ken remembered that his father used to sing something about "breaking the seal," instead of just "opening" the letter.[8] Like the chairs and instruments that he builds, or the farm he works, in music Ken takes the materials that he has inherited and reassembles them. His music acts out a process of repetition and refinement that characterizes the work that he does.

A strong part of Ken's identity as well as his repertoire is his farming background. One woman who grew up near Kane's farm, now moved off the farm and working in Cooperstown, used to like to say that "Ken liked the feeling of manure between his toes." For Ken, his farm life fostered the music and his vitality. He poignantly drives the point home with songs steeped in farmbuildings and soil such as "Stay on the Farm," "Bessie the Heifer," and "Potatoes They Grow Small." As if to sum up Ken's feelings, "Don't Go Tommy, Don't Go" often

34. Letter Edged in Black

Ken Kane, 1976

closed our recording sessions. The song begs young Tommy to fight the temptation to leave the farm for the city. It sings the praises of farm life as part of a natural order. Along with that order, Ken Kane sincerely conveys in the words of the song, is a retention of old-fashioned values:

> Be kind to your parents,
> They'll soon pass away;
> The farmer'll be heard in some great distant day,
> Eternity wants us to reap and to sow,
> I beg of you Tommy don't go.[9]

In all, I recorded 153 musical selections that included ninety distinct songs. I put down thirty-seven fiddle tunes that Ken identified as "country dance" or "square dance" tunes. Ken also volunteered two tunes that he identified as the kind that used to be played on the fife around the hills. Ken's repertoire was similar to Dorrance Weir's selection of songs, although Kane chose to play more dance tunes than Dorrance. Examining the sources of the repertoire of these men shows a close match to what emerged as the "hillbilly" repertoire.

When the old-time music was at its height in the communities around Ken Kane's home, a split existed between the traditional tunes played at dances and the songs that were played at home. With the decline after World War II of the public settings, or what writers Anne and Norm Cohen call the assembly tradition, the two traditions mixed. Anne and Norm Cohen's study of hillbilly music points out that "assembly music was much more responsive to contemporary popular musical developments than was the domestic tradition. The domestic was largely the older component, the material learned orally in the folksinger's youth without thought of commercial value or current vogue. . . . By contrast, the assembly music was greatly affected by then-current musical idioms that were enjoying national prominence, such as jazz, pop, blues, and ragtime."[10] Hillbilly music and later country music changed rapidly not only because it was commercialized, but also because it became more of an assembly tradition in an era of public change. The folk fiddle tunes of old-time music were preserved ironically by becoming a domestic tradition. In Otsego County, the favor for performances over the recordings of old-time music helped to perpetuate a community tie to the music that kept the old dances and tunes going.

Norm and Anne Cohen found that 59 percent of hillbilly recordings from 1922 to 1924 came from a folk or early minstrel origin, followed by 26 percent for Tin Pan Alley Origin (1860–1900). Ken Kane's repertoire during 1976 displayed similar tendencies. I calculated that 58 percent of his songs came from folk or early minstrel origin. 12 percent came from Tin Pan Alley sources (1860–1900) and 18 percent came from there for the period after 1900. Pop Weir, on the other hand, maintained the split between his old fiddle tunes that he played at the store and at dances and the songs that he played at home. He resisted the addition of new hillbilly songs into his public repertoire. Kane absorbed many of the songs, although he selected ones that fitted the themes or melodies of the older assembly and domestic traditions. Of the songs played by Ken Kane, 83 percent circulated in the hillbilly tradition. Although steeped in the Yankee dance heritage, Kane's music easily blended with commercial legacy of hillbilly music that swept the nation. But it was a legacy that was layered over an existing tradition rather than being one that replaced another.

Today, Ken Kane's repertoire sounds old-fashioned. He prefers to recall the work of local musicians rather than reproduce the country music hits that Dorrance Weir will sometimes play. But Ken likes to watch Grandpa Jones's playing and to hear Donna Fargo's singing when the stars appear on *Hee Haw*. To Ken, as well as to others in this region, his music is "country"; the other groups that he sees on the show are "western." For himself he has stuck with his "country" music, the evolving old-time tradition, although to do so has meant domesticating it.

Ken Kane plays fewer public events these days. On occasion he will be asked to play square dances at camps around Lake Otsego for vacationing urban children. But he lacks enthusiasm for performing at them. He misses the neighborliness of playing in the community. I asked Ken about the places that he used to play. He named the "Header Hall" in Toddsville.

"What happened to it?" I asked.

"Torn down," he replied.

"What were some others?" I continued.

"Fire Creek Grange, Quaker Valley Grange Hall, Tumble Inn," he answered.

"What happened to them?"

"They're all done."

Ken Kane at his home, 1987 (Simon Bronner)

Playing more for parlor guests, Ken renders the old fiddle tunes as songs. "Don't hold up anymore without the dance," Ken observes. Without the dance, too, the fiddle is no longer at center stage. Ken plays more guitar now. From listening to radio, Ken has picked up additional instruments such as the banjo and lap slide guitar on which to play his old fiddle tunes. But although many still admire Ken's loyalty to the old music, his children have not chosen to follow the tradition. At home he is alone; his brother and wife are both gone. The hearing that once served Ken so well in picking up tunes is failing him. Now in his sev-

35. Larry O'Gaff

Grant Rogers, 1976

enties, he intends to die where he was born. Around him will stand the products of his handiwork and the music that he hopes will "be heard in some great distant day."

In Delaware County, just south of Otsego, Grant Rogers tells me a tale that sounds much like Ken Kane's, but in Rogers's saga old-time music went public as "folk" rather than "country." In his trailer just outside of Walton, New York, Rogers describes a legacy of old-time music in the region that reaches back to the nineteenth century, but his puckish face belies his seventy years of age. He gracefully reaches for his fiddle and as he tucks it under his chin, he takes a deep breath of the fresh Catskill Mountain air. I listen to him finish off a series of fiddle tunes including "Larry O'Gaff," "Opera Reel," and "Little Red Barn."

"You'd play those at dances?" I ask.

"Oh yeah, yeah. Dances—round, square, and all that."

"Where would you get the tunes from?"

36. Opera Reel

(D tuning)
♩ = 126

Grant Rogers, 1976

"Well, that's a hard question, because it just seems that I was born and brought up in that stuff, you know, from the time I was a kid. The tunes were all over the Catskills."

"Who was playing them?"

"Well, old timers—old fiddlers. I can remember back when a guy used to take his fiddle and stand up in the corner of a room and stand there and fiddle and do his own calling and the whole mob out there was square dancing. They didn't have no great big band. Then I remember these old barn dances. I seen them bring a piano on an old wagon, bring it with a team of horses and handle it like it was an egg you know. Get it in there and get it set up for that barn dance. Word of mouth spread the news of the dance. I remember an Irishman, his name was Mullen, Thomas Mullen, and he was a fiddler and square dance caller. He was one of the type that would stand there and fiddle and do his own calling you know. He played a lot of them Irish tunes, Irish reels. He could really play with the beat, like they did then. You would have a lot of that old-time kind of waltz, called it a quadrille. This was way back in the twenties. I also learned a lot from

Grant Rogers at home, 1975 (Simon Bronner)

old Sherm Yorks. He was a peg-legged fiddler who worked the lumber camps. Some pieces you pick up just be hearing folks deedle them. You know, they'd go 'deedle-ee-deedle-dee-dee.' "

"How old are you now Grant?"

"I was born in 1907 and I played the fiddle pretty quick. I started playing the fiddle when I was around eight years old—starting playing by ear. I played some square dances where they had to stand me up on a chair. This was here; it's been my homeplace all my life."

Grant's father Delbert was a railroader and stonemason in the mountains around Walton. His father could fiddle a few tunes, although Grant claims that "you wouldn't pay a ticket to hear him." At home Grant's mother and father sang parlor songs like the ones that Emery Kane kept in his book of broadsides. He also remembered songs of lumbering and railroading that workers would introduce to the youngster. "The lumbermen used to like to make up songs and I guess I got some ideas from that." Rogers soon learned to play the guitar to accompany the family's singing at home. The phonograph provided him with songs that were similar to the ones he sang at home: Vernon Dalhart's recordings of story songs such as "Wreck of the Old 97" and "Death of Floyd Collins." Rogers eagerly learned the songs from the records, because, to hear him tell it, they had much of the flavor of the ballad tradition in the region. Rogers also cherished the radio that pulled in hillbilly programming from New York, Canada, and the South.

As a young man, Rogers found work cutting timber in the lumber camps and he followed his father into stonecutting at the quarries. Still, he found time to fiddle for dances. An accomplished fiddler with a full repertoire of British Isles jigs and hornpipes as well as American reels and waltzes, Rogers gained a reputation as an heir to the renowned old-time fiddlers of Delaware County such as Alva Belcher and Sherm Yorks. In the 1940s, a furniture company asked Rogers to organize a group for a radio spot on WVOS out of nearby Liberty, New York. Rogers formed the Delaware County Ramblers with fellow barn-dance musicians, but he realized that the group would have to play more than the old square dance numbers to hold the radio audience. Rogers arranged sentimental and humorous ballads that he knew from home for the group. The band played old familiar ballads such as "Potter County Maid," "Once More a Lumbering Go," "Jam on Gerry's Rock," and "Mother Was a Lady." The group also sang some of the songs that were being heard on the radio. "I liked to sit and listen to good ballad singers like Bradley Kincaid. He had a line of good stuff we played like 'What Will I Do With the Baby O'; and some of that Jimmie Rodgers stuff, we put some of that on the show."

Although the show tilted toward the hillbilly repertoire, a mix of the assembly and domestic traditions, Grant Rogers retained the Yankee fiddling style. "I didn't like that southern hacksaw fiddling," Rogers comments. Like Kane and Pop Weir, Rogers favored a plain bowing style with moderate, danceable tempos. Even the performance of Rogers's songs are taken at an easy pace and seemed reserved by comparison with the singing of southern songsters that Rogers admired such as Uncle Dave Macon. With his combination of old occupational ballads, Yankee square dance tunes, and new hillbilly hits, Rogers's show became a local favorite. Responding to his community, Rogers always sent greetings to neighbors and friends and he took requests for songs. The show was a regular feature on Saturday nights in the region until 1950.

Rogers was swept aside by changes in country music after World War II. As more of the music became commercialized, disk jockeys spinning records replaced live radio broadcasts like Rogers's. The music also changed as it dropped its hillbilly image. "They called it country and western," Rogers complained, "but I don't see where they get any western out of it. All these country and western so called is to me the same thing. You hear one you hear them all. All it amounts to is their teardrops and their heartaches and their sorrows, and that's the limit of the thing. There's no songs to it. You couldn't follow the song to sit down and listen to it. It's one heartache right after another. Well you take folk songs or what we did as country, there's a lot of the old folk songs that are sorrowful songs, you know, but still they got a story, they got something, they got a background there. So as you go through the years things change, songs change. I went to an advertised square dance, it was a round and square dance. My wife and I went into the place. We went into the place and you know what the orchestra was. For the square dances and round dances? Seven guitars. Seven guitars come out on the platform and they sound just like a human earthquake. And they thought they was doing a wonderful job."

Grant Rogers maintained his old-time music through this period with the encouragement of the folk music "revival." Although the heyday of the revival is usually thought of as the 1950s and 1960s, the movement had roots in the Depression era. During the 1930s, Works Progress Administration projects and Library of Congress recordings brought attention to the nation's folk music. The recorded traces of a longstanding folk tradition that undergirded the precarious nation offered the hope of an inner strength drawn from the country's primitive roots. But as World War II approached, many pundits feared that the purity and freshness of the songs would disappear as rural areas were wracked by advancing industrialization and urbanization. Downtrodden rural singers like Leadbelly, Woody Guthrie, Josh White, and Big Bill Broonzy moved to New York City where they were celebrated by a liberal circle of singers and activists. They took their music to urban folk clubs and college campuses where they appealed to socially conscious intellectuals and cosmopolitans flocking to an earthy alternative to the growing banality of popular music. During the 1950s, the Weavers, a revival folksinging group from New York City, popularized many of the old folk songs before a wider urban audience. They placed songs like "Goodnight Irene" and "Kisses Sweeter than Wine" on pop music surveys. Even as country music left the hills to embrace the image of the West, urban revival groups found success smoothing out the old mountain ballads for popular consumption. In 1958, the Kingston Trio's recording of a North Carolina murder ballad, "Tom Dooley," rode the top of the popular music charts. The success of the group with the song spawned many imitators and some renewed attention to the music's sources. As part of a continuing social concern for depressed areas of the country and a fondness for music that had not been commercialized, a fresh wave of folk song collectors descended on the southern Appalachians to record the pure strains of the common people.

Although much of the attention was pointed south, the Catskills of New York provided an important northern base for the urban folk song revival's interest in "mountain music." At Camp Woodland near Rogers's home, folk song collectors Norman Studer, Norman Cazden, and Herbert Haufrecht had during the 1940s and 1950s introduced folk songs and dances from the Catskills to vacationing New York City children. For this group, the discovery of the region's folk culture and old-time music had a social message for the city dwellers. As Norman Cazden wrote, "Camp Woodland's educational program was an outgrowth of the 1930s and '40s, two decades of turmoil and despair, yet also of renewed hope for the long-delayed fulfillment of the American promise. . . . Many turned to the more sturdy and positive aspects of the folk culture belonging to our optimistic past, for that folk culture had developed in an era in which men and women had believed in themselves, and had sensed some control over their destinies. That culture had blossomed during the age of homespun, during which even people whose outlook was limited by rural and semirural isolation found opportunities to exercise their creative potentials."[11] Norman Studer, director of the camp, recalls how the creative potentials of Rogers became involved with the camp and its folk festival.

> We met Ethel Rogers, Grant's mother, and through her met Grant and his circle of singers, square dance callers and fiddlers. Every summer since a large group of musicians from the Delaware region have come across the mountains to give a lusty and vigorous flavor to the annual Folk Festival of the Catskills. Among them are Marvin Atwell, Don McAdam and Murray Rogers. But Grant was undeniably the star of the group, and the center of every jam session and fiddling bout.[12]

Rogers drew praise from Studer for being "one of the best fiddlers of the Catskills." But when Rogers first played the Folk Festival of the Catskills, he appeared in a cowboy costume and ten-gallon hat. Soon after, Studer convinced Rogers that his old-time music tradition didn't need the western overlay. Studer describes what happened to Rogers's music after that: "The relationship with Camp Woodland and its emphasis on preserving the history and folklore of the Catskills gave Grant's music a new direction. He began to value more highly the kind of songs that related to the life of the region, and to recover forgotten segments of his own musical heritage. Over the years he began to introduce songs with roots in the folk tradition."[13]

Camp Woodland had already made a folk star out of the Catskill singer George Edwards, a charismatic personality with a long ballad repertory. From the likes of George Edwards and Grant Rogers, Studer looked to recapture the vitality of a "generation that knew all the old ballads from England, Ireland and Scotland, could sing them from sun to sun without repeating themselves once, could take these old tunes and shape new words that told stories of men and women of Livingston Manor, Roscoe and Hancock. They were a gabby, hard drinking, fiddling, singing, square dancing lot." "To know Grant Rogers," Studer pointed out, "one must know the tradition of talk and song and fiddling that flourished in the boarding houses of the bark peelers, the grim shacks of the acid factory hands, the saloons that waited at the eddies for the raftsmen who tied up their logs for the night."[14]

"Yeah, way back in them days, when-they-were-rafting days, when they rafted the logs down the river," Grant recalls, and he sings "Jam on Gerry's Rock."

> Come all you jolly river lads, I will have you to draw
>   near
> While I relate the dangers that you're about to hear
> Tis of six jolly Canadian lads who did volunteer to go
> To break the jam on Gerry's Rock with their foreman
>   young Monroe

Twas on a Sunday morning, the sixth day of July
There was a jam on Gerry's Rock, the logs piled
    mountain high
Turn out, turn out, their foreman cried, no dangers now
    to fear
We will will break the jam on Gerry's Rock, and the
    second all will steer

Some of the boys were willing to go while others they
    hung back
To work upon a Sunday they thought it hardly right
Tis of six jolly Canadian lads who did volunteer to go
And break the jam on Gerry's Rock, with their foreman
    young Monroe

They had not rolled off many a log, when their foreman
    did say
I will have you on your guard boys, the jam so will
    give way
His words were scarcely spoken when the jam did break
    and go
And carried away six jolly Canadian lads and their
    foreman young Monroe

And when the rest of the river lads this sad news they
    did hear
In search of their companions to the river they did
    steer
In search of their dead bodies in sorrow, grief, and
    woe
All dead and mangled on the beach was their foreman
    young Monroe

They carried him to the river side as his friends they
    all did stare
There was a maid amongst them whose cries did rend the
    air
There was a maid amongst them, who came from
    Saganaw Town
Her moans and cries did rend the sky for her lover
    young Monroe

This maid she had not long to live, in sorrow and in
    grief
For only three weeks later death come to her relief
Twas only three weeks later that she was called to go
Her last request was granted to be by her young Monroe

Come all you jolly river lads, if you would like to see
A mound down by the river side where grows the hemlock
    tree

37. Jam on Gerry's Rock

Song: Verse, no chorus
♩ = 80–84

Grant Rogers, 1976

A mound down by the river side where a hemlock tree
　　　does grow
You'll see the grave of Clara Brown and your foreman
　　　young Monroe.[15]

Grant pauses and then his eyes sparkle as he says, "Here's one that my dad got
from George Edwards's dad, I got it from him. It was a kind of hand-me-down
thing you know."

Got a job in Susquehanna yard where the work was a buck
　　　a day
Was so hard to make a living that I thought she'd
　　　hardly pay
They said they would raise our wages if they do I won't
　　　complain
If they don't I'll hoist my turkey and I'll hit the
　　　road again

I'll hit the road again boys, hit the road again
Be the weather fair I'll comb my hair and I'll hit the
　　　road again.[16]

38. I'll Hit the Road Again

Grant Rogers, 1976

"They don't sing songs like that anymore," Grant observes, "but they should."

Rogers provided Studer, Cazden, and Haufrecht with many songs that pre-dated his hillbilly repertoire and he reached into the lumbermen's tradition of composing new topical songs that would be sung to old melodies. Many of his songs speak the theme of changes to the old culture of the Catskills. "Pat McBrade" tells of an Irish-American woodsman who witnesses a transformation of his community:

> From me fifty years of loggin'
> I've seen a mighty change;

> From river raft to steamship
> To motor trucks and trains.

"Cannonsville Dam" is a song about the construction of a dam and reservoir being built to provide New York City residents with water. The dam would flood valley residents out of their homes and devour centuries of culture and history. Rogers gives the saga an old ballad treatment:

> Friends just lend an ear and listen,
> While our family friends and neighbors
> Search for a distant land so new;
> We've been told that we must leave our homes
> From this valley we love so dear,
> To make room for the dam they're building here.
>
> When the flood comes to the valley
> Spanning miles from shore to shore
> Then we realize as humans we could have done but little
>   more
> There will be many hearts that's broken
> Among their young as well as old
> For they'll never see the old homes anymore
> For they'll never see the old homes anymore.

Rogers added to this stock of new songs by bringing to the public stage folk songs that had once been reserved for the parlor or lumber camps. He sang traditional ballads such as "The Butcher's Boy" and "Three Nights Drunk" along with occupational folk songs such as "Jam on Gerry's Rock" and "Once More A-Lumbering Go." Nonetheless, Rogers still showed a fondness for songs from the hillbilly repertoire such as Jimmie Rodgers's "Mother the Queen of My Heart" and Vernon Dalhart's "May I Sleep in Your Barn?"

Despite its growing reputation for reinvigorating the old-time traditions of the Catskills, Camp Woodland and its Folk Festival of the Catskills closed during the 1960s. "Sadly," Louis C. Jones, director of the New York State Historical Association, observed, "in the McCarthy years the Studers were hounded out of the Catskills and the camp burned."[17] The efforts of Studer, Cazden, and Haufrecht turned to publishing the collections made around Camp Woodland. The notoriety that Grant Rogers gained from the Folk Festival of the Catskills earned him invitations to other folk festivals and college concerts.

In 1965, folk song collector Sandy Paton recorded Grant Rogers for his Folk-Legacy label. Paton recorded him in his native Walton, New York, where he still held down his stonecutting job. Paton wrote on the sleeve that "Grant Rogers stands as living proof that the art of songmaking still thrives, not only in Greenwich Village, but among the folk themselves." Paton mentioned that Rogers did not consider himself a folksinger, saving that designation for folkniks like Burl Ives or Pete Seeger. Paton released twenty-three musical selections on the album. Of that number five were fiddle tunes and the rest were songs played on guitar. Befitting his folk-revival audience, Paton emphasized Grant's composed

Grant Rogers at Mariposa Folk Festival, Toronto, Canada, 1976 (Simon Bronner)

songs such as "When a Fellow is Out of a Job," "Cannonsville Dam," "Pat McBrade," and "Tales of My Grandad." The fiddle tunes came from the old country dance tradition. He recorded "Larry O'Gaff," "The Little Red Barn," "Rogers' Hornpipe," "Kitty Sharp," and "The Canadian Rose."

In 1970, Rogers recorded another album, but it was aimed at more of an old-time music audience. Entitled "Ballads and Fiddle Tunes By Grant Rogers," the album was recorded for Kanawha Records. One side had six songs taken from the hillbilly repertoire. The other side was devoted to five fiddle tunes and a folk song. The songs were "When the Snowflakes Fall Again," a song taken from bluegrass singer Mac Wiseman, "Two Drummers," an old parlor song, "May I Sleep in Your Barn," taken from the playing of Vernon Dalhart, "Mother The Queen of My Heart," a parlor-styled Jimmie Rodgers song, "Putting on the Style," a folk song recorded by Vernon Dalhart and Carson Robison, "My Bearded Lover," a lumberman's folk song, and "The Weeping Lady," a miner's folk song. The fiddle tunes ranged from tunes that were adapted from traditional melodies such as "Conservation Hornpipe" and "Black Market Reel" to traditional country dance tunes such as "Opera Reel" and "The Little Red Barn." He penned his own notes to the album. In them he reported his roots in the Catskills and his years playing solo on the fiddle and with string bands for dances and radio broadcasts. "Since then," Rogers wrote, "I have participated in several radio and television shows throughout the U.S. and Canada, as well as many different festivals."

When I saw Rogers at his home in 1977, he made a point of telling me that cuts from the Kanawha album could occasionally be heard on a local radio station. But his music now seemed out of place on the radio. The irony for Rogers was that in preserving the old-time sound, he had carried the music away from his community. During the 1970s, I caught up with him again at the Binghamton Folk Festival at the State University of New York at Binghamton and the Mariposa Festival at Toronto, Canada. Upon spying me, he always exclaimed how good it was to see someone from "home." He always received a good reception from the crowd, and then he was alone. He told me more than once that "these kids are too quiet; they don't get up to dance or tell me what to play." Especially when he was far from Walton, he would pause to tell the audience about life in the Catskills. "It's a wonderful place with fishing, hunting, mountains, valleys, and rivers. You've never heard fiddling so fine." As the 1980s began, word of Grant Rogers's death passed around in folk music circles. Notice was made of the loss of an accomplished "songmaker of the Catskills." In Delaware County, old-timers remembered a fine dance fiddler and stonecutter who used to travel out of town.

While Grant Rogers hit the folk festival circuit with his mountain songs, Charley Hughes went western. His group, the Westernaires, has reigned since the 1950s as the best known country and western band in the region. He and the other members of the group who grew up during World War II demonstrate the path into the country and western field taken by sons of the old-time fiddlers. Their world had been opened up by the revolution in electronic communication. Radio, records, and films opened their region to a national culture. They looked

Charley Hughes at home, 1973 (Robert Sieber)

to become part of it, while maintaining the feeling of home and family. The war threw together people from all walks of life and of different tastes. The swingy beat of jazz mixed with the plaintive themes of country. With fewer families growing their food and making their goods, Americans became consumers. The gigantic leap in sales of records, radio sets, prefabricated housing, and processed food signalled the arrival of the consumer culture. For America's rural population which had felt left behind by the industrial culture, the post—World War II prosperity promised them hope of taking their belated place in modern comfort. In the new age of commercialism, music became more specialized. It too was consumed. Bands became less dependent on the family and neighborhood. They became independent organizations. Their titles bespoke restless images—the Westernaires, Ramblers, Rangers, and Driftwoods. No longer strictly commu-

39. Turkey in the Straw

Charley Hughes, 1973

nity dance groups, they were now stage and club acts. They were musical specialists in a growing consumer culture.

Charley Hughes had been reared on the old fiddle music. His father and uncles played for dances and were regular sights at Pop Weir's general store. In addition to the Hughes family, Charley also had the McLean family to count as relatives on his mother's side. Charley was born in Oneonta in Otsego County near the Delaware County line in 1935. Two years later, his father moved the family to a farm in smaller Milford in Otsego County. Some of Charley's first memories are of frolicking house parties at the farm that featured the old-time fiddle music and country dances. "I ate that music up!" Charley exclaims, as he

40. Rubber Dolly Breakdown

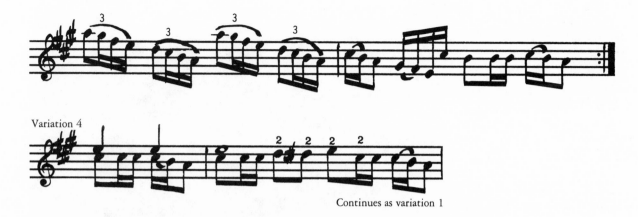

Variation 4

Continues as variation 1

recalls the farmers requesting tunes from the men in his family who all seemed to play the fiddle. He watched his father and uncles with admiration. Learning by ear from them, he took up the fiddle and he soon could reproduce the dance tunes that they played. He spent evenings by the radio listening to the hillbilly hits coming out of Utica, New York, and those further away coming from radio barn dances out of WCKY in Cincinnati, WSM in Nashville, and WWVA in Wheeling. To the fiddle tunes he learned, he added some of the flourishes that were becoming more popular in bluegrass and western swing. He added intermittent double-stopping and playing of open strings which produced harmony and droning at points in the tune. He can show all his flashy new licks and shuffles on top of the old-time fiddling he inherited with an improvisational rendition of "Rubber Dolly Breakdown." To Charley, with the additions the fiddle had a louder, fuller sound. Yet he stayed loyal to the spirit of his family's playing. Picking up the fiddle he typically begins with "Turkey in the Straw" and goes on to old favorites like "Eighth of January" and "Red Wing."

As a teenager, Charley learned to play guitar and memorized the groundbreaking songs that the young Hank Williams put out in the late 1940s. What Vernon Dalhart and Jimmie Rodgers had been to Grant Rogers, Hank Williams was to Charley Hughes. "Mansion on the Hill," "I'm So Lonesome I Could Cry," "Your Cheating Heart," and "Cold, Cold Heart" swept away the hearts of many young singers. Under the careful direction of Acuff-Rose and MGM Records, Williams' stock soared. His fame was not all hype. He had a talent for catchy melodies and rough-edged lyrics that reached for the gut. The themes of his songs had a continuity with the older heart-wrenching songs of the hillbilly period, but he sang with a novel directness about problems of love and marriage. In country music circles he quickly rose from his first appearance on the Grand Ole Opry in 1949 to become the music's premier performer. Unusual for his day, Williams sang mostly his own songs in performance. Sung by popular performers like Tony Bennett, his songs consistently made the crossover to the popular market and paved the way for the post–World War II pop-country mix. Within country music, Williams's recordings highlighted the singer backed by a swingy western beat. It was a formula that helped push the rural music past the hillbilly sound into the country and western period. When Williams died prematurely in 1953, his claim to legend was assured.[18]

"Barefoot" Bob Kinney, c. 1960 (courtesy Bob Kinney)

At the age of sixteen, Charley Hughes began performing in public. He played guitar and fiddle and was joined by a steel guitarist for parties and other social events. After high school he met "Barefoot" Bob Kinney, a hillbilly singer and guitarist who had a popular live radio show on WCHN out of Norwich, New York, in Chenango County. An upstate New York native, Kinney had moved from the Rural Radio Network in Ithaca to Norwich in 1953. His show fitted into the genre associated with Bradley Kincaid's broadcasts. In addition to music, Kinney issued greetings, plugged sponsors, and cracked jokes. Backed by his solo guitar, Kinney sang a hillbilly and old-time selection of songs. He sang the old parlor songs like "There's an Old Spinning Wheel in the Parlor," folk songs like "The Girl I Left Behind Me," hillbilly hits like "When the Roses Bloom Again," and gospel songs like "May the Good Lord Bless and Keep You." In addition to his show, Kinney operated a "hillbilly park" near Bainbridge known as Echo Lake where he would sponsor shows of local musicians. On fiddle and guitar Charley backed the older Kinney on his shows at the park and at high schools

Rhythm Rangers, 1953. Left to right: Eddie Davidovich, Neil Ralston, Clayton Loucks, Charley Hughes, Norm Van Pelt (courtesy Robert Sieber)

through Chenango, Delaware, and Otsego Counties for over a year. From Kinney, Hughes learned to entertain as well as play.

Although popular, Kinney still appeared old-fashioned to Hughes. Hughes wanted to perform some of the newer songs that were appearing on the radio with the swing beat that Williams made a trademark. In 1953, Hughes joined the Rhythm Rangers with Eddie Davidovich, Neil Ralston, Clayton Loucks, and Johnny Van Pelt. They played the Hank Williams songs while still retaining the old fiddle tunes for square dances in their repertoire. From this group, Charley spun off in 1957 to form his Westernaires. The first group had Charley on rhythm guitar, Johnny Van Pelt on steel guitar, Ken Shields on fiddle, and Dick Thompson on bass. The band received regional notice beyond their club appearances when they ably backed the country star Hawkshaw Hawkins on his tour through Central New York. Although the group had invitations to play outside the region, Charley rejected the idea of touring, preferring to work his farm and stay close to his family. In 1960 the band began playing every Saturday at the Bell Hotel (yet another bar given the hotel label) in Schenevus, New York, in Otsego County. With their combination of new hits and old squares played with youthful exuberance, the band became an institution there.

Through the early years of the Westernaires, the band went through many

The original Westernaires, 1957. Left to right: Norm Van Pelt, Dick Thompson, Charley Hughes, Ken Shields (courtesy Robert Sieber)

changes until it settled into a group that had Jimmy Wright on electric guitar, Clifford Fitch on bass, Elden "Speedy" Wyman on fiddle, and Warren Grossman on drums. Other western groups meanwhile proliferated. Dick Thompson left the Westernaires to form his own western group, the Driftwoods, which did a stint at the Wheeling (West Virginia) Jamboree on radio station WWVA, before returning home to hold court at the Butternutts Inn in Garrattsville. The Driftwoods, like the Westernaires, do renditions of the hit country songs as well as calling out the old Yankee squares. Unlike the hillbilly numbers, the hits call for a solo singer and takeoff instrumental breaks. For the Westernaires, Fitch, Wright, and Hughes take turns singing the country hits while Jimmy Wright usually does the square dance calls. Although a talented fiddler, Hughes no longer takes his fiddle out to the band's performances. In public he sticks to rhythm guitar. Wright has become the group's takeoff instrumentalist, and often his amplified guitar takes the lead position the fiddle once had.

The other members of the Westernaires share with Charley Hughes a lineage in the old-time music of the region along with a fondness for the pop country music that came to the fore after World War II. The oldest in the group is Jimmy Wright who was born in Stamford, New York, Delaware County, in 1916. His father was a fiddler and guitarist who played square dances around the county.

Westernaires, 1960. Left to right: Charley Hughes, Norm Van Pelt, Dick Thompson, Elden Wyman (courtesy Robert Sieber)

With his father's encouragement, Jimmy was proficient by the age of ten on the harmonica, guitar, and fiddle. In 1928, he won the title of Delaware County Harmonica Champion. In 1936, he moved to Corning, New York, to find work. His Saturday nights were taken up by dances at the "Old Barn" in Elmira, where Woodhull's Old Tyme Masters were the featured attraction. He listened attentively to their square dance calls and used them in his own repertoire. In 1939, he became a professional entertainer. He joined the Catskill Sodbusters, a hillbilly band that played the Smalley Theater circuit through the Otsego, Chenango, and Delaware Counties region. The band featured banjo, dobro, guitar, fiddle, and harmonica. During World War II, Wright toured army bases with the USO; he was billed as a "Cowboy Country Singer." With the USO, he heard more of the big band jazz that was popular in the country, and he incorporated some of its swinging beat and jazz phrasings into his own playing. After the war he switched to electric guitar and he played lead for a local orchestra. Finding orchestra jobs harder to get because of the tide of rock and roll, Wright moved back into the western field. Wright's abilities on lead guitar became especially important to the Westernaires on the breaks to the new hits. Playing in noisy bars and clubs, the Westernaires used the amplified power of the electric guitar to punch out the melodies of the fiddle tunes when they went through the square dances. Wright also switched to the familiar harmonica for renditions of Johnny

Westernaires at the Bell Hotel, 1965. Left to right: Warren Grossman, Clifford Fitch, Charley Hughes, Jimmy Wright, Norm Van Pelt (courtesy Robert Sieber)

Cash tunes and some square dance numbers. Wright's son, Jimmy Jr., also came in the band to play bass for a period when Clifford Fitch devoted more time to his farm, but after Jimmy Jr. went into the Navy, Fitch again stepped into the bassman's slot.

Clifford Fitch is the youngest member of the Westernaires. He is a steady bass player and he boasts a silky baritone voice. He was born near Burlington Flats in Otsego County in 1945. In his junior year of high school he joined a hillbilly group called "The Horton Valley Boys." After the group disbanded, he played rhythm guitar and sang in Oaksville with the McLean family. He knew the group through his wife who is the niece of Chub McLean. With the McLeans as well as the Westernaires, Fitch called square dances in addition to his crooning. He learned his calls from callers in the region, especially Hubert Hume, who had played with Pop Weir, and Clayton Loucks, of the old Rhythm Rangers group. His singing style, on the other hand, bears a strong resemblance to the sound of country star Jim Reeves. Fitch openly admits his admiration for the Country Music Hall of Famer. A singer who crossed over between popular and country charts, Reeves produced runaway hits such as "Four Walls" and "He'll Have to Go" in 1959–1960. Rather than being an imitation, Fitch's voice delivers Reeves's songs today with heart-tugging sincerity.

Charley Hughes singing at the Bell Hotel, 1973 (Robert Sieber)

The pressures of both running a farm and playing in a popular band have given both Hughes and Fitch second thoughts about continuing the Western-aires. In 1976, after almost twenty years in existence, Hughes considered retiring the band. But soon a call went out for them from the schools in Milford and Cherry Valley, and once again the band came out. "It's certainly not the money," Hughes insists, "because it is hardly enough to cover expenses most of the time." "It's the people. There's got to be something good about it or I wouldn't go down there, then get up the next morning and milk cows on two hours sleep. I'm not worth two hoots on Sundays."

Charley is at home on the same Milford farm that his father occupied. At home, Charley Hughes sits in his favorite chair. A pipe hangs securely from one

Jimmy Wright calling a square dance, 1973 (Robert Sieber)

side of his mouth. He picks up his fiddle and offers his father's "Rubber Dolly Breakdown." He follows with a tune from his generation, Hank Williams's "I Saw the Light." He reflects that his music will be transformed again by the children of his generation. His son is playing guitar and Dick Thompson's son is already playing in his father's band. Under the red lights at the Bell Hotel, I could barely see Charley. He leans up to the microphone and begins "I Gave Up Getting Over You Today," an old Dick Curliss song. He follows with a series of plaintive love songs. He moves through "Don't Be Angry With Me Darling" (a Stonewall Jackson hit) and "Take Me as I Am" (a song written by the famous Nashville songwriting team of Felice and Boudleaux Bryant and popularized by Jimmy Dickens). The crowd sits at tables in packs of two, three, and four. They talk quietly to one another and occasionally throw appreciative glances at Charley. A call then goes out for a square dance and suddenly the crowd comes alive. The lights go up and a ripple of laughter and voices move through the floor. Couples nudge each other and leap from their seats. A few sets are incomplete; a couple raises their hands to invite more dancers. Charley encourages a couple to join

Westernaires calling a Yankee square dance set, Milford, New York, 1977
(Simon Bronner)

them. He waves to a crowd in the corner. They answer his call. Jimmy readies
the crowd. "OK, are we ready to go?" You've been doing this one for a long
time," he chortles. His guitar picks out a familiar strain of "Irish Washerwoman" and he calls them to go "under and over, over and under." The crowd
barely hears him. They go through the movements with a relaxed grace. The
band finishes the tune off and the crowd waits for another. Charley rears his head
and laughs. "Brings you back, don't it?"

The musical conversion of old-time music in the area of Chenango, Otsego, and
Delaware counties is not unique. Over to the west near Elmira and Ithaca—in
Tompkins, Chemung, and Schuyler Counties—the family hillbilly bands had
mostly given up performing during the 1950s. Yet continuity with the old-time
traditions could be heard in the new club acts. Bands like the Boogie Masters
and the Ding-a-lings are the spinoffs from the Dingler and Kouf family groups.

William "Bill" Dingler, the patriarch of the Dingler family, was born in
rural Philipsburg, Pennsylvania, in 1895. When he was seven, his father took
the family to the burgeoning town of Elmira, New York. The town had its fair

Clifford Fitch singing in Milford, New York, 1977 (Simon Bronner)

share of talented old-time fiddlers. Young Bill especially admired Fred Wood-hull. His own fiddling had advanced enough to be called to play house dances in the region. Around 1925, Bill moved back to the country with his wife Josie. He went to her old home of Caroline Center, New York, in Tompkins County. It was a tiny hamlet where the old fiddle music was still fulfilling the old community functions at harvest parties, play-parties, weddings, and quilting bees. Bill soon met Willard Kouf, a prominent fiddler from Newfield, a few miles away. The two played together informally and found that they shared many of the old tunes such as "Money Musk," "Wilson's Clog," and "Devil's Dream."

Willard, born in 1881, had an old-time dance repertoire that he had taught to his young boys. In the late 1920s, Willard had encouraged his talented

William Dingler (center with fiddle) with Ott's Woodchoppers, c. 1930
(courtesy Milo Kouf)

sons to form Ott's Woodchoppers, a hillbilly band. When Willard died in 1933, the boys asked the elder Dingler to fill Willard's slot. Bill played the fatherly role and added authenticity to their renditions of the nineteenth-century dance tunes. Meanwhile, Bill was teaching his own boys the rudiments of the old-time repertoire.

During 1940, Bill left the Woodchoppers to lead his sons in a band. He called the band the Carolinians, named after Caroline Center. Bill played fiddle, Bob played the piano and accordion, George played the upright bass or "bullfiddle," David played the accordion, Don played the guitar, and John played the fiddle. For the next nine years William divided his time between a general store which he managed and his family band. Bill's boys were now working men with families to support, and that along with the dwindling demand for hillbilly groups in the 1950s, scattered the Carolinians. Don left for the city of Binghamton, New York, to find work and he joined a country band that played for local bars. Bob continued playing some of the newer country hits for a three-piece band in Ithaca.

Of Bill's sons, John had the highest musical aspirations. In addition to playing the fiddle, John could handle the upright bass and he could sing the new western hits with a pleasing delivery. He struck out for the Southwest joining up with a band in Texas called the Chaparrals. In the 1970s, John returned to help his brother Bob convert his father's general store into a country music bar called the 76 Bar.

William Dingler, 1977 (Simon Bronner)

John formed the Ding-a-lings with George Dingler on bass, Bob on accordion and piano, Milo Kouf on fiddle and guitar, Denny Dingler, Bill's grand-
son, on guitar, and Terry Carlisle on drums. Shirley Fox, an accordion player and
singer, joined the group later. John is the pivotal figure in the Ding-a-lings. He
creates a strong presence by his radiant personality, powerful fiddling, and long
familiarity with his community. He is constantly joking and calling out to the
crowd as he performs a repertoire of modern country hits, fiddle tunes, square
dances, waltzes, and polkas. The 76 bar sits on what used to be a secluded village
crossroads. The old man, Bill, lives in a house next door. The place is packed
when I sit in on a cool spring night in April of 1977. White middle-aged couples
wearing casual dress dominate the tables. John Dingler comes out on stage in a
gray vest, white shirt, string tie, and western boots. In the dim light I keep notes
on the band's set.

Too Fat Polka—instrumental, two women dance.
It Wasn't God Who Made Honky Angels—vocal duet by Shirley
and John.
Devil's Dream—good audience response. John plays it at a rapid
clip, much faster than the tempo that his father prefers. A young couple
come up afterwards and ask John to play their wedding.

41. Devil's Dream

John Dingler, 1977

Variation 3

Tags:

Flop Eared Mule—John also knows this as D-A Reel. Two women dance. John jokingly says, "Lift your leg up Bessie."

Tennessee Waltz—big turnout of dancers. John tucks fiddle under arm and sings with eyes closed. After the song is finished John yells greetings to someone in audience. John is the only musician to take a solo break.

I Thought I Heard You Calling My Name—another good turnout of dancers for this slow mournful country hit.

Square Dances—John calls for square dancers while playing what he calls "Boiling Cabbage." He encourages specific individuals to find partners. He kiddingly says, "Your husband won't mind!" as a woman dances with another man. As John fiddles the tune, the woman sitting next to me who has recently come to the area from North Carolina leans over and says, "He doesn't do it right." Her companion replies, "You just haven't been here long enough to know."

Lady Round the Lady—"We're going to do one you learned from your parents!" John exclaims.

Promenade in the Moonlight—this dance has one section that re-

John Dingler, 1977 (Simon Bronner)

quires a couple to kiss. Dick Thompson calls this "Kiss in the Dark."[19] John stops the dance at one point and yells at one couple, "You farmer! Do it right! Do it country style!" After they kiss intimately to the enjoyment of the crowd, John yells, "Hold it, hold it! Don't get carried away!" This gets a good laugh. John disperses dancers and tells a joke about a "Polack" who wants a "prophoplastic." After the druggist tells him how much it is, the Polack says, "To hell with it, I'll use Scotch tape."

Darktown Strutter's Ball—John ends set. William Dingler enters bar to see how things are going.

42. Flop-Eared Mule

John Dingler and Milo Kouf, 1977

Bill watches the scene silently. He thinks to himself that the music he taught his boys had been given a dramatic transformation. It was still there, but it was couched between the new hits in a place that had scant resemblance to the farmhouses and halls that Bill knew. John felt some of the tension between the old and new. John competed in the Newfield Old-Time Fiddlers Contest that summer (a contest won by a formally trained student from Cornell University), but he yearned to lead a western band that could make it in Nashville. After Bill Dingler's death a few years later, John leaves Caroline Center behind again, this time headed for work in North Carolina.

Milo Kouf and John Dingler felt close ties through the years. Sharing a bond through their fathers, John would play fiddle while Milo played guitar. Then the other would play bass while the fiddle changed hands. But while Bill Dingler's son felt the lure of success elsewhere, Willard Kouf's boy stayed close to home. After all his years of travelling through New York State with the Woodchoppers, it was probably appropriate that Milo opened an automobile parts business. When his brothers drifted away from the Woodchoppers during the

43. Wilson's Clog

Milo Kouf, 1977

transition years after World War II, Milo found that his guitar work was still in demand among some of the newer groups. He played with a rockabilly group called the Boogie Masters that later developed into a western group and he played for a pop country band called Sophisticated Country. But Milo especially enjoyed the occasional reunion of the Woodchoppers during the 1950s for a rousing encore performance at the Moose, Elk, and Eagles lodges. But Milo was able to keep up with the new sounds more easily than his brothers. "The music really hasn't changed over the years when you stop to look at it. The beat is just a little different. But you know there was something special about those old fiddle tunes." During the 1970s two of his brothers died and one retired to Florida. He too competes in the Newfield Old-Time Fiddlers Contest, a regular feature of Independence Day festivities. Once on stage, he runs through his selections of "Haste to the Wedding" and "Wilson's Clog," two tunes learned from his father, and to the surprise of the judges he engages in some tomfoolery. Two characters dressed outlandishly in outdated clothes pull up his pants and tickle him while he plays. John Dingler and Milo's other cronies get a good laugh out of it, while some of the audience from Cornell don't seem to appreciate what's going on. Rather than contesting one another, the group retires to a van on a knoll beyond the stage. There they share memories and old fiddle tunes. Today, Milo entertains senior citizens centers and family reunions with the old tunes. In his golden years, he has returned to his roots. He shows off his old fiddle that needs no amplification

Milo Kouf during World War II (courtesy Milo Kouf)

44. Farmer Had a Dog

(D tuning)
♩ = 116

Milo Kouf, 1977

to fill a room with dulcet tones. Flowery decorations jump off the neck and his name sweeps across the tailpiece. With a turn of the pegs, he turns back the clock as he demonstrates several non-standard tunings that his father used. Recalling his father, Milo moves easily from a quadrille to a jig to a clog. His daughter has picked up some of the old tunes, but he complains that she doesn't have them down because she didn't learn them the way he did. "She plays them by note rather than by rote; they don't come out sounding old-time."

Playing by ear is a dramatic symbol, rather than a definition, of the old-time sound. It points to the traditional circulation of the old music within the families and communities of upstate New York. Old-time music in the memories of Dorrance Weir, Ken Kane, Grant Rogers, Charley Hughes, John Dingler, and Milo Kouf was a family and community affair. During the hillbilly period, a change occurred from the traditional setting of the old-time music; the music from parlor and dance fused in public performance. Upstaters widened their musical culture during this period through the media. Radio helped bring in songs that had the style of their musical performance and had a bearing on their cultural conditions. After World War II, the old-time music pulled back in performance as music and culture became more nationalized and commercialized. Still, some performers found outlets. Grant Rogers brought his old-time music to a new folk revival audience; Ken Kane invigorated the dance tune and song tradition around his hearth. Others like Charley Hughes and Milo Kouf adapted to the modern sound. Trying to keep up, they eagerly played the new hits, but

45. Crockford's Jig

Milo Kouf, 1977

they found that the old-time music, albeit played with instruments and a tempo that might disturb their elders, still had an important slot in their performances. It signalled the connections between past and present in a changeful world. It allowed them to reach out to one another when commercial entertainment had made them more passive.

Like the hillbilly and western music, the old-time music had derived from popular as well as folk sources but old-time music travelled more through the intimate oral channels that flourished in a family and a work community. Still, the new hillbilly and country songs continued to be treated in the same manner

Shirley Fox, Milo Kouf, and John Dingler, 1977 (Simon Bronner)

as the broadside ballads and comic songs from the minstrel and vaudeville stage. They were incorporated into a communally shared repertoire. Bob Kinney and Grant Rogers used their radio shows to mix both the regional and national cultures and found them compatible. Although commercialism fostered a standard version of country music, it ironically also encouraged regional variations because communities sought to retain their folk imprint on the widely heard music. Areas in Texas, Canada, and Tennessee made their claims to a distinctive brand of the music.[20] In upstate New York, the distinction that was claimed owed to the occupational legacy of farming, lumbering, and railroading and the lineage back to New England Puritan roots. The new country music after World War II made a transition to a more modern sound for a more socially and geographically mobile generation once and twice removed from their secluded rural parents. Although putting them more firmly in the modern world, the modern sound dimly recognized the debt to the old fiddle music and the foundation that their parents had built.

Milo Kouf braves comic visitors to the stage at the Newfield Fiddlers Contest, 1977 (Simon Bronner)

In the move to the hillbilly repertoire, the assembly and domestic traditions met and evolved. In the shift to the western sound, the media loomed large over the influence of the family hearth. The constant reference made by Kane, Hughes, and the others to the mixed influences of the radio and family point to a fundamental social change. The radio and later television opened the homestead to a larger world; it was modern and exciting. The family was the older institution and its hold over youth seemed weakened. The radio symbolized a progressive move toward a national commercial culture. A social pattern underlies the shift from family groups to image-producing band names in country music after World War II. The structure of family relations shifted in the countryside. The decline of the farm economy that stressed family cohesiveness and regional continuity contributed to change. As a result, the value placed on individual preference and mobility upended many of the traditional rural family bonds of upstate New York. There are statistical indications of all this: on average, families became smaller, children left home sooner, and travelled further.[21] But cultural reasons go further. Fewer of the old village crossroads supported independent communities that held families for generations. Fewer children followed the ways of their fathers; they were more oriented toward the future.[22] While the new country hits sang again and again of home and family, the sons and daughters of the old order were coming to grips with their own choices, often far away from home. More and more, country composers wrote love songs that told of the tribulations of finding solace in the precarious world of strangers.

Still, old-time music takes its place in the new order. It celebrates heritage on Independence Day; it brings families together at reunions; it relives one's childhood or culture at dances; it gives a sense of home at quiet times. The old-time masters have not disappeared as the pundits have predicted, but it is true that the masters have become less visible. That's because they usually don't ride in the commercial lane. Still, their music and its youthful associations with family and community emerge frequently from the collective memory of the new generation that grew up during the changeful years of the 1940s. Even dressed in western attire, the symbol of adventurous movement, the new generation will hear an old familiar strain and importantly ask, "Brings you back, don't it?"

Epilogue

FOR A WHILE, it appeared that the line from the house parties to barn dances to hotels that Chub McLean painted would run its downward course. After the brief rush of heritage activity during the American Bicentennial, old-time fiddling was less visible in the late 1970s. More of the old rural "hotels" closed down; fewer fiddling contests were held. After forty years of working with the old fiddlers, even the dean of tune seekers Samuel Bayard noticed during the period that " 'oldtime' fiddlers were feeling rejected, while many young folks were referring to their music as 'that awful corn.' "[1] "I guess we got down on the stuff then," Marjorie Crawford of New Berlin, in Chenango County, New York, tells me. A guitarist with ties to both the old Yankee square dance tradition and the new Nashville sounds, she remembers her defensiveness about the old-time music. "We in the region became more afraid of being old-fashioned. We pushed to be modern. The music was part of it."

That was only part of it. The rural economy and social life that supported a vital regional culture threatened to come apart. Poverty was widespread; farms lay abandoned; new jobs were few. The press published grim predictions of agriculture's future in New York State. Meanwhile, the "living section" carried eye-opening articles on the supposedly last old-time fiddler, or last craftsman, or last general store. There were other signs. Where once pundits harped on the persistence of family traditions, they wrote of the "generation gap" and "embattled family." In response to this time of flux, New York's Regional Conference of Historical Agencies offered a buttressing series of "Dialogues" throughout the region on the cultural background of rural upstate New York. Undoing the forward-rushing rhetoric of the Rockefeller era in New York State politics, a new administration gave the sobering message of belt-tightening and re-tooling. There were ripples that extended to the local level. The State University of New York and the New York State Historical Association shut down the folk culture program at Cooperstown. At the same time, the New York Folklore Society al-

171

most shut down. Barefoot Bob Kinney's once-popular show, one of the last radio broadcasts with a live hillbilly singer, was cancelled by the new modern-thinking owners of Norwich's radio station. Folklorists found residents who were less willing to reveal their old traditional customs. "You might think we're backward," they frequently heard. They wanted to move ahead, and often they moved on.

But something happened in the mid-1980s. Sons and daughters who had left for the cities after high school came back to the country. They demanded to know where their culture had gone. Farmers gave dairying new life by taking other jobs to help support their farms. The "generation gap" became an outworn phrase; one heard more about "roots." New surveys revealed a renewed faith in family life and regional heritage, and as if to prove the point a wave of family reunions hit picnic grounds across upstate New York.[2] A glossy campaign to invigorate tourism in New York State splashed awe-inspiring images of rural Central New York State and its folkways. A new graduate folklore program opened at the State University of New York at Buffalo. Arts councils sponsored exhibitions of folk art that sprung from the soil of the region. New centers for regional folkways sprung up for the "North Country" in Canton, New York, and for the Catskills in Arkville. The learned bastion of the Madison County Historical Society and Fryer Memorial Library held a special evening on "Folk and Country Music in Central New York." Fire halls opened up for square dances again. Reversing his gloomy forecast, Samuel Bayard announced "genuine traditional fiddling . . . seems to be experiencing something very much like a 'comeback,' with higher technical standards than those of former times, and numerous upcoming young players appearing in towns as well as in the countryside."[3]

Dick Thompson, a country music veteran in Central New York, also noticed the trend. His son now takes his position next to his father in the band. Looking at the audience, he observes, "They seem to be going back to the old time tunes, the old time sound," he said.

"Why?" I asked.

"I think they're trying to reach for something that they think people years ago had that they don't have, a contentment that they can't find with all the modern stuff."

Residents also heard a turn from the pop sound of country music on their radios. Bill Knowlton's bluegrass and old-time music show from Liverpool, New York, began broadcasting to a wider radio and, later television, audience in the mid-1980s. The *Country Music Courier* opined, "occasionally, Bill will do a live show and it is so enjoyable to attend these shows and see the local talent we have in Central New York. As Bill says, 'With talent like that who needs Nashville?' "[4] But from Nashville, Ricky Skaggs had a hit with "Uncle Pen," an old Bill Monroe song about an old-time fiddler whose foundation of old-time music gives the young player strength. Skaggs followed that with "Country Boy," a song that celebrated rural roots, and showed the vigor of those roots with a flashy takeoff solo on acoustic guitar. Meanwhile the Judds, a harmonizing family group, had a smash hit with "Grandpa, Tell Me About the Good Ol' Days."[5] More York State entertainers are recording now. Dick Thompson and the Driftwoods put "Second to None" and Art Anderson and the Anderson Family put "I've Been Searchin' in My Dreams" on discs. Coco and the Lonesome Road Band had a regional hit with her "New England Songs." Its lyrics proclaimed, "New England is just as country as Dixie."

To balance these new songs, "Old Songs, Inc." was formed in Guilderland, New York, and in 1980 began sponsoring an annual "Old Songs Festival of Traditional Music and Dance." The old country dances and the old parlor and work songs from New York and New England were featured attractions. No longer insisting that the old-time sound was a southern one, the Ashokan Field Campus of the State University of New York offered a full week of workshops on northern fiddling and country dancing. During 1981, the young New York State Old Tyme Fiddlers Association purchased a building for the "North American Fiddlers Hall of Fame and Museum and a New York State Branch." To draw attention to the music's country roots, the organization put the museum in the rural setting of Osceola, New York. In the old-time music stronghold of Chenango, Otsego, and Delaware Counties, a new organization arose to support traditional music. Known as the "Del-Se-Nango Olde Tyme Fiddlers Association," the group began in 1978 as a spinoff from the New York State Old Tyme Fiddlers Association. It sponsored a Yankee square dance caller's contest, an old-fashioned waltz contest, and a fiddlers festival. During the mid-1980s the group found more and more adherents, many from faraway counties and states. The group explains itself this way: "The purpose of our organization is to preserve, perpetuate, and promote the art of old tyme fiddling as well as keep alive and record for posterity the songs, melodies, and dances of our ancestors. This music was brought to the area by hardy, pioneering people that carved a livelihood from the wilderness, settled and civilized this country. We are endeavoring to maintain this as a part of our heritage."[6] As the membership grew, the list of events expanded. The group's calendar for July and August 1986, for example, read like this:

> July 12–13—Fifth Annual Fiddlers Festival at the Chenango County Fairgrounds; July 19–20—Del-Se-Nango Fiddlers Country Picnic at Arkville; July 25–27—New York State Old Tyme Fiddlers Picnic at Osceola; August 9—Del-Se-Nango Fiddlers Concert at Richfield Springs; August 4—Fiddling at Delaware County Fair; August 16—Square Dance at Margaretville; and August 23–24—Square Dance at Cooperstown.

"These dances," a report in the *Country Music Courier* pointed out, "are something that rural New York used for entertainment prior to the days of improved, faster travel. Neighbors got together, rolled back the rug, danced and helped provide the evening's repast." The piece continued to explain that although contra dancing disappeared by World War II and the popularity of square dancing suffered during the rock and roll period, the "traditional dances" are back, and residents are again thinking of the region as the "Heartland," not backlands, "of the Empire State."[7] Maybe it's because the music provides active entertainment for a health-conscious society, maybe it just prevents life from getting electronically homogeneous and dull; maybe it's because it provides a participatory connection with authentic heritage in the midst of a passive, plastic age; or maybe it gives a sense of community in an overbearing mass culture, a

Del-Se-Nango Old Tyme Fiddlers picnic gathering, 1982. Left to right, kneeling: Butch Minor, Bob Dougherty. Left to right, standing: Bill Pompeii, Ray Lewis, Claude Sherwood, Carl Hedges, John Coss, Bob Jacobs, Stella Kelly, Hilton Kelly, Marjorie Crawford, Dave Scudder, Ernie Shultis (courtesy Marjorie Crawford)

new form of regional pride. For one or all of these reasons old-time fiddling and dancing in New York State is enjoying a resurgence.

This resurgence does not mean that the old order has come back. The new context of association-sponsored contests and picnics has put an organizational structure on what was once a spontaneous family and community setting for old-time music. Associations have taken the lead in maintaining tradition because they connect scattered networks of old-time-music devotees into a cohesive group.[8] The public displays of dance and music are less spontaneous than they once were, but they lack none of the vitality. The associations work at the grass-roots level and often awaken some spontaneous celebrations of the old music within the crossroads communities. In at least one place that I know of, the tiny Otsego County hamlet of Salt Springville, residents pitched in to restore a large Dutch barn which they then used for regular barn dances as well as housing for a food cooperative and community meetings. With this awakening comes a new, more open attitude toward culture. Where once residents might have believed that the new order, including modern commercial music, discards with the old,

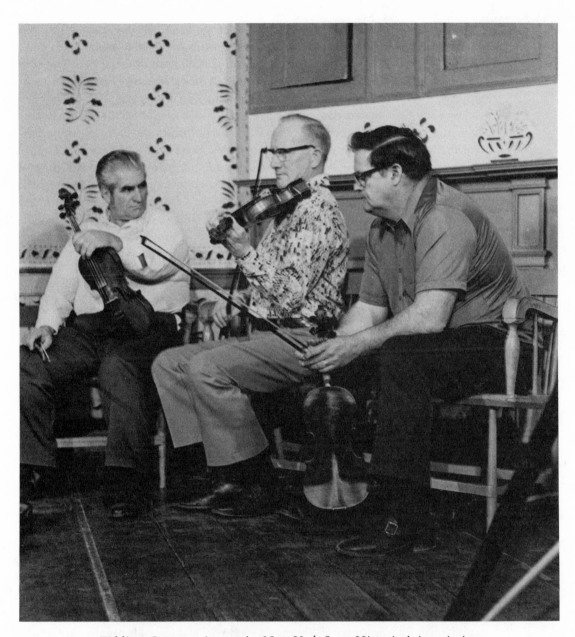

Fiddlers Conversation at the New York State Historical Association, Cooperstown, New York, 1978. Left to right: Bill Shampine from Delhi, Hilton Kelly from Fleischmanns, and Les Weir from Oaksville (courtesy Roderick Roberts)

they have found it possible, indeed desirable, to have the old visible for the new. Residents can listen to a variety of music and appreciate without embarrassment both daddy's folksy fiddling and a slick country star's hits. And with that freedom comes a cultural strength built of variety and continuity.

The recent wave does not have the sponsorship of a looming figure like Henry Ford, but it has found support from the New York State Council on the

Arts, the National Endowment for the Arts, and the National Council for the Traditional Arts. In our mass culture, presenting traditional music holds challenges for our society. It is non-tangible and it is non-commercial. The frequent response of producing festivals can become artificial and impersonal. But some intervention from grass-roots organizations and cultural agencies is necessary to allow the music to breathe in the open air, for traditional fiddling and country dancing are still endangered species. Festivals, exhibits, recordings, and publications sponsored by the new cultural organizations have the significant result of preserving heritage and offering the development of regional understanding and pride. Moreover, they involve people with their communities. They promote the old kind of intimate cultural communication that technological innovations have not provided. With funding from the New York State Council on the Arts, folklorists in Delaware, Onondaga, Allegany, and Wyoming Counties, among others, find new appreciation for their efforts to collect the songs and crafts born of tradition. While these efforts contribute to the preservation of and education from the cultural heritage, other directions see to it that the heritage comes alive and continues to develop. To encourage the perpetuation of old-time fiddling as a living force, an apprenticeship program encourages old-time fiddling masters to pass their knowledge to another generation.[9] Aided by a grant from the National Council for the Traditional Arts, a "Fiddlers' Conversation" took place at the New York State Historical Association at Cooperstown. Traditional fiddlers from throughout the state met to get acquainted and offer their music to townsfolk who had rarely heard it outside of their homes in recent years. "So many people crowded into the tavern to enjoy the music," a report stated, "that at closing time the museum staff had a difficult time trying to coax people out so that the museum could close for the day."[10]

The appeal of the old music has responded time and again to different generations. It has been the tool of nation-makers and community-boosters, industrialists and farmers, fathers and sons. Its cultural role for an agrarian nation has changed, but its lessons remain. Its continuance reminds us of the homespun diversity that exists below mass culture. It reminds us of the need for reaching back into the cradle of our regional cultures, of our families and communities. As much as we speed headlong into the technological future, old-time music still has something to offer. It offers a familiar strain and a continuity of culture. With the helping hand given by fiddlers' organizations, arts councils, and cultural agencies, communities can go beyond regional festivals to reinvigorate the sense of tradition at their crossroads, in their fire halls, in their homes. Or there are simply the quiet personal benefits. Lyle Miles at the ripe age of eighty-four wrote me to announce, "I play on occasion with different local bands (I enjoy that) . . . I feel fine as a fiddle." Ken Kane's daughter now knows more of what her father wrought, and Marjorie Crawford proudly kicks her heels to the lively scrapings of hometown fiddlers. I mourn the loss of John McDermott, Jehile Kirkhuff, Gib Bourne, Pop Weir, Grant Rogers, and William Dingler, but I can pass the word that their craft has not died with them.

Appendix—Tables

Table 1

"Turkey in the Straw" and "Arkansas Traveller" on Edison Records Before 1919

Title-Artist	Number	Date
1. Turkey in the Straw—Billy Golden	Standard Cylinder 8293	Jan.–Feb. 1903
2. Turkey in the Straw Medley—Edison Male Quartet: John Bieling, S. H. Dudley, William F. Hooley, Harry MacDonough	Standard Cylinder 8698	May 1904
3. Turkey in the Straw—Billy Golden and the Empire Vaudeville Company	Diamond Disc 50605	1919
1. Arkansas Traveller—Len Spencer	Standard Cylinder 8202	Oct. 1902
2. Return of the Arkansas Traveller—Len Spencer	Standard Cylinder 10356	May 1910
3. Devil's Dream Medley—Joseph Samuels	Diamond Disc 50653	Nov. 7, 1919

Source: Edison Archives

Table 2
John H. Kimmel on Edison Records

Title	Serial	Date	Diamond Disc No.	Blue Amberol Cylinder No.
Kimmel March	6043	3/4/18	50604	3493
Bonnie Kate Medley Reels*	6044	3/4/18	50604	3577
Connaught Man Medley Jigs	6045	3/4/18	50692	3521
Haste to Wedding Jigs†	7115	1/17/20	50653	4194
Oh Gee-Medley Reels‡	7116	1/17/20	50870	3985
Haley's Fancy Medley Jigs	7117	1/17/20		4076
Homeward March	7118	1/17/20	50674	4111
Stack o' Barley-Medley§	8567	8/11/22	51041	4688
Contentment-Medley‖	8568	8/11/22	51041	
Bryant's Favorite Hornpipe#	18968	12/27/28	52488	
Fitzmaurice's Polka	18969	12/27/28	52488	
Floggan Reel	18982	1/3/29	52499	
The Trip to the Cottage	18983	1/3/29	52499	

*Medley includes "Bonnie Kate," "Green Fields of America," "Swallow Tail."
†Medley includes "Corlairne," "Haste to the Wedding," "Larry O'Gaff."
‡Medley includes "Maid of Kildare."
§Medley includes "Blackberry Blossom," "Green Fields of America.
‖Medley includes "Father Jack Walsh." Title issued as "Contentment is Wealth."
#Guitarist Andy Fiedler replaced regular Joe Linder on the 1928 session.

Source: Edison Archives

Table 3
Joseph Samuels on Edison Records

Title	Serial	Date	Diamond Disc. No.	Blue Amberol Cylinder No.
St. Patrick's Day Medley*	7013	11/7/19	50870	3995
Devil's Dream Medley†	7014	11/7/19	50653	4000
Witch of Wave Medley	7473	8/4/20	50900	4161
Miss Johnson's Party Medley‡	7474	8/4/20	50900	4222
Land of Sweet Erin Medley Erin Medley	7553	9/30/20		4199

*Medley includes "Garry Owen," "Jackson's Fancy," "Moll in the Wad," "Mysteries of Knock," "Tivoli."
†Medley includes "Arkansas Traveller," "Chicken Reel," "Devil's Dream," "Fairy Dance," "Half Penny," "Old Zip Coon."
‡Medley includes "Durang's Hornpipe," "Irish Hornpipe," "Ladies Triumph Hornpipe," "Mississippi Hornpipe," "Saratoga Hornpipe."

Source: Edison Archives

Table 4
Discography of John Baltzell

Master No.	Title	Recording Date	Record No.*
(Fiddle solos, with John F. Burckhardt, piano, New York City)			
9144-A	Money Musk Medley	9/7/23	Ed 51354
9145-A, B, C	Durang Hornpipe Medley†	9/7/23	Ed 51236, 4918
9148-A, C	Old Red Barn Medley Quadrille‡	9/8/23	Ed 51236, 4914
9149-A	Buckeye Medley Quadrille§	9/8/23	Ed 51354
9150-B, C	Farmer's Medley Quadrille‖	9/10/23	Ed 51548
9151-A, C	Drunken Sailor Medley#	9/20/23	Ed 51548, 5454
(Fiddle solos with "Mr. Shields, piano")**			
	Sand Class Reel (two recordings)	6/19/24	unissued
	Pearl Quadrille (two recordings)	6/19/24	unissued
	Ada's Quadrille	6/19/24	unissued
	Levison Reel	6/19/24	unissued
(No piano)			
72613-A	John Baltzell's Reel	June/July '24	Ok 40206 Pa 33094
72614-A	Mandlyn Quadrille Medley	June/July '24	Ok 40206 Pa 33094
7134	Arkansas Traveler††	3/27	Ba 2159, Or 917 Pm 3015, Bw 8051, Hs 16496
7135-2	Turkey in the Straw‡‡	3/27	Ba 2151, Or 945, Hs 16492, Pm 3015, Bw 8052, Cq 7741

(Table 4, cont'd.)

7136	Sailor's Hornpipe	3/27	Ba 2159, Or 945, Hs 16492, Pm 3017, Bw 8051
7137-1	The Girl I Left Behind Me	3/27	Ba 2151, Or 917, Hs 16496, Pm 3017, Bw 8052, Cq 7741

(Burckhardt on piano)

11606	Electric Light Schottische	3/24/27	Ed 51995
11607	London Polka	3/25/27	Ed 51995
11608	Gilderoy's Reel	3/25/27	Ed 52022
11609	Clinton's Quadrille	3/29/27	Ed 52022
11610	Tramp Waltz	3/29/27	5411
11611	Mocking Bird	3/29/27	5362
11612	Sand Reel	3/29/27	unissued
11613	New Century Hornpipe	3/29/27	unissued

(Other)

18378	Ginger Ridge Quadrille[+]	4/28	Ed 52450, 5672
18379	Soldier's Joy Hornpipe[+]	4/28	Ed 52370, 5634
18380	S. J. Rafferty Reel	4/28	Ed 52450
18381	Hills Quadrille	4/28	Ed 52370
18382	Flowers at Edinburgh	4/28	Ed 52313
18383	Wooten Quadrille	4/28	Ed 52425
18384	Emmett Quadrille[+]	4/28	Ed 52281, 5562
18385	Arkansas Traveler[+]	4/28	Ed 52294, 5538
18386	Scotch Reel[§§]	4/28	Ed 52395, 5521
18387	Paddy Ryan's Favorite Irish Jig[§§]	4/28	Ed 52313, 5633
18388	Kenion Clog	4/28	Ed 52281, 5522
18391	Highland Fling	4/28	Ed 52395

| 18392 | Starlight Waltz | 4/28 | Ed 52425, 5703 |
| 18393 | Pandora Waltz | 4/28 | Ed 52294 |

*Abbreviations used are: Ed (Edison Diamond Disc), no prefix (Edison Blue Amberol Cylinder), Bw (Broadway), Cq (Conqueror), Hs (Homestead), Pm (Paramount), Ok (Okeh), Or (Oriole).

†Medley includes "Ohio Hornpipe," "Mountain Hornpipe."

‡Medley includes "Buckboard," "Whiffle Tree."

§Medley includes "Hoosier," "Red Ear."

ǁMedley includes "Cows in the Corn Quadrille," "Kentucky Quadrille."

#Medley includes "Indian Fancy," "Leather Breeches."

**These recordings were made by Victor in New York City at a trial session. No master numbers were assigned and no records were issued from the session. According to discographer Tony Russell who informed me of the session, Mr. Shields "is presumably the Victor house accompanist and conductor Leroy (Roy) Shield" (correspondence of December 6, 1986).

††Broadway labels list Baltzell as John Barton; Homestead and Oriole labels list him as Hiram Jones.

‡‡Some pressings of Cq 7741 (credited to John Baltzell) and Bw 8052 (credited to John Barton) of "Turkey in the Straw" and "The Girl I Left Behind Me" actually carry American Record Company's masters of southerner Doc Roberts's recordings.

§§E. S. C. "Samuel" Schults playing fiddle.

⁺E. S. C. "Samuel" Schults calling calls.

Source: Edison Archives and Tony Russell, *Old-Time Music* Magazine

Table 5
Jasper Bisbee on Edison Records

Title	Serial	Date	Diamond Disc No.	Blue Amberol No.
Money Musk	8794	11/23/23		
Girl I Left Behind Me	8795	11/23/23		
College Quadrille	8796	11/23/23		
Money Musk*	9259	11/24/23	51381	
Girl I Left Behind Me†	9260	11/24/23	51381	
College Hornpipe	9261	11/24/23	51382	
McDonald Reel	9262	11/24/23	51278	4916
Opera Reel (With Calls)	9263	11/24/23	51278	4912

*Label lists title as "Money Musk With Variations."

†Medley includes "Arkansas Traveller," "St. Patrick's Day," "Turkey in the Straw."

Source: Edison Archives

Table 6
Mellie Dunham's Repertoire Compared with "New York's Favorite Tunes"

"Mellie" Dunham's Fiddlin' Dance Tunes*	"New York's Favorite Tunes"†
1. Rippling Waves Waltz	1. Arkansas Traveller
2. Happy Hours Waltz	2. Bonnie Dundee
3. Norway Schottische	3. Captain Jinks
4. Haywood Schottische	4. Coming Through the Field
5. The Little Stack of Barley	5. Delaware Hornpipe
6. Old Zip Coon	6. Devil's Dream
7. Arkansas Traveler	7. Dick Sand's Hornpipe
8. Turkey in the Straw	8. Durang's Hornpipe
9. The Ripple	9. Emerald Isle
10. Irish Washerwoman	10. Emigrant's Reel
11. The Tempest	11. First Two Gents-Square Dance
12. Fisher's Hornpipe	12. Fisher's Hornpipe
13. Chorus Jig-Square Dance	13. Flogging Reel
14. Portland Fancy	14. Flower of Donnybrook
15. Boston Fancy-Square Dance	15. Flower of Edinburgh
16. Durang's Hornpipe	16. Galway Reel
17. Lamp Lighter's-Hornpipe	17. Garry Owen
18. Hull's Victory-Hornpipe	18. Girl I Left Behind Me
19. Liverpool-Hornpipe	19. Golden Slippers
20. McDonald's Reel	20. Haste to the Wedding
21. Rustic Reel	21. Highland Fling
22. Pop Goes the Weasel	22. Irishman's Heart to the Ladies
23. Jingle Bells-Galop	23. Irish Washerwoman
24. Old Times-Schottische	24. Kerry Dance
25. Rory O'More-Jig	25. Kingdom Coming
26. Larry O'Gaff-Jig	26. Lamplighter
27. St. Patrick's Day in the Mornin'	27. Larry O'Gaff
28. Money Musk	28. Little Brown Jug
29. Rakes of Mallow	29. Liverpool Hornpipe
30. White Cockade	30. Low-Back Car
31. Soldier's Joy	31. Marching Through Georgia
32. The Devil's Dream	32. McDonald's Reel
33. Fred Wilson's Clog Dance	33. Miss McLeod's Reel
34. Ned Kendall's Hornpipe	34. Money Musk
35. Miss McLeod's Reel	35. Moonlight Clog
36. Girl I Left Behind Me	36. My Love is But A Lassie Yet
37. Forest de Bondi-Square Dance	37. New Century Hornpipe
38. Lannigan's Ball	38. Oh Susanna
39. Haste to the Wedding	39. Old Crow
40. Speed the Plough	40. Old Rosin the Bow (Beau)
41. Over the Waves-Waltz	41. Opera Reel

(Table 6, cont'd.)

42. Mountain Hornpipe
43. Buy a Broom-Waltz
44. Seaside Polka
45. Steamboat Waltz
46. Old Southern Waltz
47. Eliot's Schottische
48. Varsovienne
49. Heel and Toe Polka
50. Do You See My New Shoes-Varsovienne

42. Paddy Whack
43. Pop Goes the Weasel
44. Praties are Dug
45. Rakes of Mallow
46. Rickett's Hornpipe
47. Rory O'Moore
48. Sailor's Hornpipe
49. Soldier's Joy
50. Speed the Plough
51. St. Patrick's Day in the Morning
52. Ta-ra-Ra-Ra Boom De Ay
53. Top of Cork Road
54. Turkey in the Straw
55. Virginia Reel
56. White Cockade
57. Wind that Shakes the Barley

*This heading is the title of a book published in 1926 by Carl Fischer, Inc. "Rippling Waves Waltz," "Happy Hours Waltz," "Norway Schottische," and "Highway Schottische" are apparently Dunham's compositions while the others are older or traditional tunes. According to Paul Wells, the list "is a good grouping of standard New England tunes, and probably represents Mellie's repertoire fairly well."

†In response to an inquiry to the *New York Folklore Quarterly* in 1952 about New York's favorite fiddle tunes, Editor Louis C. Jones published this list given by Lettie Osborne of Orange County, New York, who learned the tunes traditionally (vol. 8, pp. 213–15). Although some Tin Pan Alley tunes creep into her list and although the list shows some personal preferences, the repertoire shows remarkable continuities with Dunham's New England repertoire. They share at least twenty-three tunes. The same number of tunes is shared between Dunham's list and a list compiled by musicologist Norman Cazden in *Dances from Woodland: Square Dances from the Catskills* (1955).

Table 7
Discography of Mellie Dunham

Title	Date	Master No.	Victor Record No.
Chorus Jig (With Calls)	1/19/26	34338-1	Vi 40131
Lady of the Lake* (With Calls)	1/19/26	34339-2	Vi 19940
Mountain Rangers† (With Calls)	1/19/26	34340-3	Vi 19940
Hull's Victory (With Calls)	1/19/26	34341-1	Vi 40131
Boston Fancy (With Calls)	1/19/26	34344	unissued
Boston Fancy‡ (With Calls)	1/26/26	34344-7	Vi 20001
Rippling Waves Waltz	1/26/26	34440-2	Vi 20001
Medley of Reels‖	2/3/26	34440-4	Vi 20537
Medley of Reels§	2/3/26	34528-4	Vi 20537

*The title on label may refer to a dance that is being called rather than the fiddle tune; the tune is "Portsmouth Hornpipe." This recording and the others on 1/19/26 took place in New York City. The personnel on all of Dunham's recordings is Dunham, fiddle; M. A. Noble, violoncello; Cherrie Nobel (Dunham's granddaughter), piano.

†The tune on the recording is "Haste to the Wedding."

‡The tune on the recording is "The Tempest"; the recording along with "Rippling Waves Waltz" was made in Camden, New Jersey. The recording of "The Tempest" was also issued as part 2 of "Barn Dance on the Mountain" (MW M-8137); part 1 was a number by the Crook Brothers String Band.

‖The two medleys recorded on this day include "Miss McCloud's Reel," "White Cockade," "Johnny Coakley," and "Irish Washerwoman" (actually a jig), "Lannigan's Ball," "Campbells are Coming." The first medley was recorded in New York City.

§Brian Rust reports in *The Victor Master Book* that this recording was made in Camden, New Jersey, but in his discography of Dunham, Paul Wells states that "it seems unlikely that Dunham recorded in both New York and Camden on the same day, especially since he also had to play a date in Newark, New Jersey, that day.

Source: Paul Wells, *John Edwards Memorial Foundation Quarterly*, No. 43, 1976.

Table 8
Chronology of the Performing Bands for the Woodhull Family

Date	Personnel
1. 1896–1916	Fred Woodhull: fiddle Elizabeth Woodhull: guitar, vocals
2. 1916–1928	Fred Woodhull: fiddle Floyd Woodhull: piano, accordion, vocals *Billy Held: steel guitar *Herb Woodhull: harmonica
3. October 1928–late 1940	"Woodhull's Old Tyme Masters" Fred Woodhull: fiddle Herb Woodhull: plectrum banjo John Woodhull: guitar Floyd Woodhull: accordion, degan bells, vocals John Taggart: bass
4. 1941–1947	"Woodhull's Old Tyme Masters" Ransom Terwilliger: fiddle Herb Woodhull: plectrum banjo John Woodhull: guitar Floyd Woodhull: accordion, degan bells, organ, vocals *Tommy Wood: guitar (replacing John Woodhull)
5. 1947–1949	"Woodhull's Old Tyme Masters" Eddie Pettingill: fiddle Herb Woodhull: plectrum banjo Carl Zagadusky: guitar John Taggart: bass Floyd Woodhull: accordion, degan bells, organ, vocals
6. 1949–July 1953	"Woodhull's Old Tyme Masters" Eddie Pettingill: fiddle Herb Woodhull: plectrum banjo Carl Zagadusky: guitar Bob Regan: bass Floyd Woodhull: accordion, degan bells, organ, vocals
7. July 1953–1983	"Sammy and Woody" Sam Rossi: drums and vocals Floyd Woodhull: accordion, organ, vocals
8. 1975–1981	"Floyd Woodhull with the McNett Family" Eddie Pettingill: fiddle Kenny Marsh: bass Dean McNett: banjo Bob McNett: guitar

*Sometimes appearing

Table 9
Discography of Woodhull's Old Tyme Masters and Floyd Woodhull

---

1. "Woodhull's Old Tyme Masters," Band 4 (see Table 8 for personnel). Recorded in New York City, Studio #2, 9 A.M. to 12 noon, 14 July 1941. Released in 1948 on four 10-inch 78 rpm discs. Reissued in August 1952 as RCA Camden LP CAL 220 with new serial and release numbers assigned. In the table below, for every title the numbers on the same line are those assigned in 1941. Those on the line below are those assigned in 1952.

Master No.	Title	Release No.	Album No.
CS 066812-1	Oh Susanna	36400A	C36-1
DIVC-0076-1		E4DP-6238	
CS 066813-1	Pop Goes the Weasel	36400B	C36-2
DIVC-0080-1		E4DP-6238	
CS 066814-1	Captain Jinks	36401A	C36-3
DIVC-0077-1		E4DP-6238	
CS 066815-1	Wearing of the Green	36401B	C36-4
DIVC-0079-1		E4DP-6238	
CS 066816-1	The Girl Behind Me	36402A	C36-5
DIVC-0078-1		E4DP-6238	
CS 066817-1	Triple Right and Left Four	36402B	C36-6
DIVC-0081-112		E4DP-6239	
CS 066818-1	Blackberry Quadrille	36403A	C36-7
DIVC-0013		E4DP-6239	
CS 066819-1	Soldier's Joy	36403B	C36-8
DIVC-0012-1		E4DP-6239	

2. "Woodhull's Old Tyme Masters," Band 6 (see Table 8 for personnel). Recorded in New York City, 1949, master numbers not known. Released on three 12″ 78 rpm discs in 1950 (Album No. DC 45) and also on three 45 rpm discs. The number for the 45 rpm discs appears below the 78 rpm release number. All the selections from this session with the exception of "Take Me Out to the Ballgame" and "The Bum Song" appeared on the second side (E4DP-6239) of the RCA Camden LP released in 1952.

Title	Release No.
Take Me Out to the Ball-game	28-0439A
	48-0156A
Ann Green	28-0439B
	48-0156B
The Bum Song	28-0438A
	48-0155A
Bloom is on the Sage	28-0438B
	48-0155B
Irish Washerwoman	28-0437A
	48-0154B
Pony Boy	28-0437B
	48-0154B

3. "Woodhull's Old Tyme Masters," *Square Dance Party* (Library of International Folk Dances, Volume 18), Band 6 (see table 9), Folkraft records. Recorded in Newark, New

(Table 9, cont'd.)

Jersey, in 1950. Released on three 10-inch 78 rpm records in 1950.

Master No.	Title	Record No.
KW 324	Hinky Dinky Parley Voo	F 1023A
KW 325	Last of the Lancers	F 1023B
KW 326	Forward All-Kick in the Middle	F 1024A
KW 327	Wabash Cannonball	F 1024B
KW 328	Hot Time	F 1025A
KW 329	Promenade in the Moonlight	F 1025B

4. "Floyd Woodhull," *Called Square Dances,* Folkraft LP-7, Accordion-Floyd Woodhull, guitar-Frank L. Kaltman, fiddle-James Hammond, unidentified banjo and bass. Master numbers unknown, 12-inch 33 rpm record. In interviews, Floyd Woodhull recalled that the sides were recorded and released in 1952. At the bottom of the record purchased in the 1960s are the words "Golden Anniversary," and the notes indicate that they refer to fifty years in Woodhull's career. That would place the second release date at 1966.

Title	Record No.
Where Do We Go From Here	F-LP-7A-1
Nellie Bly	F-LP-7A-2
The Old Pine Tree	F-LP-7A-3
Casey Jones	F-LP-7A-4
Lady Round the Lady	F-LP-7A-5
Bum Song	F-LP-7B-1
Take Me Out to the Ball Game	F-LP-7B-2
Pony Boy	F-LP-7B-3
The Bloom is on the Sage	F-LP-7B-4
The Old Apple Tree	F-LP-7B-5

5. "Floyd Woodhull," *Called Square Dances, Volume II,* Folkraft LP-30, 12-inch 33 rpm record. The second of the Golden Anniversary records was also thought to be recorded in 1953, and it was probably also re-released in 1966. Master numbers unknown. Personnel same as for LP-7.

Title	Record No.
New York Star	F-LP-30A-1
Around the Corner	F-LP-30A-2
Red Wing	F-LP-30A-3
Nellie Gray	F-LP-30A-4
John Brown's Body	F-LP-30A-5
Little Log Cabin	F-LP-30B-1
Two Little Girls in Blue	F-LP-30B-2
Four Way Star	F-LP-30B-3
Sashay By Your Partner	F-LP-30B-4
Bird in the Cage	F-LP-30B-5

Notes to the Chapters

Preface

1. The relationship of old-time music to traditional fiddling is evident from Michael Mendelson, "A Bibliography of Fiddling in North America" *John Edwards Memorial Foundation Quarterly* 11 (1975): 104–11, 153–60, 201–4, and 12 (1976): 9–14, 158–64; see also the chapter "Old-Time Music" in Douglas B. Green, *Country Roots: The Origins of Country Music* (New York: Hawthorn Books, 1976), pp. 19–48, and the introduction in R. P. Christeson, *The Old-Time Fiddler's Repertory* (Columbia: University of Missouri Press, 1973). Recordings of "old-time music" also emphasize fiddling: see anthologies such as *The Wonderful World of Old Time Fiddlers,* 2 vols. (Vetco 104, 106), and *Old Time Fiddle Classics* (County 514), and the listing under "old-time music" in Dean Tudor and Nancy Tudor, *Grass Roots Music* (Littleton, Colorado: Libraries Unlimited, 1979), pp. 101–40. For attempts at the definition of "old-time music," see Robert E. Nobley, "What is Old Time Music?" *Devil's Box,* no. 20 (1 March 1973): 19–20; Nowell Creadick, "What is Old Time Music?" *Devil's Box,* no. 21 (1 June 1973): 2–3. Although old-time music is a generally recognizable category, residents of some other states may understand the meaning of "old-time music" slightly differently than New Yorkers, who associate it most closely with the old Anglo-American dance tradition. I have used the term because it is familiar to residents and scholars alike, and as Neil Rosenberg points out in *Bluegrass: A History* (Urbana: University of Illinois Press, 1985), "there were many similarities, enough so that individuals raised on the old-time music of one region could appreciate and recognize at least some parts of the old-time music of another region" (p. 19). The use of "old-time music" to refer to the playing, and especially fiddling, associated with country dances dates at least to 1895; see N. H. Allen, "Old Time Music and Musicians," *Connecticut Quarterly* 1 (1895): 368–73. According to the *Oxford English Dictionary,* the use of "old-time" standing for something old-fashioned was especially pronounced in the United States. Supporting the argument that "old-time music" came to represent rural values to an industrializing country is that the dictionary places this use to the height of American industrialization end of the nineteenth century with four references between 1882 and 1894.

2. Bill C. Malone, *Country Music, U.S.A.: A Fifty Year History* (1968; rev. ed., Austin: University of Texas Press, 1985); Charles K. Wolfe, *Tennessee Strings: The Story of Country Music in Tennessee* (Knoxville: University of Tennessee Press, 1977) and *Kentucky Country: Folk and Country Music of Kentucky* (Lexington: University Press of Kentucky, 1982); Ivan M. Tribe, *Mountaineer Jamboree: Country Music in West Virginia* (Lexington: University Press of Kentucky, 1984). The

approach that I take comes from my training in folklore and American studies; it works on the role of folk and popular culture in American civilization and uses interdisciplinary methods. My aim is to set old-time music in a cultural and historical context; see Simon J. Bronner, " 'I Kicked Three Slats Out of My Cradle First Time I Heard That': Ken Kane, Country Music, and American Folklife," *New York Folklore* 3 (1977): 53–81; Charles Wolfe, "Toward A Contextual Approach to Old-Time Music," *Journal of Country Music* 5 (1974): 65–75; Patricia Averill, "Can the Circle Be Unbroken: A Study of the Modernization of Rural Born Southern Whites Since World War I Using Country Music" (Ph.D. diss., University of Pennsylvania, 1975).

3. Simon J. Bronner, *Chain Carvers: Old Men Crafting Meaning* (Lexington: University Press of Kentucky, 1985) and *Grasping Things: Folk Material Culture and Mass Society in America* (Lexington: University Press of Kentucky, 1986). See also Simon J. Bronner, ed., *American Material Culture and Folklife* (Ann Arbor: UMI Research Press, 1985); John Michael Vlach and Simon J. Bronner, eds., *Folk Art and Art Worlds* (Ann Arbor: UMI Research Press, 1986).

Chapter 1—Strike Up a Familiar Strain

1. For more discussion of the distinct geographic features that help make Central New York State a natural region, see John H. Thompson, ed., *Geography of New York State* (Syracuse: Syracuse University Press, 1966; rev. ed. 1977). The observation by James Fenimore Cooper comes from *The Pioneers, or The Sources of the Susquehanna* (1859; rpt. ed., New York: New American Library, 1964), p. 13.

2. Ulysses Prentiss Hedrick, *A History of Agriculture in the State of New York* (1933; rpt. ed., New York: Hill and Wang, 1966), p. 90.

3. Arthur C. Cole, "The Puritan and Fair Terpsichore," *Mississippi Valley Historical Review* 29 (1942): 3–34. See also Philip J. S. Richardson, *The Social Dances of the Nineteenth Century in England* (London: Herbert Jenkins, 1960); S. Foster Damon, *The History of Square Dancing* (Barre, Mass.: Barre Gazette, 1957), pp. 1–31; Charles Hamm, *Music in the New World* (New York: W. W. Norton, 1983), pp. 65–76; Paul Wells, *New England Traditional Fiddling* (John Edwards Memorial Foundation JEMF-105, 1978), pp. 1–6; Richard Nevell, *A Time to Dance: American Country Dancing from Hornpipes to Hot Hash* (New York: St. Martin's Press, 1977), pp. 32–39. For samples of the music and dance from the late eighteenth century, see Kate W. Keller and Ralph Sweet, *A Choice Selection of American Country Dances of the Revolutionary Era* (New York: Country Dance and Song Society, 1975); for performed examples from Keller and Sweet's book, listen to Rodney Miller's recording of the "country fiddle" on *Instrumental Dance Music 1780s–1920s* (New World Records NW 293, 1978).

4. June Biggar, "The Journal of Richard Weston (1836): An Example of Foreign Travel Literature as Source Material in Folklife Studies" (M.A. thesis, Cooperstown Graduate Programs, 1974), p. 187.

5. Willis King, *Stories of a Country Doctor* (Philadelphia: Hummel and Parmele, 1891), p. 48.

6. David Winslow, "The Rural Square Dance in the Northeastern United States: A Continuity of Tradition" (Ph.D. diss., University of Pennsylvania, 1972), p. 93. "Skimmelton" dances and tunes are included in Norman Cazden, *Dances from Woodland: Square Dances from the Catskills* (Ann Arbor, Mich.: Cushing-Malloy, 1955), p. 40. A "shivaree" is described in Ellen Gray Massey, *Bittersweet Country* (Garden City, N.Y.: Doubleday, 1978), pp. 230–32. See also, E. Bagby Atwood, "Shivarees and Charivaris: Variations on a Theme," *Publications of the Texas Folklore Society* 32 (1964): 64–71.

7. Letter from Atwood Manley, 19 March 1976. For the background of fiddling and dance in Manley's home county, see Robert D. Bethke, "Old-Time Fiddling and Social Dance in Central St. Lawrence County," *New York Folklore Quarterly* 30 (1974): 163–84. The "kitchen junket" and rural dance in New England and New York State similar to the one that Manley remembers is also described in Nevell, *A Time to Dance,* pp. 38, 93–95; for a re-creation of the music from Yankee junkets, listen to Yankee Ingenuity, *Kitchen Junket* (Fretless 200A).

8. The photograph of a Christmas sleigh ride party and country dance is from the col-

lection of David Winslow, Oswego, New York, who gave permission for its use. Despite some clerical objections during the eighteenth century, Christmas was traditionally a time to hold a community dance. For recorded examples, see Damon, *History of Square Dancing*, pp. 4, 22, 28.

9. Alfred Frankenstein, *William Sidney Mount* (New York: Harry N. Abrams, 1975), p. 79; Janice Gray Armstrong, ed., *Catching the Tune: Music and William Sidney Mount* (Stony Brook, N.Y.: The Museums at Stony Brook, 1984).

10. Martin Welker, *Farm Life in Central Ohio Sixty Years Ago* (Wooster, Ohio: Clapper's Print, 1892), pp. 49–50. See also, Howard Sacks, Jeff Goehring, and Susan Colpetzer, "Traditional Fiddling in Ohio History," especially the section on "Fiddle Music on the Frontier," pp. 1–2, included in *Seems Like Romance to Me: Traditional Fiddle Tunes from Ohio* (Gambier Folklore Society, GFS 901, 1985). For a later chronicle of old-time music carried along the Yorker path of migration to the Midwest, see James P. Leary, "Old Time Music in Northern Wisconsin," *American Music* 2 (1984): 71–87.

11. Hamlin Garland, *A Son of the Middle Border* (New York: Macmillan, 1917), p. 94.

12. For "Haste to the Wedding," see William Chappell, *A Collection of National English Airs* (London: Chappell, 1840), I, no. 163; Cecil J. Sharp, *Country Dance Tunes* (London: Novello, 1909), pp. 8–9; Samuel Preston Bayard, *Hill Country Tunes: Instrumental Folk Music of Southwestern Pennsylvania* (Philadelphia: American Folklore Society, 1944), no. 22 and *Dance to the Fiddle, March to the Fife: Instrumental Folk Tunes in Pennsylvania* (University Park: Pennsylvania State University Press, 1982), pp. 420–28, 585–86; R. P. Christeson, *The Old-Time Fiddler's Repertory* (Columbia: University of Missouri Press, 1973), tune no. 167; Peter Kennedy, *The Fiddler's Tune-Book* (New York: Hargail Music Press, 1951), p. 40; Eloise Hubbard Linscott, *Folk Songs of Old New England* (New York: Macmillan, 1939), pp. 87–89; Miles Krassen, *Appalachian Fiddle* (New York: Oak Publications, 1973), p. 86; Maud Karpeles and Lois Blake, *Dances of England and Wales* (New York: Chanticleer Press, 1951), pp. 26–28; "Haste to the Wedding," *Journal of the English Folk Dance and Song Society* 3 (1938): 208–10; Alan Jabbour, *American Fiddle Tunes from the Archive of Folk Song* (Washington, D.C.: Music Division, Library of Congress, Album AFS L62, 1971), pp. 9–10. For "Hull's Victory," see Linscott, *Folk Songs of Old New England*, pp. 86–87; Wells, *New England Traditional Fiddling*, p. 20; Jabbour, *American Fiddle Tunes*, pp. 12–13; *Gems of the Ball Room, No. 8* (Chicago: E. T. Root and Sons, 1899), no. 9; Harold W. Thompson, *A Pioneer Songster: Texts from the Stevens-Douglass Manuscripts of Western New York, 1841–1856* (Ithaca, N.Y.: Cornell University Press, 1958), pp. 118–20; Dudley T. Briggs, *Thirty Contras from New England* (Burlington, Mass.: Dudley T. Briggs, 1953), pp. 69–71; Robert W. Neeser, *American Naval Songs and Ballads* (New Haven: Yale University Press, 1938), p. 95; John Harrington Cox, *Folk-Songs of the South* (Cambridge, Mass.: Harvard University Press, 1925), p. 257; Joanna C. Colcord, *Songs of American Sailormen* (New York: W. W. Norton, 1938), p. 130; John Anthony Scott, *The Ballad of America* (New York: Bantam Books, 1966), pp. 108–10; Anne Schley Duggan, Jeanette Schlottmann, and Abbie Rutledge, *Folk Dances of the United States and Mexico* (New York: Ronald Press, 1948), pp. 71–74; Elizabeth Burchenal, *American Country Dances* (New York: G. Schirmer, 1918), pp. 30–31; Mellie Dunham, *"Mellie" Dunham's Fiddlin' Dance Tunes* (New York: Carl Fischer, 1926), tune no. 18.

13. Olive Dame Campbell and Cecil J. Sharp, *English Folk Songs from the Southern Appalachians* (New York: G. P. Putnam's Sons, 1917); Emelyn Gardner, *Folklore from the Schoharie Hills, New York* (Ann Arbor: University of Michigan Press, 1937). Gardner's book was based on fieldwork conducted in 1912. Sharp's collection gave the impression that the Appalachian culture stopped at the Pennsylvania border, although he noted that his cut-off at the Pennsylvania border was arbitrary; for a continuation of the collection north, see Henry W. Shoemaker, *Mountain Minstrelsy of Pennsylvania* (rev. ed., Philadelphia: Newman F. McGirr, 1931); Samuel Preston Bayard, "The British Folk Tradition," in *Pennsylvania Songs and Legends*, ed. George Korson (Philadelphia: University of Pennsylvania Press, 1949), pp. 17–61. Other field collections of British ballads in New York and New England are reported in Norman Cazden, Herbert Haufrecht, and Norman Studer, *Folk Songs of the Catskills* (Albany: State University of New York Press, 1982); Phillips Barry, Fannie Hardy Eckstorm, and Mary Winslow Smyth, *British Ballads from Maine* (New Haven: Yale University Press, 1929); Helen Hartness Flanders, *Ancient Ballads Traditionally Sung in New England* (Philadelphia: University of Pennsylvania Press, 1965); Helen Hartness

Flanders, Elizabeth Flanders Ballard, George Brown, and Phillips Barry, *The New Green Mountain Songster: Traditional Folk Songs of Vermont* (Hatboro, Pennsylvania: Folklore Associates, 1966); Helen Hartness Flanders and Marguerite Olney, *Ballads Migrant in New England* (1953; rpt. ed., Freeport, N.Y.: Books For Libraries Press, 1968). See also, Tristram Potter Coffin, *The British Traditional Ballad in North America* (rev. ed., Austin: University of Texas Press, 1977). For an insightful commentary on the neglect of the trove of northeastern folk singing, see Robert D. Bethke, "New England Singing Tradition," *Journal of American Folklore* 97 (1984): 466. For background on Sharp's collecting in the southern Appalachians, see Tony Scherman, "A Man Who Mined Musical Gold in the Southern Hills," *Smithsonian* 16 (April 1985), 173–96; David E. Whisnant, *All That Is Native & Fine: The Politics of Culture in an American Region* (Chapel Hill: University of North Carolina Press, 1983), pp. 113–27. See also, D. K. Wilgus, *Anglo-American Folksong Scholarship since 1898* (New Brunswick, N.J.: Rutgers University Press, 1959).

14. G. Malcolm Laws in *Native American Balladry* (rev. ed., Philadelphia: American Folklore Society, 1964) recognizes the wide circulation of the ballad "Mary Wyatt" by assigning it a place in his canon as F14 "Henry Green (The Murdered Wife)," where he cites a dozen versions of the ballad collected from oral tradition. The version of "Mary Wyatt" printed here comes from Louis C. Jones, "The Berlin Murder Case," in *Three Eyes on the Past: Exploring New York Folk Life* (Syracuse: Syracuse University Press, 1982), pp. 97–110. Harold Thompson in *Body, Boots, and Britches: Folktales, Ballads and Speech from Country New York* (1939; rpt. ed., Syracuse: Syracuse University Press, 1979), devotes an entire chapter to murder ballads including "Mary Wyatt" in the oral tradition of New York State (pp. 427–48). "Murder in Cohoes" comes from a broadside I found in the possession of Ken Kane, Hartwick, New York. He told me that the broadside was given to him by his father. Other versions from oral tradition collected in Troy and Castleton, New York (c. 1930s), are found in the Harold Thompson Collection (New York State Historical Association, Cooperstown). Originally set in Wilbraham, Massachusetts, in 1761, "Springfield Mountain" tells the story of a farmer's son who is bitten by a rattlesnake while mowing his father's field. No one comes to his aid despite his desperate cries and he tragically dies. The moral message of this ballad is usually carried by the verse "May this a warning be to all, To be prepared when God doth call." Laws lists "Springfield Mountain" as G16 (pp. 213–14) and cites five sources for the ballad stretching from New England across to Ohio. For a variant from New York State, see Anne Warner, *Traditional American Folk Songs from the Anne and Frank Warner Collection* (Syracuse: Syracuse University Press, 1984), pp. 91–92.

15. See Warner, *Traditional American Folk Songs*, pp. 76–78, 104–106, 112–13; Cazden, Haufrecht, and Studer, *Folk Songs of the Catskills;* Thompson, *Body, Boots and Britches*, pp. 220–83; Robert D. Bethke, *Adirondack Voices: Woodsmen and Woods Lore* (Urbana: University of Illinois Press, 1981), pp. 55–79; Edith E. Cutting *Lore of an Adirondack County* (1944; rpt. ed., Elizabethtown, N.Y.: Denton Publications, 1972). The extent of the folk singing tradition is evident from Joseph C. Hickerson and William Thatcher, comps., "A Brief List of Material Relating to New York State Folk Music" (Washington, D.C.: Archive of Folk Song, Library of Congress, 1975).

16. For discussions of nineteenth-century brass bands, see H. W. Schwartz, *Bands of America* (Garden City, N.Y.: Doubleday, 1957); Charles Hamm, *Music in the New World*, pp. 279–306; Alan C. Buechner, "Long Island's Early Brass Bands," *Long Island Forum* (June 1982): 106–11; John Newsom, "The American Brass Band Movement" on *Yankee Brass Band: Music from Mid-Nineteenth-Century America* (New World Records 312, 1981); Richard Franko Goldman, *The Pride of America: The Golden Age of the American March* (New World Records 266, 1976). The description of Lafe Hornbeck comes from Thomas F. O'Donnell, ed., *Harold Frederic's Stories of York State* (Syracuse: Syracuse University Press, 1966), p. 239. An extensive literature exists on minstrelsy; for accounts supporting the discussion that I presented, see Francis Hodge, *Yankee Theatre: The Image of America on the Stage, 1825–1850* (Austin: University of Texas Press, 1964); Alan W. C. Green, " 'Jim Crow,' 'Zip Coon': The Northern Origins of Negro Minstrelsy," *Massachusetts Review* 2 (1970): 385–97; Robert C. Toll, *Blacking Up: The Minstrel Show in Nineteenth-Century America* (New York: Oxford University Press, 1974), p. 27; Hans Nathan, *Dan Emmett and the Rise of Early Negro Minstrelsy* (Norman: University of Oklahoma Press, 1961), p. 167; Sam Dennison, *Scandalize My Name: Black Imagery in American Popular Music* (New York: Garland Publishing, 1982), pp. 87–156; Charles Hamm, *Yesterdays: Popular Song in America*

(New York: W. W. Norton, 1979), pp. 109–40; David Ewen, *All the Years of American Popular Music* (Englewood Cliffs, N.J.: Prentice-Hall, 1977), pp. 36–50. A list of "Favorite Early American Minstrel Songs" is found in Edward B. Marks, *They All Had Glamour: From the Swedish Nightingale to the Naked Lady* (New York: Julian Messner, 1944), pp. 361–65. Collections of "Old Zip Coon" in oral tradition are documented in Bayard, *Dance to the Fiddle*, pp. 276–80; Linscott, *Folk Songs of Old New England*, pp. 101–3; Vance Randolph, *Ozark Folksongs*, 4 vols. (1946–50; rpt. ed., Columbia: University of Missouri Press, 1980), II, p. 378; H. M. Belden, *Ballads and Songs Collected by the Missouri Folk-Lore Society* (1940; rpt. ed., Columbia: University of Missouri Press, 1973), pp. 505–506; Henry M. Belden and Arthur Palmer Hudson, eds., *Frank C. Brown Collection of North Carolina Folklore: Folk Songs from North Carolina* (Durham, N.C.: Duke University Press, 1952), pp. 503–4. The language of "The Siege of Plattsburgh" is discussed in William J. Mahar, "Black English in Early Blackface Minstrelsy: A New Interpretation of the Sources of Minstrel Show Dialect," *American Quarterly* 37 (1985): 268–69; Frank Luther, *Americans and Their Songs* (New York: Harper and Brothers, 1942), p. 98. "Boyne Water," the tune to "The Siege of Plattsburgh," is documented with numerous sources in Bayard, *Dance to the Fiddle*, pp. 271–74, 582.

17. The account of dancing masters in Hartford comes from Cole, "The Puritan and Fair Terpsichore," pp. 20–21; N. H. Allen, "Old-Time Music and Musicians," *Connecticut Quarterly* 1 (1895): 371–72. William Sidney Mount's transcription of "Rustic Reel" and his letter to Robert Mount are discussed in Armstrong, *Catching the Tune*, pp. 17–19; "Rustic Reel" also is described in Elias Howe, *Howe's Complete Ball-Room Hand Book* (Boston: Oliver Ditson, 1858), p. 23. Howe makes the claim that the dance to the tune was popular around 1808. His description of the dances of the period may help explain the folk reference to sore feet attached to "Rustic Reel": "It was then the custom to take all the steps in each of the different dances, and to introduce the 'Pigeon's Wing' or some other flourish, as often as possible; dancers at that time often boasted that they 'put in so much work' as to wear out a pair of dancing slippers in one evening. The walking or sliding through the different changes, so fashionable at the present day, would have filled our forefathers with horror and disgust." Bayard in *Dance to the Fiddle* reports eleven versions of "Rustic Reel" in oral tradition as "O Dear Mother My Toes Are Sore" pp. 435–38. Other versions of "Rustic Reel" (which sometimes carry the title "Rustic Dance" or "Old Virginia Reel") are found in Elias Howe, *Howe's School for the Violin* (Boston: E. Howe, Jr., 1851), p. 39; *Gems of the Ball Room, No. 8* (Chicago: E. T. Root and Sons, 1899), no. 16; R. P. Christeson, *Old-Time Fiddler's Repertory, Volume 2* (Columbia: University of Missouri Press, 1984), tune no. 157; *Harding's All-Round Collection of Jigs, Reels and Country Dances* (New York: Harding's Music House, 1905), no. 191; Ira W. Ford *Traditional Music of America* (New York: E. P. Dutton, 1940), p. 52; Mellie Dunham, *"Mellie" Dunham's Fiddlin' Dance Tunes*, no. 21.

18. Pauline Hovemeyer, *100 Years in the History of Delhi, New York* (Delhi, N.Y.: *Delaware Republican-Express*, 1960); Letters from John E. Raitt, 17 August 1977, 7 July 1977, 26 July 1977.

19. "Happy Bill Daniels Quadrille" was recorded on Brunswick 20053, a 12-inch 78 rpm record, on two sides (Part 1-Master Number EX 21084, Part 2-Master Number EX 21085). "Virginia Reel Medley" was recorded on Brunswick 20050, a 12-inch 78 rpm record, on two sides (no master numbers available). Discographical information on McDermott was provided in a letter from Paul Wells printed in the *John Edwards Memorial Foundation Quarterly* 12 (1976): 174. There he also mentions two other recording fiddlers who were probably Yorkers: Colonel John A. Pattee and Frank E. "Dad" Williams, who like McDermott, recorded for Brunswick. Williams' sides were recorded on 30 January 1929: "The Dutchman's Serenade" (Brunswick 306) and "Money Musk, Introducing Opera Reel" (Brunswick 306). For a comparison of folk fiddling styles displayed by McDermott with other regional performers, see Cazden, *Dances from Woodland*, pp. 4–5; Kennedy, *The Fiddler's Tune-Book*, pp. v–vi; Samuel P. Bayard, *Hill Country Tunes*, pp. xi–xxvii, and "Some Folk Fiddlers' Habits and Styles in Western Pennsylvania," *Journal of the International Folk Music Council* 8 (1956): 15–18; Joan Moser, "Instrumental Music of the Southern Appalachians: Traditional Fiddle Tunes," *North Carolina Folklore* 12 (1964): 1–8; Marion Thede, "Traditional Fiddling," *Ethnomusicology* 6 (1962): 19–24; Linda C. Burman-Hall, "Southern American Folk Fiddle Styles," *Ethnomusicology* 19 (1975): 47–65, and "The Technique of Variation in an American Fiddle Tune: A Study of 'Sail Away Lady' As Performed

in 1926 by Uncle Bunt Stephens," *Ethnomusicology* 12 (1968): 49–71; George A. Proctor, "Old-Time Fiddling in Ontario," *National Museum of Canada Bulletin*, no. 190 (1963): 173–208; Matthew G. Guntharp, *Learning the Fiddler's Ways* (University Park: Pennsylvania State University Press, 1980); Larry V. Shumway and Tom Carter, "The History and Performance Style of J. W. 'Babe' Spangler, The 'Old Virginia Fiddler,' " *John Edwards Memorial Foundation Quarterly* 14 (1978): 198–207; John A Cuthbert, "A Musicological Look at John Johnson's Fiddling," *Goldenseal: West Virginia Traditional Life* 7 (Winter 1981): 16; Earl V. Spielman, "The Texas Fiddling Style," *Devil's Box* 14 (1 September 1980): 24–32. "The Girl I Left Behind Me" ranks as one of America's most collected folk songs. Extensive notes on the tune and song in the Northeast can be found in Bayard, *Dance to the Fiddle*, pp. 322–25; Linscott, *Folk Songs of Old New England*, pp. 79–80; Norman Cazden, Herbert Haufrecht, and Norman Studer, *Notes and Sources for Folk Songs of the Catskills* (Albany: State University of New York Press, 1982), pp. 31–32. Sources in the British Isles include Richard Henebry, *A Handbook of Irish Music* (London: Longmans Green & Co., 1928), pp. 291, 301; William Chappell, *A Collection of National English Airs*, 2 vols. (London: Chappell, 1840), I, no. 172, II, p. 134; John Ord, *The Bothy Songs and Ballads of Aberdeen, Banff and Moray, Angus and the Mearns* (Paisley, Scotland: Gardner, 1930), pp. 45–47. Prominent field collections of the tune and song in folk tradition are Cazden, Haufrecht, Studer, *Folk Songs of the Catskills*, pp. 159–61; Belden, *Ballads and Songs*, 198–200; Alan Lomax, *The Folk Songs of North America* (1960; rpt. ed., Garden City, New York: Doubleday, 1975), pp. 318–20; Henry W. Shoemaker, *Mountain Minstrelsy of Pennsylvania* (rev. ed., Philadelphia: Newman F. McGirr, 1931), pp. 155–56; Patrick W. Gainer, *Folk Songs from the West Virginia Hills* (Grantsville, W.V.: Seneca Books, 1975), pp. 173–74; Randolph, *Ozark Folk Songs*, I, pp. 283–88, III, pp. 352–54; Jan Philip Schinhan, ed., *Frank C. Brown Collection of North Carolina Folklore: The Music of the Ballads* (Durham, N.C.: Duke University Press, 1957), p. 213; David S. McIntosh, *Folk Songs & Singing Games of the Illinois Ozarks* (Carbondale: Southern Illinois University Press, 1974), pp. 76–77.

20. Bayard in *Dance to the Fiddle* reports that "Shall We Gather by the River" is included in the fiddle tune "Ellsworth's Funeral March" and "The Old Churchyard" is included in the fiddle tune "Band of Freemen" pp. 84–86, 287; even the favorite folk tune "Girl I Left Behind Me" appears as a hymn in John Gordon McCurry, *The Social Harp* (1855; rpt. ed., Athens: University of Georgia Press, 1973); George Pullen Jackson, *Spiritual Folk Songs of Early America* (New York: J. J. Augustin, 1937), no. 83. The reference to William Mahar comes from his "March to the Music," *Civil War Times* 23 (1984): 41–42.

21. "John A. McDermott, 87, Well Known Conservationist and Old Time Fiddler, Dies Here," *Cortland Standard* (24 June 1957), p. 2.

22. See "From the Archives: 'The Arkansas Traveller,' " *John Edwards Memorial Foundation Quarterly* 6 (1970): 51–57; Mike Yates and Tony Russell, "Tracing the Arkansas Traveler," *Old Time Music*, no. 31 (Winter 1978/79): 14.

23. Jim Walsh, "John H. Kimmel, 'The Irish Scotchman,' " *Hobbies* (February 1958): 34.

24. Howard L. Sacks, "John Baltzell, A Country Fiddler from the Heartland," *Journal of Country Music* 10 (1985): 18–24; Simon J. Bronner, "John Baltzell: Champion Old Time Fiddler," *Old Time Music*, no. 27 (Winter 1977/78): 13–14. For contemporary interpretations of Baltzell's playing, listen to "Baltzell's Tune" played by Rollie Hommon on *Seems Like Romance to Me: Traditional Fiddle Tunes from Ohio* (Gambier Folklore Society, GFS 901, 1985).

25. David L. Lewis, "The Square Dancing Master," *Devil's Box*, no. 17 (1 June 1972): 4–6; Richard Blaustein, "Traditional Music and Social Change: The Old-Time Fiddlers Association Movement in the United States" (Ph.D. diss., Indiana University, 1975), pp. 35–53. For coverage of Bisbee's notoriety, see "16 Old Fiddlers in Hot Contest for Ford's Cup," *Variety* (27 January 1926): 48.

26. "Fiddling to Henry Ford," *Literary Digest* 88 (2 January 1926), p. 33; Lewis, "The Square Dancing Master," p. 5.

27. "Fiddling to Henry Ford," p. 33. For information on "Uncle" Bunt Stephens, see Don Roberson, "Uncle Bunt Stephens: Champion Fiddler," *Old Time Music* 5 (Summer 1972): 4–6. For the story of "Uncle" John Wilder, see Sally Thompson, "Plymouth Old-Time Dance

Orchestra," *Vermont History* 40 (1972): 185–89; Wilder's obituary is reprinted in Wayne W. Daniel, "Fiddling in North America: A Selected Annotated Bibliography," *Devil's Box* 18 (Fall 1984): 38–39.

28. Ibid., p. 34. The wide coverage given Mellie Dunham and Ford's promotion of old-time fiddle music is indicated by the thirty-eight newspaper and magazine articles devoted to him between 1925 and his death in 1931 (Information from Paul Wells, "Mellie Dunham: 'Maine's Champion Fiddler,' " *John Edwards Memorial Foundation Quarterly* 12 (1976): 117–18.

29. Ibid., pp. 34–35.

30. See Wayne W. Daniel, "Old-Time Fiddling on Early Radio," *Devil's Box* 17 (Spring 1983): 3–9; "The Country Fiddler Boom," *Etude* (January 1929): 55; James F. Evans, *Prairie Farmer and WLS* (Urbana: University of Illinois Press, 1969), p. 154; Avis D. Carlson, "Cowboy Ballads at Our Own Firesides," in *A History and Encyclopedia of Country, Western, and Gospel Music,* ed. Linnell Gentry (1961; rpt. ed., St. Clair Shores, Mich.: Scholarly Press, 1972), p. 33; "All States Broadcast Except Wyoming," *Literary Digest* (11 November 1922): 29; Ivan M. Tribe, "The Economics of Hillbilly Radio: A Preliminary Investigation of the 'P. I.' System in the Depression Decade and Afterward," *John Edwards Memorial Foundation Quarterly* 20 (1984): 76–83; Mary Latus, "Country Music Performers in the Utica Area" (typescript, Archive of New York State Folklife, 1976).

31. D. K. Wilgus, "Introduction to the Study of Hillbilly Music," *Journal of American Folklore* 78 (1965): 196.

32. Bill C. Malone, *Country Music, U.S.A.* (Austin: University of Texas Press, 1968), pp. viii, 3–5.

33. Henry Glassie, " 'Take That Night Train to Selma': An Excursion to the Outskirts of Scholarship," in *Folksongs and Their Makers* (Bowling Green, Ohio: Bowling Green University Popular Press, 1971), p. 47.

34. The collections of Jones and Thompson date from the 1940s and 1950s. They are now housed in the New York State Historical Association at Cooperstown, New York; see Louis C. Jones, "Farmers' Museum Folklore Archive," *Folklore and Folk Music Archivist* 2 (Summer 1959): 2. Thompson published his collections of the 1930s in *Body, Boots and Britches.* He also published a manuscript collection of western New York State ballads and songs, *A Pioneer Songster: Texts from the Stevens-Douglass Manuscript of Western New York, 1841–1856* (Ithaca, N.Y.: Cornell University Press, 1958). Jones reported his collections in a series of articles published in the late 1950s and early 1960s; several have been reprinted in his *Three Eyes on the Past: Exploring New York Folk Life* (Syracuse: Syracuse University Press, 1982).

35. Cooper, *The Pioneers,* p. 14.

36. Richard Petersen and Russell Davis, "The Fertile Crescent of Country Music," *Journal of Country Music* 6 (1975): 19–27. Further evidence of the contrasting progressive and primitive images of the North and South in the American consciousness is found in Joel Garreau, *The Nine Nations of North America* (Boston: Houghton Mifflin, 1981); Henry D. Shapiro, *Appalachia on Our Mind: The Southern Mountains and Mountaineers in the American Consciousness, 1870–1920* (Chapel Hill: University of North Carolina Press, 1978). For texts that explore the cultural split between the city and country during the early twentieth century, see D. K. Wilgus, "Country-Western Music and the Urban Hillbilly," in *The Urban Experience and Folk Tradition,* ed. Américo Paredes and Ellen J. Stekert (Austin: University of Texas Press, 1971), pp. 137–59; Ivan Tribe, "The Hillbilly Versus the City: Urban Images in Country Music," *John Edwards Memorial Foundation Quarterly* 10 (1974): 41–50; Alan Trachtenberg, *The Incorporation of America: Culture and Society in the Gilded Age* (New York: Hill and Wang, 1982); Warren Susman, *Culture as History: The Transformation of American Society in the Twentieth Century* (New York: Pantheon, 1984); Blake McKelvey, *The Urbanization of America, 1860–1915* (New Brunswick, N.J.: Rutgers University Press, 1963).

37. Archie Green, "Hillbilly Music: Source and Symbol," *Journal of American Folklore* 78 (1965): 205; Malone, *Country Music, U.S.A.,* pp. 3–5. Malone later expanded the argument to suggest that all American forms of music derived from southern music; see his *Southern Music, American Music* (Lexington: University Press of Kentucky, 1979) and *Country Music, U.S.A.* (rev. ed., Austin: University of Texas Press, 1985).

38. Roderick J. Roberts, "An Introduction to the Study of Northern Country Music," *Journal of Country Music* 7 (1978): 24. The aesthetic that Roberts refers to is described in Roger D. Abrahams and George Foss, *Anglo-American Folksong Style* (Englewood Cliffs, N.J.: Prentice-Hall, 1968). For an excellent case study of the acceptance of commercial country music based on a prevailing local British-American aesthetic, see Neil V. Rosenberg, " 'Folk' and 'Country' Music in the Canadian Maritimes: A Regional Model," *Journal of Country Music* 5 (1974): 76–83.

39. "Country Music is Big Business and Nashville is its Detroit," which originally appeared in *Newsweek* (11 August 1952) is reprinted in *A History and Encyclopedia of Country, Western, and Gospel Music,* ed. Linnell Gentry (1961; rpt. ed., St. Clair Shores, Mich.: Scholarly Press, 1972), pp. 108–14. For a discussion of the effect of the southeastern market for commercial hillbilly recordings on other regional old-time musicians, see W. K. McNeil, "Five Pre–World War II Arkansas String Bands: Some Thoughts on Their Recording Success," *John Edwards Memorial Foundation Quarterly* 20 (1984): 68–75. For discussion of the commercialization and transformation of old time music into country music, see Charles K. Wolfe, "That Old-Time Music," *Devil's Box* no. 22 (1 September 1973): 6–9.

40. For details of the challenge by Dunham, see Charles K. Wolfe, *The Grand Ole Opry: The Early Years* (London: Old-Time Music, 1975), pp. 57–60. Dunham's role is chronicled in Paul Wells, "Mellie Dunham: 'Maine's Champion Fiddler,' " pp. 112–15 (Wells suggests that Dunham was actually answering a challenge by Thompson rather than issuing it). The premier of the movie *Grand Ol' Opry* in 1940 is pictured in the *Pictorial History of Country Music, Volume 2,* ed. Thurston Moore (Denver: Heather Publications, 1969), p. 42; see also "Country Music Goes to the Movies," in *Country-Song Round-Up Annual* (1965), pp. 50–52. Studies of radio station WSM include Charles K. Wolfe, "Early Nashville Media and Its Response to Old Time Music," *Journal of Country Music* 4 (1973): 2–16; Richard A. Petersen, "Single-Industry Firm to Conglomerate Synergistics: Alternative Strategies for Selling Insurance and Country Music," in *Growing Metropolis: Aspects of Development in Nashville,* ed. James F. Blumenstein and Benjamin Walter (Nashville: Vanderbilt University Press, 1975); John W. Rumble, "The Emergence of Nashville as a Recording Center: Logbooks from the Castle Studio, 1952–1953," *Journal of Country Music* 7 (1978): 22–41.

41. See Wells, "Mellie Dunham," p. 114; Charles K. Wolfe, "Uncle Jimmy's Repertoire," *Devil's Box* 9 (1 September 1975): 53–54.

42. Daniel, "Old-Time Fiddling on Early Radio," pp. 5–7.

43. For some regional differences of fiddling and a statement of the scarcity of tunes in 6/8 time, see Miles Krassen, *Appalachian Fiddle,* p. 86; Jabbour, *American Fiddle Tunes,* p. 11. On the record that Jabbour edited, Side A is devoted to northern performers while side B features southern performers. For the regionalization of early American material culture, see Henry Glassie, *Pattern in the Material Folk Culture of the Eastern United States* (Philadelphia: University of Pennsylvania Press, 1968). For settlement pattern and its relation to a national culture, see John R. Stilgoe, *Common Landscape of America, 1580–1845* (New Haven, Ct.: Yale University Press, 1982). For the nationalization of speech, see Daniel Boorstin, *The Americans: The Colonial Experience* (New York: Vintage/Random House, 1958), pp. 271–77, from which my quoted examples are taken, and Peter Benes and Jane Montague Benes, eds., *American Speech: 1600 to the Present* (Boston: Boston University Scholarly Publications, 1985). My reference to the correspondence of Robert Mount comes from Janice Gray Armstrong, *Catching the Tune,* p. 19; for commentary on the sweeping "Americanness" of fiddling, see also, Louie W. Attebery, "The Fiddle Tune: An American Artifact," in *Readings in American Folklore,* ed. Jan Harold Brunvand (New York: W. W. Norton, 1979), pp. 324–33.

44. Bayard, *Dance to the Fiddle,* p. 571.

45. Sacks, "John Baltzell," p. 34. For the recordings of Emmett W. Lundy, see Tom Carter's notes to *Emmett W. Lundy: Fiddle Tunes from Grayson County, Virginia* (String 802). For another provocative comparison of fiddling in North America across an even wider expanse, see Earl V. Spielman, "The Fiddling Traditions of Cape Breton and Texas: A Study in Parallels and Contrasts," *Yearbook for Inter-American Musical Research* 8 (1972): 39–47. The pattern of nationalization giving way to later regionalization is also found in the closely related tradition of dance. The "pioneer" dances were fairly uniform but later branched off into "eastern," "southern," and

"western" styles. See Damon, *History of Square Dancing*, pp. 51–52; Grace L. Ryan, *Dances of Our Pioneers* (New York: A. S. Barnes, 1939). For the cultural background of the nineteenth-century "national experience," see Daniel J. Boorstin, *The Americans: The National Experience* (New York: Vintage Books/Random House, 1965); Russel Blaine Nye, *Society and Culture in America, 1830–1860* (New York: Harper & Row, 1974).

46. Mahar, "March to the Music," p. 16.

Chapter 2—It Just Leaned Naturally Toward a Farmer or Hillbilly Image

1. Richard M. Dorson, "Dialect Stories of the Upper Peninsula," reprinted in his *Folklore and Fakelore: Essays Toward a Discipline of Folk Studies* (Cambridge, Mass.: Harvard University Press, 1976), pp. 223–68.

2. Richard M. Dorson, *America in Legend: Folklore from the Colonial Period to the Present* (New York: Pantheon, 1973), 108–21; the playbill for the musical comedy *Saw Mill* is illustrated in Janice Gray Armstrong, ed., *Catching the Tune: Music and William Sidney Mount* (Stony Brook, N.Y.: The Museums at Stony Brook, 1984), p. 30. Other examples of the legacy of the Yankee country bumpkin are found in Dorson's "Yorker Yarns of Yore," *New York Folklore Quarterly* 3 (1947): 5–27; *Jonathan Draws the Long Bow* (1946; rpt. ed., New York: Russell and Russell, 1969). For a discussion of "Yankee Doodle" on the American stage and its possible origins, see Sigmund Spaeth, *A History of Popular Music in America* (New York: Random House, 1948), pp. 15–22; John Tasker Howard, *Our American Music* (New York: Thomas Y. Crowell, 1965), pp. 113–18; Gustav Kobbe, *Famous American Songs* (New York: Thomas Y. Crowell, 1906), pp. 125–40. See also the listing of versions of "Yankee Doodle" in oral tradition in Samuel Bayard, *Dance to the Fiddle, March to the Fife: Instrumental Folk Tunes in Pennsylvania* (University Park: Pennsylvania State University Press, 1982), pp. 24–25. For the text and music of "Corn Cobs Twist Your Hair" and other early printings of variations on "Yankee Doodle," see Harry Dichter and Elliott Shapiro, *Handbook of Early American Sheet Music, 1768–1889* (1941; rpt. ed., New York: Dover, 1977), pp. 17–22; B. A. Botkin, *A Treasury of New England Folklore: Stories, Ballads, and Traditions of Yankee Folk* (1947; rpt. ed., New York: Bonanza Books, 1955), pp. 7–9.

3. Archie Green, "Hillbilly Music: Source and Symbol," *Journal of American Folklore* 78 (1965): 204–28.

4. Rufus Jarman, "Country Music Goes to Town," *Nation's Business* (1953) reprinted in *A History and Encyclopedia of Country, Western, and Gospel Music*, ed. Linnell Gentry (St. Clair Shored, Mich.: Scholarly Press, 1972), p. 120.

5. Green, "Hillbilly Music," p. 213.

6. Ibid., 214. The simultaneous use of "Hill Billies" in the names of groups during early 1925 seemed to have been more widespread than Alderman's group claimed. A case for the popularization of the label "hillbilly" by another band, for example, is made in Wayne W. Daniel, "George Daniell's Hill Billies: The Band That Named the Music?" *John Edwards Memorial Foundation Quarterly* 19 (1983): 81–84.

7. Maurice Zolotow, "Hayride," *Theatre Arts* (1954) reprinted in *A History and Encyclopedia of Country, Western, and Gospel Music*, ed. Linnell Gentry (St. Clair Shores, Mich.: Scholarly Press, 1972), p. 132.

8. Nelson King, "Hillbilly Music Leaves the Hills," *Good Housekeeping* (1954) reprinted in *A History and Encyclopedia of Country, Western, and Gospel Music*, ed. Linnell Gentry (St. Clair Shores, Mich.: Scholarly Press, 1972), p. 127.

9. Ibid., pp. 127–28; "Bull Market in Corn," *Time* (4 October 1943), and "Corn of Plenty" *Newsweek* (13 June 1949), reprinted in *A History and Encyclopedia of Country, Western, and Gospel Music*, ed. Linnell Gentry (St. Clair Shores, Mich.: Scholarly Press, 1972), pp. 52, 75.

10. Maurice Zolotow, "Hillbilly Boom," *Saturday Evening Post* (12 February 1944), pp. 22–23, 36, 38.

11. *Historical Memories of Otsego County*, 2nd ed. (Otsego County Council of Senior Citizens, 1976), p. 56.

12. Warren Susman, "The People's Fair: Cultural Contradictions of a Consumer Society," reprinted in his *Culture as History: The Transformation of American Society in the Twentieth Century* (New York: Pantheon, 1984), pp. 226–27. The importance of the New York World's Fair in 1940 is also mentioned in S. Foster Damon, *The History of Square Dancing* (Barre, Mass.: Barre Gazette, 1957), pp. 50–51.

13. Esther G. Grayson, "The Country Dance Goes To Town," *New York Times Magazine* (31 March 1940), reprinted in *A History and Encyclopedia of Country, Western, and Gospel Music,* ed. Linnell Gentry (St. Clair Shores, Mich.: Scholarly Press, 1972), pp. 46–47.

14. "Country Musicians Fiddle Up Roaring Business," *Life* (19 November 1956) reprinted in *A History and Encyclopedia of Country, Western, and Gospel Music,* ed. Linnell Gentry (St. Clair Shores, Mich.: Scholarly Press, 1972), p. 152.

15. Jim Jennings, "For Woody, It's . . . ," *Elmira Star-Gazette* (19 November 1977), p. 16.

16. Personal communication with Roderick Roberts, Cooperstown, New York, 8 July 1986. Supported by the Arts Council for Wyoming County with funding from the New York State Council on the Arts, the project included a survey of folk and country music. For more information, see Paula Tadlock Jennings, "One Year Later: NYSCA's Folk Arts Program," *New York Folklore Newsletter* 7 (May 1986): 3–4.

17. It was a common practice for bands having a radio spot to come up with a theme song. Although the theme of the Hillbillies uses snatches from other hillbilly songs, it also contains a fragment of an old play-party game. The theme song of the Hornellsville Hillbillies uses a reference to a play-party song that contains the line "Here We Come, Bum Bum Bum." William Wells Newell calls it "Comes, it Comes" and states that it is "familiar to children in New England." See *Games and Songs of American Children* (1883; rpt. ed., New York: Dover, 1963), p. 150. Words are provided to a version collected in Alabama; "Bum, bum, bum, Here we come" one group cries while the other replies "Where are you from?" See Jack and Olivia Solomon, *Zickary Zan: Childhood Folklore* (University: University of Alabama Press, 1980), p. 28. "Black Cat" was a standard tune at New England dances during the 1930s; see Beth Tolman and Ralph Page, *The Country Dance Book* (New York: A. S. Barnes, 1937), pp. 62–70.

18. The circulation of "Bye Bye Blues" is discussed in Sigmund Spaeth, *A History of Popular Music in America* (New York: Random House, 1948), pp. 310, 483; Roger D. Kinkle, *The Complete Encyclopedia of Popular Music and Jazz, 1900–1950* (New Rochelle, N.Y.: Arlington House, 1974), I, p. 214, 226.

19. Archie Green, "Hillbilly Music: Source and Symbol," *Journal of American Folklore* 78 (1965): 223.

20. John H. Braunlein, " 'Is That Hillbilly Enough For You?': The Northern Country Music Tradition in Madison County," *Madison County Heritage,* no. 10 (July 1981): 14–17.

21. Ibid., p. 17. Before his death in 1981, Bourne made up a list of "Leading Fiddle Tunes for the Country Bands of George (Gib) Bourne": Little Brown Jug, The Campbells Are Coming, Golden Slippers, Oh Susanna, Climbing Up the Golden Stairs, Irish Washerwoman, Arkansas Traveler, Devil's Dream, Lamplighters Hornpipe, Soldier's Joy, White Cockade, Turkey in the Straw, Darling Nellie Gray, The Wind that Shook the Barley, Up Jumped the Devil, The Old Spinning Wheel, Buffalo Girls, Marching Through Georgia, Old Dan Tucker, Durang's Hornpipe, The Girl I Left Behind Me, Leather Breeches, Gray Eagle, Pop Goes the Weasel, Arkansas Traveler, Cackling Hen, Going to Boston, Skip to My Lou, Miller Boy, Old Brass Wagon, Bully of the Town, Casey Jones, Wreck of the Old 97, Bill Bailey, Wabash Cannonball. At the end of the list, Bourne attached a note: "This is not all of them, just the best known."

22. Bradley Kincaid, *My Favorite Mountain Ballads and Old Time Songs* (Rochester: WHAM, 1940), p. 7. For discussion of Kincaid's influence, see D. K. Wilgus, "Bradley Kincaid," in *The Stars of Country Music,* ed. Bill C. Malone and Judith McCulloh (New York: Avon, 1975), pp. 93–102; Loyal Jones, *Radio's "Kentucky Mountain Boy" Bradley Kincaid* (Berea, Ky.: Berea College Appalachian Center, 1980).

Chapter 3—Brings You Back, Don't It?

1. Almost every book on bluegrass music discusses the debt of the new style to old-time music. For texts that cover the relation of old-time music to bluegrass and its role in bluegrass's future development, see Neil V. Rosenberg, *Bluegrass: A History* (Urbana: University of Illinois Press, 1985); Robert Cantwell, *Bluegrass Breakdown: The Making of the Old Southern Sound* (Urbana: University of Illinois Press, 1984); Marilyn Kochman, ed., *The Big Book of Bluegrass* (New York: Quill, 1984); Matthew G. Guntharp, *Learning the Fiddler's Ways* (University Park: Pennsylvania State University Press, 1980), pp. 112–33; Bill C. Malone, *Country Music, U.S.A.* (rev. ed., Austin: University of Texas Press, 1985), pp. 322–67.

2. Quoted in John H. Braunlein, " 'Is That Hillbilly Enough For You?': The Northern Country Music Tradition in Madison County," *Madison County Heritage*, no. 10 (July 1981): 9–10.

3. Henry Glassie, " 'Take That Night Train to Selma': An Excursion to the Outskirts of Scholarship," in *Folksongs and Their Makers* (Bowling Green, Ohio: Bowling Green University Popular Press, 1971), p. 41.

4. Ibid., p. 3.

5. This song is a folk variation of a composition published in 1907 by Benjamin Hapgood Burt; see Sigmund Spaeth, *Read 'Em and Weep: The Songs You Forgot to Remember* (Garden City, N.Y.: Doubleday, Page and Co., 1926), pp. 255–57. The words went through many alterations as the song travelled in oral tradition; see the version in Ira W. Ford, *Traditional Music in America* (1940; rpt. ed., Hatboro, Pa.: Folklore Associates, 1965), pp. 273–76. Bradley Kincaid also sang a version; in Loyal Jones, *Radio's 'Kentucky Mountain Boy' Bradley Kincaid* (Berea, Ky.: Appalachian Center, 1980), he is quoted as saying, "If there ever was a 'hillbilly' song, this is it. I don't know its origin" (p. 150).

6. This song was, in Dorrance Weir's words, a "Weir family song." It was a favorite around his family parlor and it continues to be song by the Weir siblings. Its words tell of a man who plans to sell his pasture to the railroad, buy "a high silk hat and a gold top walking cane, and a watch you can twist right around your wrist that don't need any chain," and return to his mountain shack after mixing with the gentry. Henry Glassie in "Take That Night Train to Selma" reports that Sarah Cleveland, a noted traditional singer from upstate New York, recognized it as a song sung by the older people in her family (p. 55). Glassie also locates the song as "A High Silk Hat and a Walking Cane" on a commercial recording by Frank Crumit from the late 1920s or early 1930s.

7. I recorded these verses from Ken Kane on 1 April 1976 and 13 April 1976; Henry Glassie recorded Kane singing the song with only the first verse on 9 July 1965 which he reported in "Take That Night Train to Selma," pp. 24–25. Apparently the song has a wide Anglo-American folk circulation. For discussion of the song's variants, see Vance Randolph, *Ozark Folksongs*, 4 vols. (Columbia: University of Missouri Press, 1980), III, pp. 117–19; Anne Warner, *Traditional American Folk Songs from the Anne & Frank Warner Collection* (Syracuse: Syracuse University Press, 1984), pp. 376–79; Alan Lomax, *The Folk Songs of North America* (Garden City, New York: Doubleday, 1975), pp. 375; Lester A. Hubbard, *Ballads and Songs from Utah* (Salt Lake City: University of Utah Press, 1961), pp. 232–33; MacEdward Leach, *Folk Ballads and Songs of the Lower Labrador Coast* (Ottawa: National Museum of Canada, 1965), p. 286. A British Isles version is reported in Peter Kennedy, *Folk Songs of Britain and Ireland* (London: Cassell, 1975), p. 469.

8. On January 5, 1987, Ken Kane added the following verses to the version reported here.

> I was sitting by the window yesterday morning
> Without a thought of worry or of care
> When I saw the postman coming up the pathway
> With such a happy face and merry air

With trembling hands I took this letter from him
I opened it and this is what it said
Come home my boy, your dear old father wants you
Come home my boy, your old mother is dead

You know those words over in anger I wish I had never spoken
You know I never meant them don't you Jack
The angels bear me witness I'm asking you forgiveness
For this letter edged in black

The original tearful song "Letter Edged in Black" is credited to Hattie Nevada (1897), a professional composer and entertainer. A full text with music was published in Sigmund Spaeth, *Weep Some More My Lady* (New York: Doubleday, Page and Co., 1927), pp. 38–39. After its publication on broadsides and performance on the vaudeville stage, the song quickly entered oral tradition in the countryside. It was picked up in the 1920s and 1930s by folk-styled recording artists Vernon Dalhart, Fiddlin' John Carson, Frank Luther, and Bradley Kincaid. It is reported in its folk forms in Randolph, *Ozark Folksongs,* IV, pp. 162–63; Ethel Park Richardson, *American Mountain Songs* (Ellicott City, Maryland: Greenberg, 1927), p. 35; *Carson J. Robison's World's Greatest Collection of Mountain Ballads and Old Time Songs* (Chicago: M. M. Cole, 1930), pp. 12–13; *Smith's Collection of Mountain Ballads and Cowboy Songs* (New York: Wm. J. Smith Music, 1932), pp. 22–23. Richardson's comment on the song is instructive: "This song once had a wide vogue all over America, but may well have been of mountain origin. Its melody contains suggestions of the modern "Prisoner's Song," and its words employ more than ordinary art in the telling of the story" (p. 107). The song is one of many popular compositions from the late Victorian period that persisted in country music as folk-styled ballads or fiddle tunes; see Gene Wiggins, "Popular Music and the Fiddler," *John Edwards Memorial Foundation Quarterly* 15 (1979): 144–56.

9. On January 5, 1987, Ken sang an additional verse:

We're feeble and old, but your mother and me
We watched over your cradle in sweet infancy
Oh that night that we knelt by your cradle so low
I beg of you Tommy don't go

On this occasion, he was alone with me. In performances with his family and friends, he tends to drop this verse and end the song with a yodel. Longer versions of "Don't Go Tommy" are reported in Randolph, *Ozark Folksongs* IV, pp. 385–86; Henry Glassie, "Jesse Wells" (typescript, Archive of New York State Folklife, 1965). An older version of the song, dating to 1917, was collected by Josiah H. Combs; see the notes in Josiah H. Combs, *Folk-Songs of the Southern United States,* ed. D. K. Wilgus (Austin: University of Texas Press, 1967), p. 221. Folklorist Robert Bethke mentions "Stick To Your Mother, Tom," a variant circulating in the North Country of New York, in *Adirondack Voices: Woodsmen and Woods Lore* (Urbana: University of Illinois Press, 1981), p. 57.

10. Anne and Norm Cohen, "Folk and Hillbilly Music: Further Thoughts on Their Relation," *John Edwards Memorial Foundation Quarterly* 13 (1977): 52–53.

11. Norman Cazden, Herbert Haufrecht, and Norman Studer, *Folk Songs of the Catskills* (Albany: State University of New York Press, 1982), p. 1. For further discussion of the folk music revival's relation to country music, see Malone, *Country Music, U.S.A.,* pp. 278–83; Rosenberg, *Bluegrass,* pp. 143–202; R. Raymond Allen, "Old-Time Music and the Urban Folk Revival" (M.A. thesis, Western Kentucky University, 1981); Eric von Schmidt and Jim Rooney, *Baby Let Me Follow You Down* (Garden City, N.Y.: Doubleday, 1979); Ellen Stekert, "Cents and Nonsense in the Urban Folksong Movement: 1930–1966," in *Folklore and Society: Essays in Honor of Benj. A. Botkin,* ed. Bruce Jackson (Hatboro, Pennsylvania: Folklore Associates, 1966), pp. 153–68; Andrew Smith, "The New Lost City Ramblers," *Country and Western Spotlight,* n.s., no. 15 (June 1978): 6–8; Mark Schoenberg, "The Plum Creek Boys: College Bluegrass in the Early Sixties," *Bluegrass Unlimited* 21 (December 1986): 28–32; Jack Bernhardt, "The Hollow Rock

String Band," *Bluegrass Unlimited* 21 (December 1986): 74–81; Robert Shelton, "Old-Time Fiddlers," *New York Times* (9 April 1961), sec. 2, p. 13.

12. Norman Studer, "Grant Rogers: Folksinger of the Delaware Valley," *Sing Out* 12 (Summer 1962): 30.

13. Ibid.

14. Ibid., p. 29. For background on George Edwards, a singer celebrated by the staff at Camp Woodland, see Marilyn Kimball, "George Edwards, Catskill Folksinger" (M.A. thesis, Cooperstown Graduate Programs, State University of New York at Oneonta, 1966).

15. "Jam on Gerry's Rock" circulates in lumbering regions from Maine to Michigan and beyond. Extensive discussion of the song is found in Cazden, Haufrecht, and Studer, *Folk Songs of the Catskills,* pp. 46–52; Norman Cazden, Herbert Haufrecht, and Norman Studer, *Notes and Sources for Folk Songs of the Catskills* (Albany: State University of New York Press, 1982), pp. 8–9; Fannie Hardy Eckstorm and Mary Winslow Smyth, *Minstrelsy of Maine* (Boston: Houghton Mifflin, 1927), pp. 176–98. Variants of the song are reported in Warner, *Traditional American Folk Songs,* pp. 76–78; Henry W. Shoemaker, *Mountain Minstrelsy of Pennsylvania* (rev. ed., Philadelphia: Newman F. McGirr, 1931); Emelyn Elizabeth Gardner and Geraldine Jencks Chickering, *Ballads and Songs of Southern Michigan* (1939; rpt. ed., Hatboro, Pennsylvania: Folklore Associates, 1967), pp. 270–73; Robert Bethke, *Adirondack Voices: Woodsmen and Woods Lore* (Urbana: University of Illinois Press, 1981), pp. 64–67; Harold W. Thompson, *Body, Boots, and Britches: Folktales, Ballads and Speech from Country New York* (1940; rpt. ed., Syracuse: Syracuse University Press, 1979), pp. 259–60; Phillips Barry, *The Maine Woods Songster* (Cambridge: Harvard University Press, 1939), pp. 52–53; E. C. Beck, *Lore of the Lumber Camps* (Ann Arbor: University of Michigan Press, 1948), pp. 194–97; Edith Fowke, *Lumbering Songs from the Northern Woods* (Austin: University of Texas Press, 1970), pp. 95–99; Johnny Crockett, *Log Cabin Songs* (New York: Universal Music, 1930), pp. 6–7; Helen Hartness Flanders, Elizabeth Flanders Ballard, George Brown, and Phillips Barry, *The New Green Mountain Songster: Traditional Folk Songs of Vermont* (1939; rpt. ed., Hatboro, Pennsylvania: Folklore Associates, 1966), pp. 44–46; Carl Sandburg, *The American Songbag* (New York: Harcourt, Brace, 1927), pp. 394–95; Roland P. Gray, *Songs and Ballads of the Maine Lumberjacks* (Cambridge: Harvard University Press, 1924), pp. 3–9; Richard Dorson, George List, and Neil Rosenberg, "Folksongs of the Maine Woods," *Folklore and Folk Music Archivist* 8 (Fall 1965): 3–33; Edward Ives, *Joe Scott: The Woodsman Songmaker* (Urbana: University of Illinois Press, 1978), pp. 314–15; Helen Creighton, *Songs and Ballads from Nova Scotia* (1932; rpt. ed., New York: Dover, 1966), pp. 267–68; William Main Doerflinger, *Songs of the Sailor and Lumberman* (New York: Macmillan, 1972), pp. 238–40; Eloise Hubbard Linscott, *Folk Songs of Old New England* (New York: Macmillan, 1939), pp. 217–20.

16. "I'll Hit the Road Again" is a variant of "I'll Walk the Road Again," a song credited to nineteenth-century singer Jehila "Pat" Edwards from the Catskills of New York. I recorded this version from Grant Rogers on 17 November 1976. Sandy Paton recorded a fuller version of the song during April 1975 and included it on *Brave Boys: New England Traditions in Folk Music* (New World Records NW 239, 1977). The phrase "hoisting the turkey" refers to a carrying a little bundle of belongings carried over the shoulder at the end of the stick. Rogers has not used the modal tune sung by George Edwards, but rather has used a major-scale tune that he commonly sets to ballads. As for the text, despite claims for its originality, it shows thematic and linguistic connections to folk songs such as "The Rock Island Line" and "The National Line"; see Norman Cazden, ed., *The Abelard Folksong Book* (New York: Abelard Schuman, 1958), pp. 52–53. For an extensive discussion of "I'll Walk the Road Again," see Cazden, Haufrecht, and Studer, *Folk Songs of the Catskills,* pp. 518–20, 637–44.

17. Louis C. Jones, "Early Days of the Folklore Renaissance in New York State," *New York Folklore* 11 (1985): 33.

18. For further discussion of Hank Williams's role in propelling country music into the modern period, see Roger M. Williams, *Sing a Sad Song: The Life of Hank Williams* (Garden City, N.Y.: Doubleday, 1970; Chet Flippo, *Your Cheating Heart: A Biography of Hank Williams* (New York: Simon and Schuster, 1981); Jerry Rivers, *Hank Williams: From Life to Legend* (Denver: Heather Enterprises, 1976); Bill C. Malone, *Country Music, U.S.A.* (rev. ed., Austin: University of Texas Press, 1985), pp. 239–43.

19. This dance has a connection to British Isles tradition and apparently derives from a play-party kissing game. The dance is called "Kiss Under the Stairs" and is done to "any good jig" according to Jean C. Milligan, *99 More Scottish Country Dances* (Glasgow: Collins, 1963). A similar play-party kissing game from the nineteenth century was recorded by William Wells Newell in *Games and Songs of American Children* (1883; rpt. ed., New York: Dover, 1963), p. 231; W. H. Babcock, "Games of Washington Children," *American Anthropologist* 1 (1888): 255–56; Alice Bertha Gomme, *The Traditional Games of England, Scotland, and Ireland,* 2 vols. (1894; rpt. ed., New York: Dover, 1964), I, pp. 312–13. Kissing dances were also reported in the early country dance tradition; see Elias Howe, *Howe's Complete Ball-Room Hand-Book* (Boston: E. Howe, 1858), which includes "The Cushion Dance."

20. For Texas's claim, see Nicholas Spitzer, " 'Bob Wills Is Still the King': Romantic Regionalism and Convergent Culture in Central Texas," *John Edwards Memorial Foundation Quarterly* 11 (1975): 191–96; Nelson Allen, "Texas Revisited," *Country Music Magazine* (October 1977): 38–40, 60–61; Douglas B. Green, *Country Roots: The Origins of Country Music* (New York: Hawthorn Books, 1976), pp. 131–43; Charles R. Townsend, *San Antonio Rose: The Life and Music of Bob Wills* (Urbana: University of Illinois Press, 1976). For Tennessee, see Charles K. Wolfe, *Tennessee Strings: The Story of Country Music in Tennessee* (Knoxville: University of Tennessee Press, 1977); Malone, *Country Music, U.S.A.,* pp. 245–68; Peter Guralnick, *Feel Like Going Home* (New York: Outerbridge & Dienstfrey, 1971), pp. 139–79; "Sunrise in Memphis," *Country Music Magazine* (March 1977): 26. For Canada, see Fred Roy, "A Pictorial Review of Country Music in Canada, From 1922 to 1965," in *Pictorial History of Country Music, Volume 2,* ed. Thurston Moore (Denver: Heather Enterprises, 1969), pp. 1–8; Peter Narvaez, "Country Music in Diffusion: Juxtaposition and Syncretism in the Popular Music of Newfoundland," *Journal of Country Music* 7 (1978): 93–101; Neil V. Rosenberg, *Country Music in the Maritimes: Two Studies* (St. John's: Memorial University of Newfoundland Reprint Series, No. 2, 1976).

21. For social statistics showing the dramatic change in family relations after World War II, see Paul C. Glick, *American Families* (New York: John Wiley & Sons, 1957); Nelson Foote, "The Old Generation and the New," in *The Nation's Children: Problems and Prospects,* ed. Eli Ginsberg (New York: Columbia University Press, 1960); Robert F. Winch, *The Modern Family* (New York: Holt, Rinehart and Winston, 1964); Anne Foner, "Age Stratification and the Changing Family," *American Journal of Sociology,* supplement, 84 (1978): 340–66; Kenneth Keniston, *All Our Children: The American Family Under Pressure* New York: Harcourt Brace Jovanovich, 1977). The trend for the rural family, which occurred after similar patterns had taken place among urban dwellings at the turn of the century, is discussed in Paul H. Landis, *Rural Life in Process* (New York: McGraw-Hill, 1940), pp. 335–53.

22. For the cultural influence of the changing American family, see Andrew G. Truxal and Francis E. Merrill, *The Family in American Culture* (New York: Prentice-Hall, 1947); James H. S. Bossard and Eleanor S. Boll, *Ritual in Family Living: A Contemporary Study* (Philadelphia: University of Pennsylvania Press, 1950); Edward Shorter, *The Making of the Modern Family* (New York: Basic Books, 1975); Robert S. Pickett, "The American Family: An Embattled Institution," *The Humanist* 35 (May/June 1975): 5–8; Michael Gordon, ed., *The American Family in Social-Historical Perspective* (New York: St. Martin's Press, 1978); Christopher Lasch, *Haven in a Heartless World: The Family Besieged* (New York: Basic Books, 1977). For a discussion of the selfward, futuristic orientation of the new generation, see Wilbur Zelinsky, "Selfward Bound? Personal Preference Patterns and the Changing Map of American Society," *Economic Geography* 50 (1974): 144–79; Alan Dundes, "Thinking Ahead: A Folkloristic Reflection of the Future Orientation in American Worldview," *Anthropological Quarterly* 42 (1969): 53–71.

Epilogue

1. Samuel Bayard, "Foreword," in Matthew G. Guntharp, *Learning the Fiddler's Ways* (University Park: Pennsylvania State University Press, 1980), p. 11.

2. A popular report on the renewed strength of the family during this period was Theodore Caplow, Howard M. Bahr, Bruce A. Chadwick, Reuben Hill, and Margaret Holmes Wil-

liamson, *Middletown Families: Fifty Years of Change and Continuity* (New York: Bantam Books, 1983); another upbeat report was "Family Horizons, 1980," in *America's Families: A Documentary History,* ed. Donald M. Scott and Bernard Wishy (New York: Harper and Row, 1982). For evidence of the "Roots" movement inspired by Alex Haley's novel of the same name published in 1976, see Irving Howe, *World of Our Fathers* (New York: Harcourt Brace Jovanovich, 1976); Ellen Robinson Epstein and Rona Mendelsohn, *Record and Remember: Tracing Your Roots Through Oral History* (New York: Monarch, 1978); Jim Watts and Allen F. Davis, *Generations: Your Family in Modern American History* (New York: Knopf, 1978); Barbara Allen and Lynwood Montell, *From Memory to History: Using Oral History Sources in Local Historical Research* (Nashville: American Association for State and Local History, 1981); Steven J. Zeitlin, Amy J. Kotkin, Holly Cutting Baker, *A Celebration of American Family Folklore* (New York: Pantheon, 1982).

3. Bayard, "Foreword," p. 11. For a review of the spate of reissues that accompanied the "comeback" of old-time fiddling, see Burt Feintuch, "The Fiddle in North America: Recent Recordings," *Journal of American Folklore* 95 (1982): 493–500. That same year, *The Bluegrass Alternative and the National Fiddler* published an extensive list of new "fiddle records" (June 1982), p. 23. See also, Norm Cohen, "Anglo-American Music: Field Recorded and Otherwise," *Journal of American Folklore* 100 (1987): 80–88.

4. "Bill Knowlton," *Country Music Courier* (May 1986), cover page.

5. Bill C. Malone comments on the new wave of traditionalists in country music in *Country Music, U.S.A.* (rev. ed., Austin: University of Texas Press, 1985), pp. 411–15; a review that expands on Malone's discussion of the traditionalist movement is Charlie Seemann, "Review of *Country Music, U.S.A.,*" *Journal of American Folklore* 99 (1986): 356–58. For more information on the success of traditionalist Ricky Skaggs, see Jim Hatlo, "Ricky Skaggs: Nashville's Latest Star Paid His Dues in the Trenches of Bluegrass," *Frets* (March 1985): 30–45.

6. The quote comes from the brochure for the Del-Se-Nango Olde Tyme Fiddlers Association (New Berlin, N.Y.: n.d.) sent to me by Marjorie Crawford, 8 July 1986.

7. "Old Time Dance Series," *Country Music Courier* (May 1986): 17.

8. See Richard Blaustein, "Traditional Music and Social Change: The Old Time Fiddler Association Movement in the United States" (Ph.D. diss., Indiana University, 1975); Burt Feintuch, "The Fiddle in the United States: An Historical Overview," *Kentucky Folklore Record* 29 (1983): 34–35; Delores DeRyke, "American Old Time Fiddlers Association," *The Devil's Box,* no. 18 (1 September 1972): 6–7; George Kenneth Leivers, "Structure and Function of an Old-Time Fiddlers Association" (M.A. thesis, California State University—Chico, 1974). For the New York State Old Tyme Fiddlers Association and the North American Fiddlers Hall of Fame and Museum, see Joyce Newberry Rudnick, "Alice Clemens: Tug Hill Virtuoso," *Bluegrass Unlimited* (August 1986): 62–66. For discussion of the effects of the associations in one particular locale, the "North Country" of New York, see Robert D. Bethke, "Old-Time Fiddling and Social Dance in Central St. Lawrence County," *New York Folklore Quarterly* 30 (1974): 163–84.

9. For reports on apprenticeship programs, see Pennsylvania Council on the Arts, *Apprenticeships in Traditional Arts* (Harrisburg: Pennsylvania Council on the Arts, 1986); Debbie Felton, "Folk Art Apprenticeships: America Preserves its Crafting Legacy," *Needlecraft Ideas* (Fall 1986): 66–67. A provocative series of articles on the future preservation of old-time fiddling is found in *The Devil's Box,* a magazine devoted to old-time fiddling. See Kelley Kirksey, "The Future of Old-Time Fiddling," no. 5 (22 July 1968): 8–12; Richard Blaustein, "Preservation of Old Time Fiddling as a Living Force," no. 13 (September 1970): 6–8; Neil Johnston, "Folk Fiddling: Which Direction—Preservation or Development?" no. 21 (1 June 1973): 5–6, and "Preservation and Development in the Next Decade," no. 23 (1 December 1973): 17–19. For a general background on the movement to conserve culture, see Ormond H. Loomis, *Cultural Conservation: The Protection of Cultural Heritage in the United States* (Washington, D.C.: Library of Congress, 1983).

10. " 'Fiddlers' Conversation' at Cooperstown," *Quarterly Newsletter of the Center for the Study of North Country Folklife* (Spring 1978): 9.

Notes to the Musical Transcriptions

THESE notes provide information that should be useful to appreciating the performance, function, and circulation of these tunes. First, I document the performance from which the transcription was taken. Second, I offer a commentary on the style or technique of playing and some historical and comparative notes on the tune. Third, I give places to find the tune in books and articles, and some recently available records. While I cannot be comprehensive, I hope that by giving this bibliographic discussion, I will suggest the spread, or at least the record of collection, of the tunes. Last, I give information on the use of the tunes. Most often this will be in the form of references to the dances or play-party figures that accompany the tunes.

There are far more tunes in the New York old-time music repertoire than could be reproduced here, but this is a fair sampling. I was guided by several considerations in my choice of tunes. First, I wanted to give tunes that are characteristic of the musicians in this book. I also selected tunes that would give a cross-section of the types of music and instruments used in New York State. In addition, I repeated some tunes to invite comparison. The titles cited for the tunes are the ones given by the musicians.

In the background of the tunes are examples of the various sources that went into the formation of old-time music. I included tunes with roots in old British Isles folk tradition, the vogue of English and French dancing in the late eighteenth and early nineteenth centuries, minstrel shows and Yankee theaters, ballads and folk songs, children's play-parties, family and community traditions, Tin Pan Alley compositions, and barn dances. In some instances the sources for the tunes are clear, but in most others, they are not. The notes on sources are therefore meant to be suggestive and inspiring of more detective work.

The historical purpose in giving special due to transcriptions of tunes played by influential nineteenth-century fiddlers is this: In the absence of recordings from the nineteenth century, Wordell Martin's rendition of one of Alva Belcher's reels and John McDermott's tribute to Happy Bill Daniels are our only means of noting the contributions of these historic figures. These figures stood in a path of cultural migration from New England to New York across to Ohio and Michigan. To give a reference to this shared heritage, I have included some exemplary tunes from the first revival of the pioneers' music. You'll find transcriptions of the playing of Mellie Dunham of Maine, John Baltzell of Ohio, and Jasper Bisbee of Michigan. But lest you think that this legacy is a nook of still water beside a rushing stream, I show developments in New York's old-time music right up to the present. I have included transcriptions from performers like Milo Kouf and Charley Hughes who have inherited the old-time music repertoire and are active now. The notes, then, include something for the historian, musician, dancer, musicologist, and folklorist, and for those who simply want to know what these tunes are about.

1. "Haste to the Wedding," played by Milo Kouf on fiddle. Recorded by Simon Bronner, at the Newfield Old Time Fiddlers Contest, Newfield, New York, 2 July 1977. Kouf plays this jig in a standard tuning and he follows an A A B B form in performance. He creates a droning sound on the tune by playing the open A or D strings. He inserts a more complicated melody, probably for the purposes of the contest, in a variation of measure 13. Kouf said that he learned from his father and that the tune was a favorite dance tune in western New York State. British sources of the tune are William Chappell, *A Collection of National English Airs,* 2 vols. (London: Chappell, 1840), I, no. 163; Cecil J. Sharp, *Country Dance Tunes* (London: Novello, 1909), pp. 8–9; Maud Karpeles and Lois Blake, *Dances of England and Wales* (New York: Chanticleer Press, 1951), pp. 26–28; Peter Kennedy, *The Fiddler's Tune-Book* (New York: Hargail Music Press, 1951), p. 40; Miles Krassen, *O'Neill's Music of Ireland* (New York: Oak Publications, 1976), p. 49. Chappell traces the tune back at least to the eighteenth century; he writes that "this tune is more frequently to be heard upon the chimes of country churches than any other, and usually played when a wedding is about to take place. In 1767, it was introduced into a pantomime called *The Elopement,* performed at Drury Lane Theatre, and we have not yet seen any older copy" (II, p. 129). American versions of the tune are reported in Samuel Preston Bayard, *Hill Country Tunes: Instrumental Folk Music of Southwestern Pennsylvania* (Philadelphia: American Folklore Society, 1944), no. 22 and *Dance to the Fiddle, March to the Fife: Instrumental Folk Tunes in Pennsylvania* (University Park: Pennsylvania State University Press, 1982), pp. 420–28, 585–86; R. P. Christeson, *The Old-Time Fiddler's Repertory* (Columbia: University of Missouri Press, 1973), p. 121; Eloise Hubbard Linscott, *Folk Songs of Old New England* (New York: Macmillan, 1939), pp. 87–89; Miles Krassen, *Appalachian Fiddle* (New York: Oak Publications, 1973), p. 86; Ira W. Ford, *Traditional Music of America* (Hatboro, Pennsylvania: Folklore Associates, 1965), p. 53; *One Thousand Fiddle Tunes* (1940; rpt. ed., Chicago: M. M. Cole, 1967); Alan Jabbour, *American Fiddle Tunes from the Archive of Folk Song* (Washington, D.C.: Music Division, Library of Congress, Album AFS L62, 1971), pp. 9–10; B. A. Botkin, *Play and Dance Songs and Tunes* (Washington, D.C.: Music Division, Library of Congress, Album AAFS L9), p. 1; Winston Wilkinson, "Virginia Dance Tunes," *Southern Folklore Quarterly* 6 (1942): 7–8; W. H. Morris, *Old Time Violin Melodies* (St. Joseph, Mo.: W. H. Morris, 1927), no. 16; E. F. Adam, *Old Time Fiddlers' Favorite Barn Dance Tunes* (St. Louis: E. F. Adam, 1928), no. 15; James C. Tyson, *Twenty Five Old Fashioned Dance Tunes for Piano Solo* (New York: Belwin, n.d.), no. 9. The tune can be heard on Jabbour, *American Fiddle Tunes;* Guy Carawan, *Jubilee* (June Appal JA 029, 1979). Descriptions of country dances that accompany the tune are found in Cecil J. Sharp, *The Country Dance Book* (rev. ed., London: Novello, 1934), pp. 48–49; Beth Tolman and Ralph Page, *The Country Dance Book* (New York: A. S. Barnes, 1937), pp. 103–4.

2. "Belcher's Reel," played by Wordell Martin on fiddle. Recorded by Sam Eskin, Prattsville, Greene County, 1948. Martin plays this unusual setting of "Mason's Apron," a reel usually traced back to Scotland and Ireland, with fast separate bows. In America, variants of the tune also go by the name of "Wake Up Susan" and "Hell on the Potomac." Playing each note in this clean manner makes this tune difficult to execute. In addition to "Belcher's Reel," Eskin recorded Martin's versions of "Haste to the Wedding," "Irish Washerwoman," "Mrs. McLeod's Reel," "Larry O'Gaff," "Jolly Blacksmith," "Opera Reel," "Turkey in the Straw," "Dusty Miller," "Soldier's Joy," "Durang's Hornpipe," "Over the Waves," and "Nellie Gray." Martin's repertoire gives at least a glimpse of the musical tradition in the Catskills that Belcher probably performed. For variants of the tune, see Bayard, *Dance to the Fiddle,* pp. 76–77, pp. 185–86, 346–53; Kennedy, *Fiddler's Tune-Book,* p. 25; Krassen, *O'Neill's Music of Ireland,* p. 122; Christeson, *Old-Time Fiddler's Repertory,* p. 5; Krassen, *O'Neill's Music of Ireland,* p. 49; Ford, *Traditional Music in America,* p. 65; *One Thousand Fiddle Tunes,* pp. 21, 50; E. Gale Huntington, ed., *William Litten's Fiddle Tunes 1800–1802* (Vineyard Haven, Mass.: Hines Point Publishers, 1977), p. 12; *White's Unique Collection of Jigs, Reels, Etc.* (New York: White-Smith Music, 1896), no. 52. David Brody in *The Fiddler's Fakebook* (New York: Oak Publications, 1983), p. 185, provides a version based on the recording of the tune by Boys of the Lough (*Second Album,* Rounder 3006); other versions are heard on Jean Carignan, *French Canadian Fiddle Songs* (Legacy 120), Sean McGuire, *Ireland's Champion Traditional Fiddler* (Outlet 1031), and Graham Townsend, *Le Violon/The Fiddle* (Rounder 7002). Mention of a dance done to "Mason's Apron" is given in H. A. Thurston, *Scotland's Dances* (London: G. Bell and Sons, 1954), p. 103.

3. "Happy Bill Daniels Quadrille" played by John McDermott on fiddle. Recorded on Brunswick 20053, New York City, 30 December 1926. In naming this tune after Bill Daniels, McDermott did not make clear whether he was offering tribute by playing Daniels' tunes, his style, or both. The man McDermott honors was born in 1853 and was an active professional fiddler around Cortland by 1871; he died in 1923. Of the tunes on this recording, only one is clearly recognizable—"Turkey in the Straw." This is not surprising, because quadrilles especially, in the words of Samuel Bayard in *Dance to the Fiddle,* are characterized by being "untraceable as melodic entities, often plainly composite—but well organized, shapely, and instinct with grace and gaiety" (p. 489). In both Bayard's and Christeson's collections the largest number of unnamed tunes belong to quadrilles. Why this should be true of quadrilles can be explained by the nature of the dance. As the name suggests, the single quadrille is a dance having four sides, a couple on each side. The classic quadrille, passed to the British Isles from France, was distinguished from other square dances by having a particular series of five or six prescribed sequences, each different. The form required many different melodies of eight bars each to signal each new figure within the sequences. It became common practice to string tunes or parts of tunes together, often in new combinations, to serve the demanding purposes of the quadrille. During the nineteenth century, the music for the quadrille was published in four parts and had at least three, and sometimes more, numbers in different keys and tempos. By contrast, today's quadrille refers to a single number in 6/8 time. The recording of this quadrille is accordingly in four parts; it uses six distinct strains and a closing fiddle tune. In the quadrille, McDermott switches his time signature three times and his keys twice, all while shouting calls and keeping the rhythm absolutely steady. In its structure and performance, at least, this performance harks back to an earlier age. As can be seen, an important reason for honoring an older fiddler with a quadrille (John Baltzell in this collection also honored his mentor Dan Emmett with a quadrille) was that it was the ultimate test of the old-time fiddler's versatility and technique. In the first set of the recording, McDermott plays octaves in the B part and a long flowing, lyrical melody in the C part. The form that McDermott uses is A B A C A B A C. Apparently emphasizing the older British Isles style, McDermott emphasizes the quick 6 beats over 4 by playing in a 12/8 time signature. In the second set, McDermott switches to cut time while keeping the rhythm right on the beat. Again, McDermott relies on an impressive use of long slurs and long note values as well as a contrasting lyrical section in the B part. The third set is unusual because it is in the key of C. This is not a common fiddle key because it requires an awkward fingering pattern on the instrument's neck. The B part of this set consists of a repeated arpeggio on a G chord where the fingers are not moved but set in a pattern (similar to forming a chord on the guitar) and the bow moves over all four strings rapidly to get the effect. On "Turkey in the Straw" McDermott relies on another technique of using constant sixteenth notes. Many times he repeats the same note four or more times and adds to the rhythmic effect by forming octaves in the B part. This heavy reliance on rhythm by the melody instrument made younger players of square dances from Cortland like Larry Harrington flinch, but it was an effective means for the solo fiddler in the house-party days to achieve volume and give the dancers a sure rhythm. Indeed, McDermott demonstrates several advanced fiddling techniques that probably put him a cut above other fiddlers. His long slurs require a good balanced bow hold; it is easier to play everything in the middle of the bow rather than drawing long bows as McDermott does. Unlike many old-time fiddlers, McDermott also uses the difficult third position in the A and C part of the first set, and the A and B parts of the second set. Also impressive are his use of two-fingered double stops in the B part of the first set, long slurs in the C part of the first set and the B part of the second set, and arpeggio bowing in the B part of the third set. McDermott's playing in the key of C and his frequent shifting to third position also point out his good left hand position and secure hold on the violin. Although finding the sources for the unidentified tunes that McDermott uses is difficult, the tunes bear resemblance to strains in the collections of Bayard and Christeson. The first set is reminiscent in parts of Bayard's tune no. 561 identified simply as "Quadrille," and the third set shows some similarities to Bayard's tune no. 489 identified as an "Old Dance" in 6/8 time. There is also more than a passing resemblance between the descending passages of Christeson's tune no. 181, identified simply as "Quadrille," and the C part of McDermott's first set. I cover the background on "Turkey in the Straw" separately in the notes for my tune no. 31. For more descriptions of the music and dance of the quadrille, see Philip J. S. Richardson, *The Social Dances of the Nineteenth Century*

in England (London: Herbert Jenkins, 1960), pp. 54–74; Tolman and Page, *Country Dance Book,* pp. 56–82; Thornton Hagert, *Instrumental Dance Music 1780s–1920s* (New World 293), pp. 1–2.

      4. "Virginia Reel Medley," played by John McDermott on fiddle. Recorded on Brunswick 20050, New York City, 30 December 1926. On this dance medley, McDermott opens with a version of "Miss McLeod's Reel," followed by a sudden switch to the time of 6/8 with a tune that often goes by the name "Jesus Loves the Little Children" or "Jesus Loves the Little Ones"; see Florence E. Brunnings, *Folk Song Index: A Comprehensive Guide to the Florence E. Brunnings Collection* (New York: Garland, 1981), p. 156. An Irish-sounding shuffle then introduces "The Girl I Left Behind Me." McDermott's "Miss McLeod's Reel" bears strong similarities to a tune widely reported in America as "Hop Hi Ladies" or "Wild Horses at Stoney Point." McDermott's version is characterized by a pointed rhythm using a ♫ figure in the main motif and an interesting variation using an octave shuffle in the B part. The switch to 6/8 time jolts the listener but the beat stays steady for the dancers: ♩ becomes ♩.. "McDermott's Shuffle" has 8-bar sections played without internal repeats making the structure half as long as most fiddle tunes. It resembles the B section of a tune reported in the British Isles as "May Day" and "Miss McLeod's Reel"; Norman Cazden reports a similar B part in a version of "Miss McLeod's Reel" collected in the Catskills. See Kennedy, *Fiddler's Tune Book,* p. 24, and Norman Cazden, *Dances from Woodland: Square Dances from the Catskills* (Ann Arbor, Mich.: Cushing-Malloy, 1955), p. 29. "McDermott's Shuffle" is also in the key of D which is the dominant key of the medley (all the other tunes are in G). The shuffle therefore has the feel of a bridge or interlude and not a tune in its own right. McDermott's "Miss McLeod's Reel" resembles variant E reported in Bayard, *Dance to the Fiddle,* p. 212; Paul Wells, ed., *New England Traditional Fiddling, 1926–1975* (John Edwards Memorial Foundation JEMF-105, 1978), pp. 15–16, and "Hop High Ladies" in John Cohen and Mike Seeger, *Old-Time String Band Songbook* (New York: Oak Publications, 1976), pp. 64–65, and Marion Thede, *The Fiddle Book* (New York: Oak Publications, 1967), p. 99. Apparently, "McLeod's Reel" followed two distinct tune families; see Brody, *Fiddler's Fakebook,* p. 192. Floyd Woodhull plays a version on the accordion that is almost identical to McDermott's; Prattsville, New York, native Wordell Martin (see tune no. 2) recorded a "Virginia Reel" (New York State Historical Association, Sam Eskin Collection) which is another close relation to McDermott's tune. For a New York version of the tune family that differs sharply from McDermott's, see the notes to Les Weir's "McLeod's" (tune no. 30). Bayard recognizes that McDermott's version of the tune has a wide circulation and traces the tune as far back as 1809 when it appeared in a collection of Scottish reels under the label "Mrs. McLeod of Raasay's Reel. An original Isle of Sky Reel. Communicated by Mr. McLeod" (p. 213). For more references, see Wells, *New England Traditional Fiddling,* pp. 15–16, and Richard Spottswood, *Dance Music: Reels, Polkas, & More* (Library of Congress, Music Division, Folk Music in America Series, vol. 4, LBC 4, 1976), pp. 6–7. The tune to "The Girl I Left Behind Me" is usually credited to a song that originated in the British Isles (some insist on an Irish root) in the late eighteenth century. In the instrumental tradition, it was often used as a march tune in addition to a favorite dancing tune. Indeed, it bears a resemblance to "Brighton Camp," another old (and probably older) song, that became known as a march in Great Britain. See Bayard, *Dance to the Fiddle,* p. 325; Kennedy, *Fiddler's Tune Book,* p. 27. McDermott's rendition of "Girl I Left Behind Me" matches the tune as it is usually reported in dance collections; Tolman and Page's collection credits upstate New York with the development of the country dance to the tune (p. 78). "The Girl I Left Behind Me" ranks as one of America's most collected folk songs. Extensive notes on the tune and song in the Northeast can be found in Bayard, *Dance to the Fiddle,* pp. 322–25; Linscott, *Folk Songs of Old New England,* pp. 79–80; Norman Cazden, Herbert Haufrecht, and Norman Studer, *Notes and Sources for Folk Songs of the Catskills* (Albany: State University of New York Press, 1982), pp. 31–32. Sources in the British Isles include Richard Henebry, *A Handbook of Irish Music* (London: Longmans Green & Co., 1928), pp. 291, 301; William Chappell, *A Collection of National English Airs,* I, no. 172, II, p. 134; John Ord, *The Bothy Songs and Ballads of Aberdeen, Banff and Moray, Angus and the Mearns* (Paisley, Scotland: Gardner, 1930), pp. 45–47. Prominent field collections of the tune and song in folk tradition are Norman Cazden, Herbert Haufrecht, and Norman Studer, *Folk Songs of the Catskills* (Albany: State University of New York Press, 1982) pp. 159–61; Matthew Guntharp, *Learning the Fiddler's Ways* (University Park: Pennsylvania State University

Press, 1980), pp. 46–47; H. M. Belden, *Ballads and Songs Collected by the Missouri Folk-Lore Society* (1940; rpt. ed., Columbia: University of Missouri Press 1973), pp. 198–200; Alan Lomax, *The Folk Songs of North America* (1960; rpt. ed., Garden City, New York: Doubleday, 1975), pp. 318–20; Henry W. Shoemaker, *Mountain Minstrelsy of Pennsylvania* (rev. ed., Philadelphia: Newman F. McGirr, 1931), pp. 155–56; Patrick W. Gainer, *Folk Songs from the West Virginia Hills* (Grantsville, W.V.: Seneca Books, 1975), pp. 173–74; Vance Randolph, *Ozark Folk Songs*, 4 vols. (1946–1950; rpt. ed., Columbia: University of Missouri Press, 1980) I, pp. 283–88, III, pp. 352–54; Jan Philip Schinhan, ed., *Frank C. Brown Collection of North Carolina Folklore: The Music of the Ballads* (Durham, N.C.: Duke University Press, 1957), p. 213; David S. McIntosh, *Folk Songs & Singing Games of the Illinois Ozarks* (Carbondale: Southern Illinois University Press, 1974), pp. 76–77. The dance "Virginia Reel" is widely known on both sides of the Atlantic. In Great Britain the dance was known as "Sir Roger de Coverley" and used the "longways" formation that was popular in seventeenth- and eighteenth-century social dancing until squares became more popular. See Thurston, *Scotland's Dances*, p. 14; Richardson, *The Social Dances of the Nineteenth Century in England*, p. 57; Cecil J. Sharp, *The Country Dance Book* (1934; rpt. ed., London: EP Publishing, 1972), pp. 9–14; Elias Howe, *Complete Ball-Room Hand Book* (Boston: Oliver Ditson, 1858), p. 92. The "Virginia Reel" has been the most persistent of the old longways dances in America. "For years," Tolman and Page claim in their *Country Dance Book*, the "Virginia Reel" was the common wind-up of an evening's program (p. 114); their dance instructions, apropos McDermott's version, call for a switch from a section in 6/8 time to the more common "reel" in cut time. For other versions of the dance in America, see Howe, *Ball-Room Hand Book*, p. 87; Cazden, *Dances from Woodland*, p. 14; Jean Thomas and Joseph A. Leeder, *The Singin' Gatherin': Tunes from the Southern Appalachians* (New York: Silver Burdett, 1939), p. 89; Grace L. Ryan, *Dances of Our Pioneers* (New York: A. S. Barnes, 1939), pp. 160–63; Richard G. Kraus, *Square Dances of Today* (New York: Ronald Press, 1950), pp. 108–109; Jessie B. Flood and Cornelia F. Putney, *Square Dance U.S.A.* (Dubuque, Iowa: Wm. C. Brown, 1955), p. 46; Elizabeth Burchenal, *American Country Dances* (New York: G. Schirmer, 1918), pp. 10–11.

5. "Money Musk" played by John Baltzell on fiddle. Recorded on Edison 51354, New York City, 7 September 1923. Baltzell's style of accenting the rhythm by punching out many single notes on the fiddle resembles McDermott's playing closely. The tune is usually considered a difficult one and is played in two or four parts; Baltzell apparently plays it both ways on this recording. The label lists "Baltzell's Reel" in addition to "Money Musk." The reel appears as variations C and D. A conspicuous feature of Baltzell's playing is a high C# that requires a fast shift to the third position in part B and variations 2, 3, and 4. Baltzell, an experienced contest fiddler, apparently played this piece to show off rather than to accompany dancers. In this performance, Baltzell follows the unusual structure: A A B B A B Var-1 Var-2 Var-3 Var-4 A A B Var-1 Var-2 Var-3 C C D D C C A A B Var-1 Var-2 A. According to Bayard in *Dance to the Fiddle*, the origin of the name is in the fuller Scottish title "Sir Archibald Grant of Moniemuske's Reel" and cites a manuscript stating that the piece was composed and titled by Daniel Dow in 1776. If he did compose the tune, according to Bayard, "he certainly had his earlier models, namely the two cognate airs, 'Roy's Wife of Aldivalloch' and 'The Ruffians Rant' " (p. 331). Baltzell's version closely matches Bayard's variant A (p. 329). According to Jabbour in *American Fiddle Tunes*, the tune "has turned up regularly in twentieth-century American tradition except in the South, where evidence indicates that it was once current but passed out of circulation" (p. 10). For versions of the tune, see Christeson, *Old-Time Fiddler's Repertory*, p. 15; Krassen, *Appalachian Fiddle*, pp. 70–71; Ford, *Traditional Music in America*, p. 52; Krassen, *O'Neill's Music of Ireland*, p. 125; *One Thousand Fiddle Tunes*, pp. 28, 31; E. F. Adam, *Old Time Fiddlers' Favorite Barn Dance Tunes*, no. 59; James C. Tyson, *Twenty Five Old Fashioned Dance Tunes*, no. 17; Jean Carignan, *Jean Carignan rend hommage à Joseph Allard* (Philo FI-2012) transcribed in Brody, *Fiddler's Fakebook*, pp. 194–95; Peter Kennedy, *The Second Fiddler's Tune-Book* (New York: Hargail Music Press, 1954), p. 17; *Sym's Old Time Dances* (New York: G. T. Worth, 1930), p. 5; Paul De Ville, *The Universal Favorite Contra Dance Album* (New York: Carl Fischer, 1905), no. 63; *The Robbins Collection of 200 Jigs, Reels, and Country Dances* (New York: Robbins Musical Corp., 1933), no. 120; Alexander McGlashan, *A Collection of Reels* (Edinburgh, Scotland: Neil Stewart, n.d.), p. 19; J. O'Malley and F. Atwood, *Seventy Good Old Dances* (Boston: Oliver Ditson, 1919), p. 38; Mellie Dunham, *"Mellie" Dunham's Fiddlin' Dance Tunes* (New York: Carl Fischer, 1926), no. 28;

George Knauff, *Virginia Reels, No. 1* (Baltimore: Geog. Willig, Jr., 1839), p. 1; Paul Wells, *New England Traditional Fiddling,* pp. 13–14; H. Jarman and Bill Hansen, *Old-Time Dance Tunes* (New York: Broadcast Music Co., 1951), p. 15. The tune can be heard on Jabbour, *American Fiddle Tunes;* Wells, *New England Traditional Fiddling;* John A. MacDonald, *Marches, Strathspeys, Reels and Jigs of the Cape Breton Scot* (Rodeo RLP 75); Tommy Hunter, *Deep in Tradition* (June Appal 007, 1976). The dance called "Money Musk" ranked as one of the most popular of country dances in New England and New York. Variations of the dance are described in Howe, *Ball-Room Hand Book,* p. 82; Burchenal, *American Country Dances,* p. 55; Ryan, *Dances of Our Pioneers,* pp. 148–49; Cazden, *Dances from Camp Woodland,* p. 31; Eloise Hubbard Linscott in *Folk Songs of Old New England* (New York: Macmillan, 1939); Dudley T. Briggs, *Thirty Contras from New England* (Burlington, Massachusetts: Dudley T. Briggs, 1953), pp. 67–68; Jean C. Milligan, *101 Scottish Country Dances* (Glasgow: Collins, 1956), pp. 120–21.

    6. "Durang's Hornpipe" played by John Baltzell on fiddle. Recorded on Edison 51236, 7 September 1923. The low notes in the second measure indicates that the fiddle is in a D tuning with the G string raised to A. This tuning enables the fiddle to play the low A, B, and C# with open, first, and second fingers instead of the standard tuning which requires use of the first, second, and a raised third finger for the C#. The tune was named for the popular actor and dancer John Durang (born Lancaster, Pennsylvania, 1768; died Philadelphia, 1821). In his memoirs, *The Memoir of John Durang, American Actor 1785–1816,* ed. Alan S. Downer (Pittsburgh: University of Pittsburgh Press, 1966), Durang offers his hornpipe "as Composed by Mr. Hoffmaster, a German Dwarf, in New York, 1785." Durang describes the origin of the tune this way: "While I was in New York I took lessons on the violin of Mr. Phile, and of Mr. Hoffmaster, a dwarf, a man about 3 foot, large head, hands and feet; his wife of the same stature. A good musician, he composed the following hornpipe expressly for me, which is become well known in America, for I have since heard it play'd the other side of the Blue Mountains as well as in the cities" (p. 22). The Blue Mountains rest in central Pennsylvania. Durang may have been surprised to know that the tune has travelled much farther, and in the process the tune has been substantially altered. Bayard in *Dance to the Fiddle* points out that "true to their Anglo-American heritage," northeastern fiddlers "have eliminated the accidentals, reduced the melodic sequences, and made changes that have added considerable musical variety and interest" (p. 344). For comparison, I have included Jehile Kirkhuff's rendition of "Durang's Hornpipe" in the text (tune no. 11). Other twentieth-century versions taken from tradition are reported in Ford, *Traditional Music in America,* p. 398; Krassen, *O'Neill's Music of Ireland,* p. 215; Krassen, *Appalachian Fiddle,* p. 82; Christeson, *Old-Time Fiddler's Repertory,* p. 63; Thede, *Fiddle Book,* p. 116; Cazden, *Dances from Camp Woodland,* p. 42; Adam, *Old Time Fiddlers Favorite Barn Dance Tunes,* no. 19; Newton F. Tolman, *Quick Tunes and Good Times* (Dublin, N.H.: William L. Bauhan, 1972), p. 106; Ira W. Ford, *Traditional Music of America* (New York: Dutton, 1940), p. 53. Recordings of the tune include Paul Wells, ed., *New England Traditional Fiddling;* Alan Jabbour, ed., *American Fiddle Tunes; Seems Like Romance to Me: Traditional Fiddle Tunes from Ohio* (Gambier Folklore Society GFS 901, 1985); Earl Collins, *That's Earl Collins Family Fiddling* (Briar 0798); U.S. Senator Robert Byrd, *Mountain Fiddler* (County 769); John W. Summers, *Indiana Fiddler* (Rounder 0194); Major Franklin, *Texas Fiddle Favorites* (County 707); Clark Kessinger, *Sweet Bunch of Daisies* (County 747); Grant Lamb, *Tunes from Home* (Voyager 312-S); Benny and Jerry Thomasson, *A Jam Session with Benny & Jerry Thomasson* Voyager VRLP 309); J. T. Perkins, *Fiddle Favorites Perkins Style* (David Unlimited DU 33017). Descriptions of dances that accompany "Durang's Hornpipe" are found in Howe, *Ball-Room Hand Book,* p. 82; Burchenal, *American Country Dances,* p. 34; Briggs, *Thirty Contras,* p. 49; Tolman and Page, *Country Dance Book,* p. 124; Lee Owens and Viola Ruth, *Advanced Square Dance Figures of the West and Southwest* (Palo Alto, California: Pacific Books, 1950), pp. 36–38; Richard Nevell, *A Time to Dance: American Country Dancing from Hornpipes to Hot Hash* (New York: St. Martin's Press, 1977), pp. 139–41.

    7. "Bisbee's Waltz" played by Henry Ford's Old-Fashioned Dance Orchestra. Recorded on Columbia 877, New York City, c. 1926. Waltzes are not regularly reported in collections of old-time fiddle tunes, but they do form an important part of the old-time repertoire. To this day, many old-time fiddle contests require that the fiddler play a waltz. Often, there is great variation possible on the waltzes because measures of different waltzes can be realigned to produce a novel form. "Bisbee's Waltz" is an example. Its B part recalls "Copenhagen Waltz" in Mr. and Mrs.

Ford, *"Good Morning." Old-Time Dancing Music, Calls and Directions* (third edition, Dearborn, Michigan, n.p., 1941). It is not unlikely that Bisbee inspired the music for the book. But Bisbee's fifth and sixth measures resemble "The Portland Fancy in Waltz Time" reported in Bayard, *Dance to the Fiddle*, p. 564, while the descending passages in the B part resemble the varsovienne waltzes on p. 568. Many fiddlers refer to the waltzes as part of their "round-dance" repertoire; see Ford, *Traditional Music in America*, pp. 131–46. A description of the waltz in the country dances of New England is found in Linscott, *Folk Songs of Old New England*, pp. 118–20.

8. "Hull's Victory" played by Mellie Dunham on fiddle. Recorded on Victor 40131, New York City, 19 January 1926. This tune is characterized by ending on an A note in the A part instead of D as one would expect. This gives the A part an unfinished feeling; it eggs the dancer (or listener) to continue. Dunham shares with Baltzell and McDermott playing that is full of separate bowing and single notes. He uses shuffles similar to McDermott in the variation of the A part, but he employs no drones. The song "Hull's Victory" circulated after the sea battle in 1812 between American Isaac Hull in the *Constitution* and the British Captain R. Dacres in the *Guerrière*, but the tune going by the name "Hull's Victory" used for American country dances resembles an English drinking song and a Scottish dance tune. See S. Foster Damon, *The History of Square Dancing* (Barre, Massachusetts: Barre Gazette, 1957), pp. 24–25; John Anthony Scott, *The Ballad of America* (New York: Bantam Books, 1966), pp. 108–10. For versions of the song, see Harold W. Thompson, *A Pioneer Songster: Texts from the Stevens-Douglass Manuscripts of Western New York, 1841–1856* (Ithaca, N.Y.: Cornell University Press, 1958), pp. 118–20; Robert W. Neeser, *American Naval Songs and Ballads* (New Haven: Yale University Press, 1938), p. 95; John Harrington Cox, *Folk-Songs of the South* (Cambridge, Mass.: Harvard University Press, 1925), p. 257; Joanna C. Colcord, *Songs of American Sailormen* (New York: W. W. Norton, 1938), p. 130. As a dance tune, "Hull's Victory" is found in Ford, *Traditional Music in America*, p. 74; Krassen, *O'Neill's Music of Ireland*, p. 198; *One Thousand Fiddle Tunes*, p. 103; Wells, *New England Traditional Fiddling*, p. 20; *Gems of the Ball Room, No. 8* (Chicago: E. T. Root & Sons, 1899); Lloyd Shaw, *Cowboy Dances* (Caldwell, Id.: Caxton Printers, 1952), p. 388; Mellie Dunham, *"Mellie" Dunham's Fiddlin' Dance Tunes* (New York: Carl Fischer, 1926), tune no. 18. A version taken from the recording *New England Contra Dance Music* (Kicking Mule 216) is found in Brody, *Fiddler's Fakebook*, p. 137; for other recordings, see Wells, *New England Traditional Fiddling*; Jabbour, *American Fiddle Tunes*. The dance to "Hull's Victory" in New York and New England took a contra dance formation with six to eight couples in a set. According to Linscott in *Folk Songs of Old New England*, "no country dance would be complete without 'Hull's Victory' "; she describes the dance and gives the music on pp. 86–87. For other versions of the dance, see Howe, *Ball-Room Hand Book*, p. 82; Dudley T. Briggs, *Thirty Contras from New England* (Burlington, Mass.: Dudley T. Briggs, 1953), pp. 69–71; Anne Schley Duggan, Jeanette Schlottmann, and Abbie Rutledge, *Folk Dances of the United States and Mexico* (New York: Ronald Press, 1948), pp. 71–74; Burchenal, *American Country Dances*, pp. 30–31.

9. "Irish Washerwoman" played by Floyd Woodhull on accordion. Recorded by Simon Bronner at Floyd Woodhull's home in Elmira, New York, 5 May 1976. This rendition shows some stylistic differences between playing on the fiddle and the accordion, two popular instruments of upstate New York. Woodhull's version on accordion uses more close intervals and scale passages; on fiddle it is easier to play larger intervals rapidly by crossing strings (see tune no. 19). Woodhull divides this tune into an A and B part, and plays them in an A A B B format. Bayard in *Dance to the Fiddle* (p. 419) finds that the earliest printing of the tune (that is, its A part) is in 1609; as a dance tune it appears in John Playford's *English Dancing Master* (1651). It was also a favorite tune of American stage Yankees in the turn-of-the-eighteenth-century popular theater; it appeared in music to "The Federal Overture," published by B. Carr in 1795 and it played to theaters in Philadelphia and New York. In William Chappell's *Popular Music of the Olden Time*, 2 vols. (London: Cramer Beale & Chappell, 1855–59), the tune (under the title "Country Courtship") appears in much the same form that Woodhull and most other American players know it (II, pp. 671–72). By the time that Chappell was writing, Bayard claims, the title "Irish Washerwoman" was in vogue. The tune is widely reported as a dance and once in a while it appears as a song. For samples of the tune from tradition, see Linscott, *Folk Songs of Old New England*, p. 117; Cazden, *Dances from Camp Woodland*, p. 23; Bayard, *Dance to the Fiddle*, pp. 415–20; Randolph, *Ozark Folksongs*, III, p. 21; Kennedy, *Fiddler's Tune-Book*, p. 46; Carl Sandburg, *The American*

Songbag (New York: Harcourt, Brace, 1927), pp. 120–22. For other versions, see Tyson, *Twenty Five Old Fashioned Dance Tunes*, no. 19; Adam, *Old Time Fiddlers Favorite Barn Dance Tunes*, no. 3; *Gems of the Ball Room*, no. 11. "Irish Washerwoman" accompanies a variety of dances. The oldest references refer to a longways or contra dance, but twentieth-century dance advisers use the tune for square and circle dances as well as for a part of the Virginia Reel. See Sharp, *Country Dance Book*, p. 119; Tolman and Page, *Country Dance Book*, p. 101, 114; Linscott, *Folk Songs of Old New England*, pp. 116–17; Ryan, *Dances of Our Pioneers*, pp. 174–76; Flood and Putney, *Square Dance U.S.A.*, p. 85; Kate Van Winkle Keller and Ralph Sweet, *A Choice Selection of American Country Dances of the Revolutionary Era* (New York: Country Dance and Song Society of America, 1975), p. 31.

10. "Sailor's Hornpipe," played by Floyd Woodhull on accordion. Recorded by Simon Bronner at Floyd Woodhull's home in Elmira, New York, 5 May 1976. Woodhull plays this tune on a low register; fiddlers usually play it an octave above. The tune is also known in tradition as "College Hornpipe" and sometimes "Jack the Lad." The editor of William Chappell's *Popular Music of the Olden Time* dates the tune as no earlier than the second half of the eighteenth century (II, p. 741). It was commonly played in the turn of the eighteenth-century musical theater when the sailor was a favorite stage character. Its earliest known printing in the United States was in a book published by B. Carr (who also published the "Irish Washerwoman" and "Yankee Doodle" for musical theaters) entitled *Evening Amusements* under the title "College Hornpipe" in 1796; see James J. Fuld, *Book of World-Famous Music* (New York: Crown, 1971), p. 484. Seventeen months later, the tune was printed in Great Britain by J. Dale of London under the title "College Hornpipe." Thurston in *Scotland's Dances* also mentions that the tune became ingrained in tradition because it provided the chief dance at Highland games (p. 56). The tune was also a favorite of American dancing masters for teaching a longways dance used with hornpipes; see Arthur C. Cole, "The Puritan and Fair Terpsichore," *Mississippi Valley Historical Review* 29 (1942): 18–20. For the tune as it was known in America during the Revolutionary era, see Keller and Sweet, *A Choice Selection*, p. 20; a rendition of "College Hornpipe" taken from their collection is played by fiddler Rodney Miller on *Instrumental Dance Music, 1780s–1920s* (New World NW 293). You can compare that with a "modern" version on Bill Monroe, *Bluegrass Instrumentals* (Decca 74601). For other versions, see Ford, *Traditional Music in America*, p. 46; Krassen, *O'Neill's Music of Ireland*, p. 169; Krassen, *Appalachian Fiddle*, p. 83; Jarman and Hansen, *Old Time Dance Tunes*, p. 76; Huntington, *William Litten's Fiddle Tunes*, p. 19; *One Thousand Fiddle Tunes*, p. 87; Adam, *Old Time Fiddlers Favorite Barn Dance Tunes*, no. 44; Tyson, *Twenty Five Old Fashioned Dance Tunes*, no. 22; Brody, *Fiddler's Fakebook*, p. 243; E. F. Adam, *Old Time Fiddlers' Favorite Barn Dance Tunes* (St. Louis: Hunleth Music Co., 1928), no. 44. For the dance to "Sailor's Hornpipe," see Keller and Sweet, *A Choice Selection*, p. 20; Howe, *Ball-Room Hand Book*, p. 83; Thurston, *Scotland's Dances*, pp. 64–65; Burchenal, *American Country Dances*, p. 45; Jean C. Milligan, *99 More Scottish Country Dances* (Glasgow: Collins, 1963), pp. 29.

11. "Durang's Hornpipe" played by Jehile Kirkhuff on fiddle. Recorded by Simon Bronner at Jehile Kirkhuff's home near Lawton, Pennsylvania, 13 January 1976. Kirkhuff introduces this tune by saying that he will play it in a British Isles "hornpipe style." His playing is controlled and taken at a relatively slow pace. His use of triplets and other ornaments show the British Isles affectation. Also distinguishing Kirkhuff's performance is his ricochet bowing ♫. In this technique, the bow is lightly thrown on the string and allowed to bounce. This may be done on a down bow (⊓) so the preceding downbeat must be an up (∨) bow. This pattern is in contrast to most American old-time fiddlers who arrive at all downbeats with a down bow. What appears as a shuffle pattern in the variation of part A is really a half-bounced working of the bow to create a classical-sounding figure. Kirkhuff can be heard on a tape recording made by Alan Jabbour (8 August 1970) which is deposited in the Archive of Folk Culture, Library of Congress. For that session, Kirkhuff played "Campbells are Coming," "DA Polka Quadrille," "Sailor's Hornpipe," "Wilson's Clog," and "Larry O'Gaff." For a description of Kirkhuff's life and music, see N. DeNault Grula, "Jehile Kirkhuff: A Man and His Music," *Bluegrass Unlimited* 18 (February 1984): 18–20. For historical and musical background on "Durang's Hornpipe," see the notes to tune no. 6, a more "American" sounding rendition.

12. "Soldier's Joy" (2 versions). First version played by Woodhull's Old Tyme Masters. Recorded on Victor 36403B, New York City, 14 July 1941. Second version played by Floyd

Woodhull on accordion. Recorded by Simon Bronner at Floyd Woodhull's home in Elmira, New York, 5 May 1976. Prominent on the first version is the playing of fiddler Ransom Terwilliger and accordionist Floyd Woodhull. Terwilliger has the fiddle in standard tuning, and his playing is crisp and precise. Woodhull plays in unison with Terwilliger on the A part and switches to octaves on the B part. The band uses a standard fiddle-tune form of A A B B. The A part follows the tune as it is usually reported, but the B part varies from other collected versions in its use of arpeggios. In the second version recorded thirty-six years later, Floyd Woodhull demonstrates some features of solo playing on the accordion. He inserts an ornament in the second measure and adds a chromatic line the fourth. Floyd Woodhull will also play a medley of "Soldier's Joy" and "Sailor's Hornpipe" (tune no. 10). Most sources place this tune in the British Isles during the late eighteenth century. It occasionally goes by the name "The King's Head." It has had a vigorous life in Anglo-American tradition, and it remains a favorite with fiddlers. Bayard in *Dance to the Fiddle* alone lists 19 variants. For other versions, see Krassen, *O'Neill's Music of Ireland*, p. 183; Keller and Sweet, *A Choice Selection*, p. 42; Jarman and Hansen, *Old Time Dance Tunes*, pp. 57, 70; *One Thousand Fiddle Tunes*, p. 24; Jabbour, *American Fiddle Tunes*, pp. 2–5; Botkin, *Play and Dance Songs*, p. 3; Thede, *The Fiddle Book*, p. 118; Krassen, *Appalachian Fiddle*, pp. 15, 45; Ford, *Traditional Music in America*, p. 49; Cazden, *Dances from Camp Woodland*, p. 35; Kennedy, *Fiddle Tune Book*, p. 2; Adam, *Old Time Fiddlers' Favorite Barn Dance Tunes*, no. 2; Tyson, *Twenty Five Old Fashioned Dance Tunes*, no. 8; *Gems of the Ball Room*, no. 13; Frank Maloy, "Soldier's Joy (Traditional South Georgia Version)" *Devil's Box* 20 (Winter 1986): 48–49; R. P. Christeson, *The Old-Time Fiddler's Repertory, Volume 2* (Columbia: University of Missouri Press, 1984), p. 61; David Reiner, *Anthology of Fiddle Styles* (Pacific, Missouri: Mel Bay Publications, 1979), p. 37; Maud Karpeles and Kenworth Schofield, *A Selection of 100 English Folk Dance Airs* (London: English Folk Dance and Song Society, 1951). The playing of the tune can be seen in a film *The Country Fiddle* made by Peter Seeger (Beacon, N.Y.: Folklore Research Films, 1959). The tune is a favorite accompaniment to country dances. The dance in America usually preserves an opening circle formation that accompanied "Soldier's Joy" in British Isles tradition. Thurston in *Scotland's Dances* states that "the dance is a simple one in circular formation, the main figure being the grand chain. However, it is at least as likely that this dance derives from an Irish six-hand reel. The tune is common to both Scotland and Ireland" (p. 41). Woodhull gives the following dance to the tune: "Ladies in the center back to back—Gents march around the outside track, meet your partner, pass her by, swing the next girl on the fly. Join your hands and circle to the right, circle half way 'round, the other way back in the same old track with the finest girl in town, allemande left on the corner, now allemande right with your partner, allemande left on the corner again with grand right and left." For other American versions of the dance, see Keller and Sweet, *A Choice Selection*, p. 42; Howe, *Ball-Room Handbook*, p. 89; Tolman and Page, *Country Dance Book*, p. 148; Ryan, *Dances of Our Pioneers*, pp. 34–37; Linscott, *Folk Songs of Old New England*, pp. 109–11; Cazden, *Dances from Camp Woodland*, p. 35.

13. "Blackberry Quadrille" played by Woodhull's Old Tyme Masters. Recorded on Victor 36403, New York City, 14 July 1941. The band performs this tune very much like they did on "Soldier's Joy." The band plays the tune in a A A B B form and Terwilliger and Woodhull play in octaves. Although "Blackberry Quadrille" is a common name of this dance tune in New York State, in other areas of America and Great Britain a variant of this tune goes by the name "Off She Goes." The tune also appears to have some relation to "Rustic Reel," which I discuss in the first chapter; a characteristic transcription is in *One Thousand Fiddle Tunes*, p. 33. Woodhull's tune shows the closest resemblance to "Blackberry Reel," reported by Norman Cazden in *Dances from Camp Woodland*, p. 15. Bayard in *Dance to the Fiddle* speculates that the tune derives from late eighteenth-century British Isles tradition (p. 487). It is difficult to pinpoint a "tune type," because it is reported in various distinct forms; Bayard reports eight versions that show marked differences (pp. 485–87). For other variants, see Cazden, *Dances from Camp Woodland*, p. 13; Jarman and Hansen, *Old Time Dance Tunes*, p. 65; Ford, *Traditional Music in America*, p. 52; Kennedy, *Fiddler's Tune Book*, p. 44; Krassen, *O'Neill's Music of Ireland*, p. 41; F. O'Malley and F. Atwood, *Seventy Good Dances* (Boston: Oliver Ditson, 1919), p. 39. The dance "Blackberry Quadrille" is reported as a contra dance and a square dance. Woodhull gives the following square dance to the tune:: "First four right and left—Now balance four—Two ladies chain—Half promenade—Allemande left on the corner with the grand right and left." For other American

versions, see Briggs, *Thirty Contras from New England,* p. 42; Owens and Ruth, *Advanced Square Dance Figures,* pp. 60–61; Cazden, *Dances from Camp Woodland,* p. 14.

14. "Ann Green" played by Woodhull's Old Tyme Masters. Recorded on Victor 28-0439, New York City, 1949. The tune features the playing of the Woodhull's third and most modern-sounding fiddler, Eddie Pettingill of Elmira, New York. He learned it from the playing of Fred Woodhull. Although Pettingill plays most of the tune with the clean, single-note sound common to Yankee old-time fiddlers, he also deviates from the Yankee norm by playing cross-tuning drones and double-stops. Despite this deviation, he uses slurs sparingly and his playing bears a typical Yankee precision. This recording carries a trademark of the Woodhull band, the fiddle and accordion (played by Floyd Woodhull) played in unison. Recognizing its folk quality, the Woodhulls put down "traditional" on the record label for "Ann Green." The tune is apparently a version of a fiddle tune known widely elsewhere in America as "Wake Up Susan," "Hell on the Wabash," and "Hell on the Potomac." Jabbour in *American Fiddle Tunes* relates this group to the British Isles fiddle tune "Mason's Apron" (pp. 14–16). Of "Ann Green" Jabbour writes, "The first strain is a bit simplified and begins on the tonic instead of the octave, which might obscure its kinship for some. But other sets of the tune do just those things. The second strain sounds like one of the various strains that are customarily united with the characteristic first strain" (correspondence, 23 January 1987). Indeed, most of the sets of "Hell on the Potomac" in Bayard's *Dance to the Fiddle* contain the second strain of "Ann Green" as either the second or other strain of the piece (pp. 346–54). Bayard writes additionally that "this 'Ann' version has what I would call a 'foreshortened' or 'condensed' or 'telescoped' first part, which nevertheless appears to resemble the regular first part of the 'Hell' tune versions" (correspondence, 27 January 1987). Some resemblance exists between "Ann Green" and another "Mason's Apron" relative, "Belcher's Reel," in my collection (tune no. 2). Bayard also notices the influence of the minstrel stage on the persistence of "Hell on the Potomac," and states that probably "this is an 'American-made' piece in which strains from old-country dance music were used" (p. 353). For versions of "Hell" and "Wake Up Susan" related to "Ann Green," see *One Thousand Fiddle Tunes* (taken from William Bradbury Ryan, *Ryan's Mammoth Collection: 1050 Reels and Jigs . . . And How to Play Them,* Boston: Elias Howe, 1883), p. 81; *The American Veteran Fifer* (Cincinnati: Fillmore Music House, 1927), no. 108; *White's Unique Collection,* no. 52; Christeson, *Old-Time Fiddler's Repertory,* no. 5.

15. "Campbells are Coming" played by Floyd Woodhull on accordion. Recorded by Simon Bronner at Floyd Woodhull's home in Elmira, New York, 5 May 1976. Playing this piece solo, Floyd adds a flourish in the fourth measure. Like many musicians who played regularly for dances, he emphasizes the rhythm by playing short chords with his left hand. This is another tune that came to the American country dance tradition from eighteenth-century British Isles music. James J. Fuld in *The Book of World Famous Music,* lists the earliest version in print in a collection of Scottish tunes dated 1745 (pp. 157–58), although he cites a letter that contains a reference to the melody in a letter dated 1716. Most sources refer to this tune as an old Scottish air, and point out some relation to "Miss McLeod's Reel" (see notes to tune no. 30). "Campbells" sometimes went by the name of a British Isles country dance "Hob or Nob." For American versions of the tune, see Bayard, *Dance to the Fiddle,* pp. 478–80; Ford, *Traditional Music in America,* p. 110; Jarman and Hansen, *Old Time Dance Tunes,* p. 63; O'Malley and Atwood, *Seventy Good Dances,* p. 11; *Gems of the Ball Room,* no. 15; Tyson, *Twenty-Five Old Fashioned Dance Tunes,* no. 10; National Magazine, *Heart Songs* (Boston: Chapple Publishing, 1909), p. 37. The tune has also been adapted to different words in the folk song tradition; see John A. Lomax and Alan Lomax, *American Ballads and Folk Songs* (New York: Macmillan, 1934), p. 327; Bradley Kincaid, *My Favorite Mountain Ballads and Old-Time Songs* (Chicago: Prairie Farmer Station WLF, 1931), p. 17. A dance by the name of "Scotch Reel," used with "Campbells are Coming" is illustrated in Ryan, *Dances of Our Pioneers,* pp. 164–66; see also "Campbell's Frolic" in Milligan, *101 Scottish Country Dances,* p. 42.

16. "Pop Goes the Weasel" played by Floyd Woodhull on accordion. Recorded by Simon Bronner at Floyd Woodhull's home in Elmira, New York, 5 May 1976. The chromatic line in the variation of the eleventh and twelfth measures is typical of keyboard playing but would be unusual on the fiddle. In addition to performance on those two instruments, this tune was reported to me as an old fife tune. According to Bayard, the tune comes from a nineteenth-century English

popular ditty. The tune circulates widely as a children's play-party game as well as a fiddle dance tune. For Anglo-American versions of the tune, see Bayard, *Dance to the Fiddle*, pp. 553–54; Kennedy, *Fiddle Tune Book*, p. 20; Ford, *Traditional Music in America*, p. 50; Thomas and Leeder, *The Singin' Gatherin'*, p. 88; *One Thousand Fiddle Tunes*, p. 24; Jarman and Hansen, *Old Time Dance Tunes*, p. 17; Sharp, *Country Dance Tunes*, I, p. 10; Cazden, *Dances from Camp Woodland*, p. 6; Karpeles and Schofield, *A Selection of 100 English Folk Dance Airs*, p. 4; Linscott, *Folk Songs of Old New England*, p. 108; Adam, *Old Time Fiddlers Favorite Barn Dance Tunes*, no. 1; Tyson, *Twenty-Five Old Fashioned Dance Tunes*, no. 15; Ralph Sweet, *The Fifer's Delight* (Hazardville, Ct.: Powder Mill Barn, 1964), p. 33. "Pop Goes the Weasel" also turns up in collections as a folk song; see Henry M. Belden and Arthur Palmer Hudson, eds., *Frank C. Brown Collection of North Carolina Folklore: Folk Songs from North Carolina* (Durham, N.C.: Duke University Press, 1952), p. 130; Johnny Crockett, *Log Cabin Songs* (New York: Universal Music, 1930), p. 30. In New England and New York, the dance to this tune is a contra dance or an altered square; Tolman and Page in *Country Dance Book* state, however, that "the Devil hates holy water no less than the Yankees hate the thought of Pop Goes the Weasel done as anything but a contry" (p. 94). For other versions of the dance, see Howe, *Ball-Room Hand Book*, p. 84; Linscott, *Folk Song of Old New England*, pp. 107–8; Burchenal, *American Country Dances*, p. 22; Sharp, *Country Dance Book*, pp. 40–41; Cazden, *Dances from Camp Woodland*, p. 6. For descriptions of the children's play-party game that often accompanied this tune, see Randolph, *Ozark Folk Songs*, pp. 368–69; Leah Jackson Wolford, *The Play Party in Indiana* (Indianapolis: Indiana Historical Commission, 1916), pp. 83–84; Iona and Peter Opie, *The Singing Game* (Oxford: Oxford University Press, 1985), pp. 216–28; Alice Bertha Gomme, *The Traditional Games of England, Scotland, and Ireland* (1898; rpt. ed., New York: Dover, 1964), pp. 63–64.

17. "Captain Jinks" played by Floyd Woodhull on accordion. Recorded by Simon Bronner at Floyd Woodhull's home in Elmira, New York, 5 May 1976. This tune is known as both a song and dance tune. Randolph in *Ozark Folk Songs* makes the claim that the song derived from a popular song of the Civil War (p. 354) while Sigmund Spaeth in *A History of Popular Music in America* (New York: Random House, 1948) credits the composition of the words as well as the song's popularity to William Horace Lingard, an English music-hall singer who came to America in 1871 (p. 167–68). He gives the words and music in *Weep Some More, My Lady* (Garden City, New York: Doubleday, Page, 1927), pp. 47–48. Denes Agay in *Best Loved Songs of the American People* (Garden City, New York: Doubleday, 1975) credits the words to Lingard and the music to T. Maclagan (pp. 156–57). These sources notwithstanding, the jig tune of "Captain Jinks" bears a relation to a British tune called "A Hundred Pipers." Although the tune to "Jinks" appears to date at least to the mid-nineteenth century, according to Bayard in *Dance to the Fiddle* it derived from "The Mill Mill O," which probably has a much older ancestry (p. 524). The song as reported in National Magazine, *Heart Songs* has the chorus, "Captain Jinks of the Horse Marines; I feed my horse on corn and beans, And often live beyond my means, Tho' a captain in the army." The song's connection to a dance was reinforced by a reference to dancing in its first verse: "I teach young ladies how to dance, How to dance, How to dance, I teach young ladies how to dance, For I'm the pet of the army" (pp. 54–55). For versions of the song as a fiddle tune, see Guntharp, *Learning the Fiddler's Ways*, p. 77; Kraus, *Square Dances of Today*, p. 65; Adam, *Old Time Fiddlers' Favorite Barn Dance Tunes*, no. 11; Ford, *Traditional Music in America*, p. 120; Cazden, *Dances from Camp Woodland*, p. 15; Mr. and Mrs. Henry Ford, *Good Morning*, p. 27; Jan Philip Schinhan, ed., *The Frank C. Brown Collection of North Carolina Folklore: The Music of the Folk Songs* (Durham: Duke University Press, 1962), p. 60. "Captain Jinks" has persisted in tradition as a play-party game and square dance. For versions of the play-party fame, see Randolph, *Ozark Folk Songs*, pp. 354–56; Wolford, *Play Party in Indiana*, p. 27. For versions of the dance, see Cazden, *Dances from Camp Woodland*, p. 15; Ryan, *Dances of Our Pioneers*, pp. 55–57; Putney, *Square Dancing U.S.A.*, p. 84; Kraus, *Square Dancing of Today*, p. 64.

18. "Money Musk" played by Archie Thorpe on fiddle. Recorded by Fred Palmer at his home, Alfred, New York, c. 1940. While Palmer was recording the Hornellsville Hillbillies, Thorpe performed a solo version of one of his "really old-fashioned" tunes. Thorpe, who hailed from Jamestown, New York, gave the Hillbillies much of their old-time repertoire, and this performance gives us a chance to examine his playing more closely. Unlike Baltzell's version (tune no. 5), Thorpe doesn't tie over notes to create syncopation, yet Thorpe creates a similar effect by

putting a high "A" (third finger on the E string of the fiddle) at a different place in each figure. Thorpe's frequent repetition of the first figure (first four sixteenth notes) gives the tune its typical busy feel. The C part is probably a variation of the A part, which also appears as the first part, sometimes the second, of various composite reel and strathspey airs. See Bayard, *Dance to the Fiddle,* p. 331; *One Thousand Fiddle Tunes,* p. 125; James Aird, *A Selection of Scotch, English, Irish and Foreign Airs,* 6 vols. (Glasgow, Scotland: J. Aird, n.d.), II, no. 19; Patrick Weston Joyce, *Old Irish Folk Music and Songs* (London: Longmans Green, 1909), no. 19. As a whole, Thorpe's version of Money Musk closely resembles "Money Musk" played by Ron West (who also uses three parts to the tune) in Stowe, Vermont, and recorded and transcribed by Paul Wells in *New England Traditional Fiddling,* p. 13.

19. "Irish Washerwoman" played by the Hornellsville Hillbillies. Recorded by Fred Palmer at a dance in Lake Demmon, New York, 1943. This version of "Irish Washerwoman" features the fiddling of Archie Thorpe and Lyle Miles. The band throws in some variations on the playing of this standard tune to make it more interesting. They perform the tune according to the form A B A B and they vary the rhythm between ♫ and ♩♪ with an occasional tie across the bar line. A scale passage at the end of the A and B parts also distinguishes this version from other variants. For background on the tune, see the notes to tune no. 9.

20. "Buffalo Gals" played by the Hornellsville Hillbillies. Recorded by Fred Palmer at a dance in Lake Demmon, New York, 1943. Although the band plays this familiar tune simply, they throw in a little flourish in the eleventh and twelfth measures for some effect. The fiddlers are in standard tuning and follow the form A B. Bayard in *Dance to the Fiddle* speculates that the tune comes from Germany; see Elizabeth Burchenal, *Folk Dances of Germany* (New York: Schirmer, 1938), p. 21. Bayard is more sure in noting the international circulation of the tune, and in *Hill Country Tunes* (Philadelphia: American Folklore Society, 1944) he cites versions from Yugoslavia and France (his tune no. 1). Unlike other tunes in the country dance tradition, this one does not have a clear British Isles lineage, although as Bayard points out, "in this country it has been somewhat assimilated to the British style." Certainly the performance by the Hornellsville Hillbillies demonstrates the Anglo-American qualities of a regularized beat, a repetitive "endless" quality, and an unadorned melody; for further discussion of this style, see Roger D. Abrahams and George Foss, *Anglo-American Folksong Style* (Englewood Cliffs, New Jersey: Prentice-Hall, 1968). Although apparently steeped in folk tradition, the tune owes some of its wide circulation to the nineteenth-century popular theater. In the 1840s the minstrel Cool White (whose real name was John Hodges) sang (and he claimed, composed) a song called "Lubly Fan, Won't You Come Out Tonight?" He sang it widely in the United States with the popular Virginia Serenaders; see Spaeth, *A History of Popular Music,* pp. 100–101, and *Weep Some More My Lady,* p. 108. Harry Dichter and Elliott Shapiro, in *Handbook of Early American Sheet Music* (1941; rpt. ed., New York: Dover, 1977), list a sheet music version of the song with "author unknown" out of New York in 1848. Versions well into the twentieth century preserved some of the tune's minstrel flavor. Jabbour in *American Fiddle Tunes,* however, points out that a tune entitled "Midnight Serenade" in George Knauff's *Virginia Reels, No. 4* (Baltimore: Geog. Willig, Jr., 1839), p. 7, is an American set of "Buffalo Gals" which precedes the song's vogue on the minstrel stage, and possibly suggests circulation in the oral tradition of the Upland South at the very least (p. 27). The song has the attractive quality of fitting a location to the tune. It has been performed as Jimtown Gals, Brown Town Gals, Alabama Gals, Roundtown Girls, Johnstown Gals, Lushbaugh Girls, Louisiana Gals, Bowery Gals, Cincinnati Girls, Hagtown Gals, and Hagantown Gals, although it is probably best known as Buffalo Gals. There are six towns and one river in the United States carrying the "Buffalo" name, but the location of the tune probably refers to Buffalo, New York, the only city carrying the name. Why the title became attached to the city is uncertain, although it may very well have been that as a common terminal point for the minstrel circuit from New York City to Albany across to westernmost Buffalo, the city's name and its frontier reputation made it an easy and appropriate substitute for performances of "Lubly Fan." The words of the version in National Magazine's *Heart Songs* are "As I went lumbrin' down de street, down de street, down de street, A lubly gal I chanc'd to meet, Oh! she was fair to view. Oh! buffalo gals, will ye come out to-night, will ye come out to-night, will ye come out to-night, Buffalo gals, will ye come out to-night, And dance by de light ob de moon?" (pp. 366–67). This is a tune, however, that knows no regional boundaries; it has been collected both north and

south of the Mason-Dixon line. It is a favorite on various instruments, especially the fiddle and banjo. Its settings vary; it has been reported as a folk song, a play-party game, and a country dance tune. For collections of the fiddle tune, see Bayard, *Dance to the Fiddle*, pp. 113–17; Bayard, *Hill Country Tunes*, no. 1; Guntharp, *Learning the Fiddler's Ways*, p. 48; Jabbour, *American Fiddle Tunes*, pp. 24–25; Jarman and Hansen, *Old Time Dance Tunes*, p. 39; Kennedy, *Fiddler's Tune Book*, p. 28; Kennedy, *Second Fiddler's Tune Book*, p. 25; Krassen, *Appalachian Fiddle*, p. 65; Thede, *The Fiddle Book*, p. 119; Adam, *Old Time Fiddlers' Favorite Barn Dance Tunes*, no. 12; Ford, *Traditional Music in America*, p. 53; Cazden, *Dances from Camp Woodland*, p. 40; Mr. and Mrs. Ford, *Good Morning*, p. 47; Sweet, *Fifer's Delight*, pp. 7, 24. For collections of the song, see Belden and Hudson, *Folk Songs from North Carolina*, p. 114; Schinhan, *Music of the Folk Songs*, p. 35; Randolph, *Ozark Folk Songs*, III, pp. 332–34; John A. Lomax and Alan Lomax, *Folk Song U.S.A.* (New York: Duell Sloan & Pearce, 1947), p. 104; *The Arkansas Wood-Chopper's World's Greatest Collection of Cowboy Songs* (Chicago: M. M. Cole, 1931), pp. 36–37; Wm. J. Smith, *Smith's Collection of Mountain Ballads and Cowboy Songs* (New York: Wm. J. Smith, 1932), pp. 32–33; Henry Shoemaker, *Mountain Minstrelsy of Pennsylvania* (third ed., Philadelphia: Newman F. McGirr, 1931), 152; Frank Luther, *Americans and Their Songs* (New York: Harper and Brothers, 1942), pp. 132–33. For versions of the play-party game, see Wolford, *Play Party in Indiana*, p. 32; Lucien L. McDowell and Flora L. McDowell, *Folk Dances of Tennessee, Old Playparty Games of the Caney Fork Valley* (Ann Arbor: Edwards Brothers, 1938), p. 28; W. A. Owens, *Swing and Turn: Texas Play Party Games* (Dallas: Tardy Publishing, 1936), pp. 45, 54, 103. For square dances to the fiddle tune, see Cazden, *Dances from Camp Woodland*, p. 40; Flood and Putney, *Square Dance U.S.A.*, p. 40; Kraus, *Square Dances of Today*, pp. 96–97.

21. "Chicken Reel" played by the Hornellsville Hillbillies. Recorded by Fred Palmer at a dance in Lake Demmon, New York, 1943. This tune was often played in combination with "Black Cat" (see tune no. 22); it is done in the same key and at the same tempo. "Chicken Reel" is played in the form A B A B. An unusual feature of the rendition by the Hillbillies is the syncopation in the first and third measures achieved by fiddlers Lyle Miles and Archie Thorpe. The first published version of "Chicken Reel" was a piano composition in 1910 by then nineteen-year-old Joseph M. Daly of Boston. Yet as Bayard in *Dance to the Fiddle* points out, the tune is "most obviously made up of well-known melodic formulas" (p. 293). Bayard notes the resemblance of the tune to a much older Scottish dance air and a relation to an Irish reel. Further clouding the issue of this tune's circulation is an observation made by Gene Wiggins in "Popular Music and the Fiddler" in the *John Edwards Memorial Foundation Quarterly* (vol. 15, 1979, p. 146). The distinguishing feature of the tune in oral tradition, the opening slide in imitation of a chicken's squawk, is absent from the original composition. It also appears that the slide tends to be emphasized more in reports of the tune in the South than in the North. Fuld in *The Book of World Famous Music* concludes that "it is not clear whether the *Chicken Reel* was wholly or partially an original composition by Daly or whether he merely recorded a folk melody" (p. 169). In upstate New York, the tune has been a favorite because besides being instantly recognizable, it can be easily used in combination with a number of other tunes to provide some variety or an interlude in a long set. According to several informants, it also was played regularly by some brass bands in the towns; Bayard mentions that in Pennsylvania it was used in "martial bands." For versions from tradition, see Cazden, *Dances from Woodland*, p. 37; Ford, *Traditional Music in America*, p. 41; Thede, *The Fiddle Book*, p. 116; Sandburg, *American Songbag*, p. 116, or listen to John W. Summers, *Indiana Fiddler*; Wilson Douglas, *The Right Hand Fork of Rush's Creek: Old Time Fiddling by Wilson Douglas* (Rounder 0047); Charlie Monroe, *On the Noonday Jamboree* (County 538); Lloyd Wanzer, *Plain and Fancy Fiddlin'* (American Heritage 19A); and the Tune Wranglers on the anthology *Beer Parlour Jive* (String 801). For a square dance that uses "a special Chicken Reel step," see Cazden, *Dances from Camp Woodland*, p. 36.

22. "Black Cat" played by the Hornellsville Hillbillies. Recorded by Fred Palmer at a dance in Lake Demmon, New York, 1943. The Hillbillies made this popular tune their signature piece; they opened every dance and show with it. The fiddles are in standard tuning and play precise scale passages for this tune. The band follows the form A B A B. According to Tolman and Page, *The Country Dance Book*, pp. 62–70, "Black Cat" was a standard tune at New England dances during the 1930s. They don't print the music, but they describe various types of quadrille dances that accompanied the tune. The tune played by the Hillbillies bears some resemblance

especially in the repeated figure of the third measure to "The Cat Came Back" in Christeson, *Old-Time Fiddler's Repertory,* no. 10. Christeson states that the tune was mostly heard played by fiddlers during the 1930s. An even closer match of the Hillbillies' tune is the Henry Ford Orchestra's recording of "Black Cat Quadrille-Part II" on Ford's private label Early American Dances (Release Number 112-B). Paul Wells, Director of the Center for Popular Music, provided me with a tape of the record, and adds that the original was recorded at the Ford Engineering Laboratory in Dearborn, Michigan. Like the Hillbillies' version, Ford's tune is led by a fiddle with piano accompaniment, and the playing displays the clean, precise style of the Yankee old-time sound. Most likely the record came out during the 1930s.

23. "Marching Through Georgia" played by Clyde "Chub" McLean on the mandolin. Recorded by Simon Bronner at Chub McLean's home in Hartwick, New York, 19 March 1976. Although the mandolin is not as popular among old-time musicians in upstate New York as the fiddle, plectrum banjo, and piano accordion, McLean used the mandolin because he could imitate the picking style of the older plectrum techniques while imitating the fingering of fiddlers. To compensate for the weak throw of the mandolin's sound, McLean would electronically amplify his instrument to cut through the noisy dance halls of the "hotels." In performances that I witnessed, his mandolin would take the lead while the harmonica and guitar provided rhythm. When Les Weir played with the group, the fiddle and mandolin would often play in unison, although McLean like to play it in the key of G, which is not a preferred key of fiddlers. This tune has its origin with a composition by Connecticut's Henry Clay Work (1832–84). The original version was copyrighted 9 January 1865 and was dedicated to his cousin Mary Lizzie Work, and was composed to honor Union General Sherman's destructive march "from Atlanta to the Sea" during the Civil War. Not surprisingly, Fuld in *The Book of World Famous Music* calls the composition, "the most hated song in the South" (p. 349). But in the North, the song quickly entered folk tradition. As it did, it was subject to many alterations, most for the better according to Bayard in *Dance to the Fiddle* (p. 224). The tune in its variant forms was a common one at New York State dances; see Herbert Haufrecht and Norman Cazden, "Music of the Catskills," *New York Folklore Quarterly* 4 (1948): 44. McLean plays a fairly standard version of the tune as it was performed in Central New York State; unlike the original, McLean's avoids the ascending passage ending on a high note in the third measure in addition to giving the song a fiddle-tune quality by emphasizing the melodic formula. Like other performers that I heard in Central New York, McLean puts a stress on the B part; this was in imitation of the song's chorus which exclaims "Hurrah! Hurrah! we bring the Jubile! Hurrah! Hurrah! the flag that makes you free! So we sang the chorus from Atlanta to the sea, While we were marching through Georgia." Used as a square dance, the crowd will still sing the last line; the caller leads with "When you get back home again, everybody swing, As we go marching through Georgia." A rendition of the tune from Camp Woodland in upstate New York was filmed by Pete Seeger in *The Country Fiddler.* The original Work composition is reprinted in *Songs of Henry Clay Work* (1884; rpt. ed., New York: Da Capo Press, 1974), pp. 18–20. For variants from tradition, see Bayard, *Dance to the Fiddle,* pp. 223–24; Cazden, *Dances from Camp Woodland,* p. 9; Sweet, *Fifer's Delight,* p. 32. For a dance from New York State to the tune, see Cazden, *Dances from Camp Woodland,* p. 9.

24. "Golden Slippers" played by Clyde "Chub" McLean on mandolin. Recorded by Simon Bronner at Chub McLean's home in Hartwick, New York, 19 March 1976. Although accompanying a dance, this tune is played more as a song with a verse-chorus construction (A B A B) than a fiddle dance tune (A A B B). "Golden Slippers" was originally a composition by a prominent black minstrel songwriter, James Bland. Written during the 1870s, the tune found its way later into song folios with no credit to Bland; see *Smith's Collection of Mountain Ballads and Cowboy Songs,* pp. 12–14; Carson J. Robison, *Carson J. Robison's World's Greatest Collection of Mountain Ballads and Old Time Songs* (Chicago: M. M. Cole, 1930). It is safe to say that by the time these folios were published the song had entered folk tradition. The song appears in the field collection of folk songs by Frank C. Brown; see Belden and Hudson, *Folk Songs from North Carolina,* p. 622, and Schinhan, *The Music of the Folk Songs,* p. 361. The possibilities of variation in "Golden Slippers" as a fiddle tune are demonstrated in Guntharp, *Learning the Fiddler's Ways,* p. 54, and Michael, McCreesh & Campbell, *The Host of the Air* (Front Hall FHR-023). As a fiddle tune and dance, "Slippers" appears in Ford, *Traditional Music in America,* p. 113; Reiner, *Anthology of Fiddle Styles,* p. 77; Flood and Putney, *Square Dance U.S.A.,* p. 55; Owens and Ruth, *Advanced Square*

Dance Figures, pp. 108–10; Shaw, *Cowboy Dances*, p. 383; Kraus, *Square Dances of Today*, pp. 62–63. Clyde's brother Leonard called the following set to the tune: "I love to fan her with a wagon whirl, Ain't going to cheat against all odds, Swing to the corner and promenade all, Same old buck and a brand new girl, Swing your own and promenade all, A do-si-do with your partners all, Allemande left in the corners all, Bring in a left around that hall."

25. "Soldier's Joy" played by Pop Weir on fiddle. Recorded by Milo Stewart at Violet Weir's home near Cooperstown, New York, c. 1960. This tune was recorded during a party where music-making by the Weir clan was dominant. Joining Pop at points in the tune, and speeding up the tempo, was Pop's son Don, who played in unison. Pop played the tune several times without variation, and all the while kept the ♫♩ pattern sharp and articulated. Pop plays the tune without slurs, and uses single note shuffles to good effect (see the B part of tune no. 12 for another example). The distinctive arpeggios of the tune exactly outline the chords. But whereas most versions of the tune go to a G or IV chord at the change in the first measure of the B part, Pop's version moves from a D to an A seventh (I-V seventh). The B part in this version is distinctive; it closely matches the B part in variant E of "Soldier's Joy" in Bayard's *Dance to the Fiddle*, p. 305. For further discussion of the tune, see my notes to tune no. 12 and Jabbour's in *American Fiddle Tunes*, pp. 3–6.

26. "Rickett's Hornpipe" played by Pop Weir on fiddle. Recorded by Milo Stewart at Violet Weir's home near Cooperstown, New York, c. 1960. Pop Weir's rendition of "Rickett's Hornpipe" uses a turnaround identical to the one that he used for "Soldier's Joy," and it also shares similar rhythm and note patterns over the chords (see my tune no. 25). "Rickett's Hornpipe" (or "Ricketts' Hornpipe"), a favorite among northeastern fiddlers, is also occasionally recalled as a fife tune. Jabbour in *American Fiddle Tunes* reports that the tune was named after John Bill Ricketts, an eighteenth-century circus entrepreneur. "Ricketts came from England to America in 1792 and was active in circus promotion till about 1800. Circuses under his name appeared in New York City, Philadelphia, Norfolk, Charlestown, Albany, Boston, Hartford, and Montreal. The earliest set of the tune yet to appear is an untitled version, labeled simply "Danced by Aldridge," in McGlashan's *Collection of Scots Measures* (Edinburgh, ca. 1781). By the 1850s it had become a regular item in commercial fiddle-tune collections. It found its way onto early hillbilly recordings, and modern field collecting indicates that the tune is known in nearly every section of the United States" (p. 24). Bayard in *Dance to the Fiddle* offers 10 variants of the tune from Pennsylvania alone; of the versions, Pop's rendition appears closest to variant C. For other versions, see *American Veteran Fifer*, no. 111; Adam, *Favorite Old Time Fiddlers Barn Dance Tunes*, no. 10; Ford, *Traditional Music of America*, p. 50; Thede, *The Fiddle Book*, p. 118; *One Thousand Fiddle Tunes*, p. 89; *Sym's Old Time Dances*, p. 11; O'Malley and Atwood, *Seventy Good Old Dances*, p. 17; *White's Unique Collection*, no. 95; *Howe's School for the Violin*, p. 38; Kennedy, *Fiddle Tune Book*, no. 10; Cazden, *Dances from Woodland*, p. 43; Krassen, *Appalachian Fiddle* p. 80. For dances to "Rickett's," see Tolman and Page, *The Country Dance Book*, p. 125; Briggs, *Thirty Contras from New England*, p. 50.

27. "Get Up Napoleon (Ebenezeer Fry)" (2 versions). First version played by Dorrance Weir on guitar. Recorded by Simon Bronner at Dorrance Weir's home near Cooperstown, New York, 17 February 1976. Second version played by Les Weir on fiddle. Recorded by Simon Bronner at Les Weir's home in Oaksville, New York, 1 April 1976. Dorrance and Les Weir are brothers and they both learned this tune from the singing and playing of their father. The differences in style demonstrate the different orientations that an old-time tune can take in the second generation. Dorrance Weir was more influenced than Les by radio and the hillbilly songs that were popular during World War II. He turned his father's ditty into a country song. Les Weir followed in his father's footsteps as a dance fiddler. He preserved the feel of his father's playing in his performance of the tune. Dorrance Weir's version is in cut time (4/4 or 2/2) with a definite duple meter feel. Les Weir's version is in the jig-sounding 6/8 time with a triple-meter feel. The triple meter gives a lazier effect to the tune and the duple a more driving one. The difference between the two versions is not so much in speed or melody but rather in the ratio of short notes to long notes. Even with Les's playing, there are differences with his father's style. Les played this tune faster than his father would have. The song was written with the title "Wal I Swan" by Benjamin Hapgood Burt and published in 1907; see Sigmund Spaeth, *Read 'Em and Weep: The Songs You Forgot to Remember* (New York: Doubleday, Page & Co., 1926), pp. 255–57. Although originat-

ing on Tin Pan Alley, the song apparently entered oral tradition. The traditional theme of a rube outwitting a city slicker made the words memorable. Singing a version that he calls "Ebenezer Frye," Bradley Kincaid commented that "if ever there was a 'hillbilly' song, this is it. I don't know its origin"; see *Radio's "Kentucky Mountain Boy" Bradley Kincaid* (Berea, Kentucky: Appalachian Center, 1980), p. 150. It received at least one other hillbilly rendition before World War II by Riley Puckett (Columbia 15695). Adding to its appeal is that the tune used a melodic strain probably from the singing-game tradition. Burt was known to adapt folk melodies; his "My Gal Irene," another bit of rural humor, echoed "Turkey in the Straw" near the close (see Sigmund Spaeth, *History of Popular Music*, pp. 355, 363). At any rate, Burt's song has had a lasting power. His line "Giddap, Napoleon, it looks like rain" can be occasionally heard as a traditional saying in America. Further, Ira Ford reported the tune (played on the fiddle) and words to "Joshua Ebenezer Fry" in *Traditional Music in America*, pp. 273–76. Ford's collection of tunes and songs in the oral tradition came primarily from Missouri, so the song is apparently well-travelled. Instead of opening with the reference to Rubinville, Ford's version opens with "I'm the Constable of Pumpkinville, Jist traded hosses at the mill. My name's Joshua Ebenezer Fry." For a chorus Les Weir used a close match to Ford's last chorus: "Wal, I swan! I must be gittin' on. Giddap, Napoleon! It looks like rain. I'll be switched, And the hay ain't pitched. Drap in when yew're Over to the farm again." Nonetheless, the verses of both Weirs vary from the verses given by Ford, and the song has the markings of having entered folk tradition. Ford does not annotate his version, so I cannot compare the song's folk sources; chances are that Ford reported the song from his own experience (born in 1878 in Missouri, he was himself an old-time fiddler) or from his collecting in the Missouri Ozarks prior to 1930. The tune could have a relation to a British Isles utility tune used with a number of children's singing games or verses; see the common opening (also in 6/8) of "Wee Melodie Man" in Opie and Opie, *The Singing Game*, p. 406, and similarities to "Push the Business On" (in 6/8) in Charles H. Fransworth and Cecil J. Sharp, *Folk-Songs, Chanteys and Singing Games* (New York: H. W. Gray, 1909), pp. 96–97. The transcriber Pamela deWall remembers the tune to "Get Up Napoleon" used with different words in her Minnesota youth. Some readers may recognize the verse that she remembers: "Down by the station early in the morning, See the little pufferbellies all in a row, See the station master pull the little handle, Puff, puff, choo, choo, and off we go." Les Weir also associates the tune with a childhood verse; he sings and plays it for his daughter. The song is also given an old-time musical treatment by the Double Decker Stringband on *Giddyap Napoleon* (Fretless FR 144, 1980).

28. "Lamplighter's Hornpipe" played by Les Weir on fiddle. Recorded by Simon Bronner at Les Weir's home in Oaksville, New York, 1 April 1976. Les plays this traditional tune learned from his father in a standard tuning. Les's playing puts a heavy accent on open E downbeats and is free of any slurs and drones. This tune is more popular with old-time fiddlers in New York State than the literature on tune collecting shows. It is performed almost exclusively as a dance tune and its features suggest an eighteenth-century British Isles derivation. For variants of the tune, see Ford, *Traditional Music in America*, p. 85; *Gems of the Ball Room*, no. 24; Burchenal, *American Country Dances*, pp. 39–41; Shaw, *Cowboy Dances*, p. 389; *One Thousand Fiddle Tunes*, p. 93; Mellie Dunham, *Fiddlin' Dance Tunes*, no. 17; Ole Sandvik, *Folke-Musik i Gudbrandsdalen* (1919; rpt. ed., Oslo: Johan Gundttanum, 1948), p. 79. The tune is often used with dances that call for "Durang's Hornpipe"; Burchenal uses it with a contra dance called the "Boston Fancy" and Briggs suggests it for the easy contra dance of "Jefferson and Liberty." See Burchenal, *American Country Dances*, pp. 49–51; Briggs, *Thirty Contras from New England*, p. 33. Tolman and Page in the *Country Dance Book* have a dance that goes by the name "Lamplighter's Hornpipe," which calls for balance and swing moves to the tune (pp. 122–23). It is similar to the dance reported as "Lamp Lighter's Hornpipe" by Elias Howe in 1858; see his *Ball-Room Hand Book*, p. 85.

29. "Rakes of Mallow" played by Les Weir on fiddle. Recorded by Simon Bronner at Les Weir's home in Oaksville, New York, 1 April 1976. The B part of this tune is played in a lower octave than usual and gives more of a shuffle effect than when played entirely on the high string. The B part melody is often found in eighth notes, but Les uses sixteenths. The tag is a traditional "shave and a haircut" ending. The "Rakes" title comes from the eighteenth century when Mallow, County Cork, was a well-known spa. Some informants in New York State wrote the title of the tune for me as "Mallon," probably because in the rural reaches of the state the syllable "on"

is pronounced "awn." For variants of the tune on both sides of the Atlantic, see Kennedy, *Fiddler's Tune Book*, p. 27; Karpeles and Schofield, *Selection of 100 English Folk Dance Airs*, pp. 33, 57; Linscott, *Folk Songs of Old New England*, p. 99; Jarman and Hansen, *Old Time Dance Tunes*, p. 73; Cazden, *Dances from Camp Woodland*, p. 39; Sym's *Old Time Dances*, p. 25; Tyson, *Twenty-Five Old Fashioned Dance Tunes*, no. 12; Mellie Dunham, *Fiddlin' Dance Tunes*, no. 29. Dances to the tune usually take a contra dance form called the "Morning Star"; see Tolman and Page, *Country Dance Book*, p. 84; Linscott, *Folk Songs of Old New England*, p. 99. For a "Catskill Breakdown" from New York State that uses "Rakes," see Cazden, *Dances from Camp Woodland*, pp. 38–39.

30. "Miss McLeod's Reel" played by Les Weir on fiddle. Recorded by Simon Bronner at Les Weir's home in Oaksville, New York, 1 April 1976. The relation, or confusion, of "Campbell's are Coming" and "Miss McLeod's Reel" is apparent from Les Weir's labeling of this tune. The more conventional version of "McLeod's" is found in John McDermott's "Virginia Reel" (tune no. 4); it is a version that Floyd Woodhull also plays. They play the tune in cut time in the key of G. Yet Weir's rendition in 12/8 time, learned from his father, is not uncommon in my collecting experience. At the same party where Pop played "Soldier's Joy" and "Rickett's Hornpipe" (see my tunes 25 and 26), he also played a few measures of his "McLeod's":

These measures demonstrate Les's model for the B part of the tune. Pop uses a ♫♫ ♫♫ rhythm while Les uses a ♪♫ ♫♫ rhythm and a turnaround repeating just the ♫♫ dotted rhythm. Comparing the last measures further unveils continuities and changes between father and son. The skeleton of the phrase is:

Pop plays a melodic variation of the skeleton:

Les now plays a rhythmic variation of the skeleton

In answer to Bayard's question in *Dance to the Fiddle*, "in the McLeod tune, do we perhaps see the results of a rhythmic reworking of some set of the Campbells tune?" (p. 480), at least there is enough of a connection that fiddlers will often call this version "McLeod's." There are differences to note, however, between the renditions of the two tunes. Les Weir uses a different key and does not use the ascending scale passage that Woodhull does in his rendition of "Campbells" (see tune 15). Adding to the credence for calling Les's jig-sounding tune a "reel" is the use of tunes in 6/8 and 12/8 for the "Virginia Reel"; see Kraus, *Square Dances of Today*, pp. 108–9; Cazden, *Dances from Camp Woodland*, p. 14; Thomas and Leeder, *The Singin' Gatherin'*, p. 89; Flood and Putney, *Square Dancing U.S.A.*, p. 46. Indeed, Flood and Putney's musical example which they call "Virginia Reel" bears a strong resemblance to Weir's version as does Bayard's version A of "Campbells are Coming" (p. 478). Ryan in *Dances of Our Pioneers* gives a "Scotch Reel" to the tune of "Campbells are Coming." For background on "McLeod's" and "Campbells," see my notes to tune nos. 4 and 15.

31. "Turkey in the Straw" played by Les Weir and Ken Kane on fiddles. Recorded by Simon Bronner at Les Weir's home in Oaksville, New York, 1 April 1976. Sharing the influence of Pop Weir, it is not surprising that Weir and Kane play this tune in "Pop's style." The playing is taken at a relatively slow clip and it emphasizes the playing of each note. Weir and Kane play

in unison and use an A B form. According to Bayard in *Dance to the Fiddle*, the tune is a composite of old Scots melodies (p. 279). He gives strong evidence that the tune shows parts of "The Rose Tree" and "The Black Eagle" from the British Isles (and traced at least to the eighteenth century); he finds support for his contention from Jabbour, *American Fiddle Tunes*, pp. 31–32. Although it undoubtedly was in American folk tradition before the nineteenth century, popular theater helped to spread the popularity of the tune in America during the minstrel period of the nineteenth century. Indeed, Ken Kane and others I interviewed referred to a variant of the tune as "Old Zip Coon," a reference to the blackface minstrel song published in five editions with credits to different composers around 1834. See Fuld, *Book of World-Famous Music*, pp. 591–92; Hans Nathan, *Dan Emmett and the Rise of Early Negro Minstrelsy* (Norman: University of Oklahoma Press, 1962), p. 167; Ruth and Norman Lloyd, *The American Heritage Songbook* (New York: American Heritage Publishing, 1969), pp. 80–82. According to Fuld, the melody acquired the name in 1861 by being attached to the end of a new song entitled "Turkey in de Straw" by Dan Bryant; the tune was labeled simply as an "old melody" (p. 591). Although "Turkey in the Straw" is reported as a folk song and a dance tune, the most common use of the tune in Central New York State is to accompany dances. And performances of the tune in the region emphasize the British Isles sound of the tune. For versions of the tune on both sides of the Atlantic, see Krassen, *O'Neill's Music of Ireland*, p. 155; Kennedy, *Fiddler's Tune Book*, p. 9; Ford, *Traditional Music in America*, p. 59; Adam, *Old Time Fiddlers' Favorite Barn Dance Tunes*, no. 22; Schinhan, *Music of the Folk Songs*, p. 72; Linscott, *Folk Songs of Old New England*, pp. 84–85; Cazden, *Dances from Camp Woodland*, p. 26; Sweet, *Fifer's Delight*, p. 51; Sandburg, *American Songbag*, pp. 94–97; O'Malley and Atwood, *Seventy Good Dances*, pp. 13, 40; Randolph, *Ozark Folk Songs*, II, pp. 353–55; Tyson, *Twenty-Five Old Fashioned Dance Tunes*, no. 25; Burchenal, *American Country Dances*, p. 20; Shaw, *Cowboy Dances*, p. 389; Mellie Dunham, *Fiddlin' Dance Tunes*, no. 8; W. H. Morris, *Old Time Violin Melodies* (St. Joseph, Missouri: W. H. Morris, 1927); Don Messer, *Way Down East Fiddlin' Tunes* (Toronto: Gordon V. Thompson, 1948), no. 52. The tune is used behind a variety of dances. For some descriptions of common dances, see Howe, *Ball-Room Hand Book*, p. 87; Linscott, *Folk Songs of Old New England*, pp. 84–85; Cazden, *Dances from Camp Woodland*, p. 26; Ryan, *Dances of Our Pioneers*, pp. 109–12; Putney and Flood, *Square Dancing U.S.A.*, pp. 45–46; Burchenal, *American Country Dances*, p. 20.

32. "Nellie Gray" played by Ken Kane on fiddle. Recorded by Simon Bronner at Ken Kane's home in Hartwick Township, New York, 13 April 1976. In his performance, Kane demonstrates techniques that are characteristic of old-time fiddling. The second and third time through the tune, he varies the rhythm more than the melody. The rhythm is strong but varied; he uses long notes such as ♩ and ♩ as well as ♫, ♪, ♬, and ♪♫ . Later styles of fiddling tend to emphasize ♫♫ and ♬♬ ; the fiddler finds new combinations of notes to play while keeping a constant rhythm pattern. Kane plays the tune as a song in an A B A B form. "Darling Nelly Gray" was composed by Benjamin Russel Hanby and published out of Boston in 1856. According to Charles Hamm in *Yesterdays: Popular Song in America* (New York: W. W. Norton, 1979), the song was the most popular of a new type of " 'plantation song,' with musical and poetical ties to sentimental balladry, and with gentler and more sympathetic treatment of black characters" (p. 137). Hanby's lyrics told a tragic tale of a slave woman sold away from her home plantation in Kentucky. It had a memorable ending of "Hark! There's somebody knocking at the door, Oh! I hear the angels calling and I see my Nelly Gray." Besides these memorable words, the tune used a harmonic, tonal chord progression which was sophisticated for its day. "Nelly Gray" was written for the minstrel stage, but it also became popular through sales of broadsides and family performances in American parlors. Old-timers in New York State also remember that the tune was used to accompany some children's games at play-parties. The result, as Spaeth points out in *A History of Popular Music*, was that the song and tune quickly entered American folk tradition (pp. 131–32). "Nellie Gray," performed mostly as a dance tune, certainly was one of Ken Kane's favorites; he played it for me on six different occasions—twice on banjo, once on guitar, once on accordion, and twice on the fiddle. It was also prominent in the dance-tune performances of Floyd Woodhull, Lyle Miles, Gib Bourne, and indeed most York State old-time fiddlers who worked during the hillbilly period. The usually conservative country dance tradition accepted the tune as one of its standards later than the folk song tradition did. Newton F. Tolman in *Quick Tunes and Good Times* recalls country dances in New Hampshire, and states that "Darling Nelly

Gray" irrevocably represented square dance music in the mind of New England enthusiasts (p. 30). To make the point, Tolman tells this anecdote: "We had one caller for two or three seasons who was actually a pretty fair singer, but soon got the obsession that the dancers came mainly to hear him perform. His theme song was "Darling Nellie Gray" which he always used for the last dance of the evening, and we would have to play it, over and over, for about twenty minutes, while he displayed his vocal virtuosity" (p. 31). Tolman and Page in *Country Dance Book* make the claim that "Darling Nellie Gray and The Girl I Left Behind Me are two square dances which originated in New York State. They were danced to countless tunes before a final version was settled upon and they were ready to migrate into New England. The country west of the Green Mountains and along the Berkshires happened to like these squares, but elsewhere they were regarded with contempt reserved for the foreigner. And the old folks thought them on a par with London Bridge Is Falling Down or any of the kids' games of the day. The newer generation found them fun to do, however, and so they became established throughout southern New England. In Darling Nellie Gray four couples make up the set formed as for a plain quadrille" (p. 78). For variations of the tune from dance tradition, see Cazden, *Dances from Camp Woodland*, p. 7; Putney and Flood, *Square Dance U.S.A.*, p. 83; Kraus, *Square Dances of Today*, p. 59. For additional examples of dances to the tune, see Tolman and Page, *Country Dance Book*, pp. 78–79; Ryan, *Dances of Our Pioneers*, pp. 107–9.

33. "Pop Weir Tune" played by Ken Kane on guitar. Recorded by Simon Bronner at Ken Kane's home in Hartwick Township, New York, 13 April 1976. Kane plays the guitar with a downward frailing motion of his right hand. He uses open tunings adapted from his knowledge of fiddling in addition to standard tuning on the guitar. He beats out the melody in much the same fashion as one would expect a frailed old-time banjo to be played. He developed this way of playing after losing part of the thumb on his right hand in a shotgun accident. After talking with me of the fiddling at Pop Weir's general store in Oaksville during the 1950s, Kane offered this tune. He could not recall the name and said that it was just a "Pop Weir Tune" to him. Pop would lead the fiddling sessions at his store and he would play several tunes without giving their titles, waiting to see on which tunes the other fiddlers followed (a technique still used by Les Weir and Ken Kane at music-making sessions). "Pop Weir's Tune" contains several commonplace strains probably of nineteenth-century vintage. The first few measures resemble the opening phrase of the song "Polly-Wolly-Doodle," discussed in Fuld, *Book of World Famous Music* (pp. 434–35). Fuld puts the tune in G, but a transposition to A would be common for the fiddle. The song suggests a minstrel-stage origin, although as musicologist William Mahar suggests, "various versions of the tune probably existed in the oral tradition as well as different published versions" (correspondence, 2 February 1987). Mahar speculated that the song in its folk forms dates from the antebellum period, but Fuld found its first appearance in *Students' Songs* published and arranged by Harvard Students (copyrighted June 9, 1880 in Boston). The closest relative to "Pop Weir's Tune" in tradition that I have found is "The Old Cow Crossed the Road" in Bayard's *Dance to the Fiddle* (pp. 83–84). Bayard commented that "this piece affords a good example of how a tune, doubtless a song air to begin with, and by no means very old, can get transformed by folk musicians. Here, it looks as though a first strain, recognizably derived from some single original, has been strongly modified and furnished independently with two quite different strains to serve as second parts" (p. 84). In correspondence, Bayard wrote me that indeed, "Pop Weir's Tune" appears to be a simplified set of "The Old Cow Crossed the Road" (27 January 1987). The tune also bears some resemblance, at least in the opening measures, to Bayard's no. 216 (identified simply as "Dance Tune") in *Dance to the Fiddle* (p. 172). Pop died in 1965 but his influence remains in tunes like this that remain in the repertoires of local fiddlers who gathered around his store. Talking with Dorrance Weir about such tunes, he pointed out that his father brought many tunes to the area from the "North Country" (in St. Lawrence County). The fiddlers in Otsego County knew most of the old-time tunes that Pop played, but when a group of fiddlers didn't recognize one of the tunes, on the strength of Pop's reputation they would just label it "Pop Weir's Tune" when they replayed it. This process is not unusual as Bayard's notes to "Sam King's Tune" in *Dance to the Fiddle* bear out (pp. 313–14). Characteristic of Pop's insistence on stylistic consistency among the fiddlers playing with him, Ken Kane takes the tune at an easy clip and emphasizes each note in the melody. Showing some of the versatility of these traditional airs, Kane pointed out that the last line of the melody can also be used as an introduction.

34. "Letter Edged in Black" played by Ken Kane on guitar. Recorded by Simon J. Bronner at Ken Kane's house in Hartwick Township, 13 April 1976. Kane learned this song from his father and has passed it on to his daughter. It has a simple tune punctuated with some syncopation and chromatic tones. The original tearful song "Letter Edged in Black" is credited to Hattie Nevada (1897), a professional composer and entertainer. After its publication on broadsides and performance on the vaudeville state, the song quickly entered oral tradition in the countryside. It was picked up in the 1920s and 1930s by folk-styled recording artists Vernon Dalhart, Fiddlin' John Carson, Frank Luther, and Bradley Kincaid. Sigmund Spaeth reports a complete version of the words and music in *Weep Some More My Lady,* pp. 38–39. The song is reported in its folk forms in Randolph, *Ozark Folksongs,* IV, pp. 162–63; Ethel Park Richardson, *American Mountain Songs* (Ellicott City, Maryland: Greenberg, 1927), p. 35; *Carson J. Robison's World's Greatest Collection of Mountain Ballads and Old Time Songs* (Chicago: M. M. Cole, 1930), p. 12–13; *Smith's Collection of Mountain Ballads and Cowboy Songs* (New York: Wm. J. Smith Music, 1932), pp. 22–23. Richardson's comment on the song is instructive: "This song once had a wide vogue all over America, but may well have been of mountain origin. Its melody contains suggestions of the modern "Prisoner's Song," and its words employ more than ordinary art in the telling of the story" (p. 107). The song is one of many popular compositions from the late Victorian period that persisted in country music as folk-styled ballads or fiddle tunes; see Gene Wiggins, "Popular Music and the Fiddler," pp. 144–56. Ken associated this song with a group of parlor songs in what he calls the "old-time singing" tradition, such as the "Baggage Coach Ahead," "Old Grey Bonnet," and "Ship That Never Returned." Indeed, the connection is common; see the version of "Letter Edged in Black" in the magazine *Old Time Songs and Poems,* no. 3 (January–February 1968). For a commentary on the relation of this form of old-time singing to old-time music, see Robert Nobley, "Old-Time Singing Versus Folk Singing," *Devil's Box,* no. 15 (20 August 1971), pp. 9–10.

35. "Larry O'Gaff" played by Grant Rogers on fiddle. Recorded by Simon Bronner at Grant Rogers' home near Walton, New York, 17 November 1976. Rogers gives this tune an Irish accent by playing it throughout with separate bows. An unusual feature of the tune is the required shift to third position in the second measure of the B part. This move requires a steady hold on the violin and sure fingering. Rogers plays the tune in a standard dance-tune form of A A B B, and being an experienced dance fiddler, his rhythm is steady as a rock. He differed from other renditions of this tune that I collected by playing it at a relatively fast tempo, but his melody is close to a version from the Catskills of New York reported in Cazden's *Dances from Camp Woodland,* p. 30. The fiddle tune "Larry O'Gaff" takes its name from a nineteenth-century stage-Irish song; by 1858 it appeared as a country dance in Howe's *Ball-Room Hand Book,* p. 85. The words to the old song are rarely reported, although they can found in folk variants in Helen Creighton, *Songs and Ballads from Nova Scotia* (Toronto: Dent & Sons, 1933), nos. 113–33. Bayard in *Dance to the Fiddle* states that sometimes the name of an old British Isles dance "Hob or Knob" is given for "Larry O'Gaff." That suggests a connection to "Campbells are Coming" and Les Weir's version of "Miss McLeod's Reel," which also went by the name "Hob or Knob." Chances are that at least part of the reason that "Larry O'Gaff" became popular is because it could replace the other two tunes at contra dances. Its use for these dances also might explain why this tune is usually associated with players in northeastern America. A spate of printings of "Larry O'Gaff" occurs in the first decade of the twentieth century. See Paul De Ville, *The Universal Favorite Contra Dance Album* (New York: Carl Fischer, 1905), no. 51; T. H. Rollinson, *Favorite Reels, Jigs and Hornpipes for the Violin* (Boston: Oliver Ditson, 1907), p. 6; *Harding's All-Round Collection of Jigs, Reels and Country Dances* (New York: Harding's Music House, 1905), no. 105; *Jigs and Reels,* 2 vols. (New York: Academic Music Co., 1908), I, p. 28; Francis O'Neill and James O'Neill, *O'Neill's Music of Ireland* (Chicago: Lyon & Healy, 1903), nos. 869, 870; *White's Excelsior Collection of Jigs, Reels* (New York: White-Smith Music Publishing Co., 1907), p. 74. For more recent versions, see Wells, *New England Traditional Fiddling,* pp. 22–23; Dunham, *Fiddlin' Dance Tunes,* no. 26; Jarman and Hansen, *Old Time Dance Tunes,* p. 63; Mr. and Mrs. Ford, *Good Morning,* pp. 17, 66; Adam, *Old Time Fiddlers' Favorite Barn Dance Tunes,* no. 55; Sweet, *Fifer's Delight,* p. 63; O'Malley and Atwood, *Seventy Good Old Dances,* p. 4; Brody, *Fiddler's Fakebook,* p. 164; *One Thousand Fiddle Tunes,* p. 59. A recording of Rogers' "Larry O'Gaff" is available on Grant Rogers, *Songmaker of the Catskills,* ed. Sandy Paton (Folk-Legacy FSA-27, 1965); other per-

formers' versions are available on Wells, *New England Traditional Fiddling;* Albert Cyr, *Old Time Fiddling* (Century 36464, 1969); Graham Townsend, *Down Home Fiddlin'* (Audat 477-9048); Roma McMillan, *Old Time Fiddling 1976* (Fretless 122). Tolman and Page in the *Country Dance Book* list the contra dance that commonly accompanies "Larry O'Gaff": First two couples right and left for 8 bars, followed by the first couple down center and turn half round and back for 8 bars, followed by cast off and ladies chain for 8 bars, and finally all forward and back and key couples cross to place for 8 bars. A less traditional square-dance version is given in Cazden, *Dances from Camp Woodland,* p. 30.

36. "Opera Reel" played by Grant Rogers on fiddle. Recorded by Simon Bronner at Grant Rogers' home near Walton, New York, 17 November 1976. Rogers plays this tune at a relatively fast clip, yet still punctuates all the notes crisply. The A part is a standard fiddle-tune length, but the other parts of the tune are one-half as long. He plays the tune according to the form A A B B C C D D. Although the tune is not as widely reported in folk fiddling collections as some of the other tunes in this book, it certainly ranks as a standard of the upstate New York old-time repertoire. Grant Rogers pointed out that many fiddlers he knew in the region considered it their favorite. Fiddlers might boast of the tune because of its several parts and its complex figures in the B and C parts. The operatic triplet pattern in the C part probably suggested the name of "Opera Reel" in its early forms. According to Bayard in *Dance to the Fiddle,* the tune does not appear earlier than the first part of the nineteenth century. Bayard's version from Pennsylvania also contains four parts, although he cites other versions that have two or three parts. Linscott in *Folk Songs of Old New England* states that "the air, 'Opera Reel,' . . . was fitted for a contra dance performed on the stage" (p. 70). It may very well be that the tune has a stage origin, because besides producing light operas, popular theaters and chautauquas often did vernacular versions or even parodies of opera. But the overall feel of the tune is Scottish or Irish, and it is often used in New York and New England as a substitute for the Scottish "Lady Walpole's Reel" and the probably Irish "Pig Town Fling"; see Linscott, *Folk Songs of Old New England,* p. 71. Variants of "Opera Reel" can be found in Ford, *Traditional Music in America,* p. 69; Christeson, *Old-Time Fiddler's Repertory,* p. 56; Linscott, *Folk Songs of Old New England,* p. 70; *Jigs and Reels,* I, p. 15; Adam, *Old Time Fiddlers' Favorite Barn Dance Tunes,* no. 63; Jarman and Hansen, *Old Time Dance Tunes,* p. 79; *Sym's Old Time Dances,* p. 12; De Ville, *Universal Favorite Contra Dance Album,* no. 32; *One Thousand Fiddle Tunes,* p. 31; Brody, *Fiddler's Fakebook,* p. 209; Ryan, *Dances of Our Pioneers,* p. 150. Grant Rogers recorded "Opera Reel" on *Ballads and Fiddle Tunes* (Kanawha 313); other recorded versions are found on John Summers, *Indiana Fiddler;* Grant Lamb, *Tunes from Home* (Voyager 312-S); Norman Blake, *Rising Fawn String Ensemble* (Rounder 0122); Arm and Hammer String Band, *Stay on the Farm* (Fretless 136). The tune is usually associated with the Northeast because of its common use with contra dances that go by the name of "Opera Reel," "Lady Walpole's Reel," and "Boston Fancy." See Howe, *Ball-Room Hand Book,* p. 87; Linscott, *Folk Songs of Old New England,* pp. 69–70; Tolman and Page, *Country Dance Book,* pp. 113–14; Ryan, *Dances of Our Pioneers,* pp. 151–52.

37. "Jam on Gerry's Rock" played by Grant Rogers on guitar. Recorded by Simon Bronner at Grant Rogers' home near Walton, New York, 17 November 1976. Rogers plays this song in the relaxed manner that characterizes his fiddling. But although his rhythm is steady, he occasionally holds some notes for a varying number of beats (⌢). Rogers' tune resembles most closely version 4B as sung by George "Dick" Edwards in Cazden, Haufrecht, and Studer, *Folk Songs of the Catskills,* p. 50. This version, according to the trio of editors, "is essentially the characteristic one belonging, among others in the lumber-camp repertory" (p. 47). Norman Cazden published a composite text and tune to "Jam on Gerry's Rock" from the Catskills in *The Abelard Folk Song Book* (New York: Abelard Schuman, 1958). Cazden puts the song in the key of G, and notes that "the tune strain shows but minor variations among the forms sung by George 'Dick' Edwards, Etson Van Wagner, and Walden Van Wagner, and it has been widely used elsewhere for this song as well as for many other lumber camp favorites" (p. 115). Although commonly collected in New York State, the original location or composition of the song "Jam on Gerry's Rock" is obscure; it is listed as one of America's most collected native ballads (see Laws, *Native American Balladry,* p. 147). Extensive discussion of the song is found in Cazden, Haufrecht, and Studer, *Folk Songs of the Catskills,* pp. 46–52; Norman Cazden, Herbert Haufrecht, and Norman Studer, *Notes and Sources for Folk Songs of the Catskills,* pp. 8–9; Fannie Hardy Eckstorm and Mary

Winslow Smyth, *Minstrelsy of Maine* (Boston: Houghton Mifflin, 1927), pp. 176–98. Variants of the song are reported in Warner, *Traditional American Folk Songs*, pp. 76–78; Helen Creighton, *Songs and Ballads from Nova Scotia*, pp. 267–68; Henry W. Shoemaker, *Mountain Minstrelsy of Pennsylvania* (rev. ed., Philadelphia: Newman F. McGirr, 1931); Emelyn Elizabeth Gardner and Geraldine Jencks Chickering, *Ballads and Songs of Southern Michigan* (1939; rpt. ed., Hatboro, Pa: Folklore Associates, 1967), pp. 270–73; Robert Bethke, *Adirondack Voices: Woodsmen and Woods Lore* (Urbana: University of Illinois Press, 1981), pp. 64–67; Harold W. Thompson, *Body, Boots, and Britches: Folktales, Ballads and Speech from Country New York* (1940; rpt. ed., Syracuse: Syracuse University Press, 1979), pp. 259–60; Phillips Barry, *The Maine Woods Songster* (Cambridge: Harvard University Press, 1939), pp. 52–53; E. C. Beck, *Lore the Lumber Camps* (Ann Arbor: University of Michigan Press, 1948), pp. 194–97; Edith Fowke, *Lumbering Songs from the Northern Woods* (Austin: University of Texas Press, 1970), pp. 95–99; Johnny Crockett, *Log Cabin Songs* (New York: Universal Music, 1930), pp. 6–7; Helen Hartness Flanders, Elizabeth Flanders Ballard, George Brown, and Phillips Barry, *The New Green Mountain Songster: Traditional Folk Songs of Vermont* (1939; rpt. ed., Hatboro, Pa.: Folklore Associates, 1966), pp. 44–46; Carl Sandburg, *The American Songbag* (New York: Harcourt, Brace, 1927), pp. 394–95; Roland P. Gray, *Songs and Ballads of the Maine Lumberjacks* (Cambridge: Harvard University Press, 1924), pp. 3–9; Richard Dorson, George List, and Neil Rosenberg, "Folksongs of the Maine Woods," *Folklore and Folk Music Archivist* 8 (Fall 1965): 3–33; Edward Ives, *Joe Scott: The Woodsman Songmaker* (Urbana: University of Illinois Press, 1978), pp. 314–15; William Main Doerflinger, *Songs of the Sailor and Lumberman* (New York: Macmillan, 1972), pp. 238–40; Eloise Hubbard Linscott, *Folk Songs of Old New England* (New York: Macmillan, 1939), pp. 217–20; J. Herbert Walker, "Lumberjacks and Raftsmen" in *Pennsylvania Songs and Legends*, ed. George Korson (Philadelphia: University of Pennsylvania Press, 1949), pp. 345–46.

38. "I'll Hit the Road Again" played by Grant Rogers on guitar. Recorded by Simon Bronner at Grant Rogers' home near Walton, New York, 17 November 1976. This song is a variant of "I Walk the Road Again," a song credited to nineteenth-century singer Jehila "Pat" Edwards from the Catskills of New York. Sandy Paton recorded a version with an altered tune to this one during April 1975 and included it on *Brave Boys: New England Traditions in Folk Music* (New World Records NW 239, 1977). In both versions, Rogers has not used the modal tune sung by George Edwards, but rather has applied a major-scale tune similar to the one he uses on "Jam on Gerry's Rock" (see tune no. 37), although on "Hit the Road," he uses a more restricted range and adds a chorus. Rogers' melody to "Hit the Road" employs only 5 notes: A C# D E F#. For an extensive discussion of "I Walk the Road Again," see Cazden, Haufrecht, and Studer, *Folk Songs of the Catskills*, 637–44.

39. "Turkey in the Straw" played by Charley Hughes on fiddle. Recorded by Robert Sieber at Charley Hughes's home near Milford, New York, 11 April 1973. Hughes learned to fiddle and to play this particular tune from his father and uncles, but this transcription shows marked differences from "pioneer" versions of "Turkey in the Straw" (see tune nos. 3 and 31). Hughes shows off some of the new stylish overlays put on top of the old-time musical inheritance by many post–World War II fiddlers. Taking the tune at a fast clip, Hughes relies heavily on double-string playing and he flirts with a rhythmic syncopation in parts of the tune. He quotes the shuffle from the bluegrass number "Orange Blossom Special" in a variation of the first and second measures of the B part. To achieve many of his double-string effects, Hughes uses the key of A, while most old-time players will play this tune in G. Playing in A opens strings for the double-stops and multiple-string playing that Hughes employs. Indeed, on the variation of the first and second measures of the A part Hughes employs the rarely-played lowest string on a shuffle. Matthew Guntharp in *Learning the Fiddler's Ways* discusses some of these stylistic overlays, and he includes some variations of "Turkey in the Straw"; see pp. 53–56, 112–32. The influence of some of these "new licks to oldtime fiddling," as Matthew Guntharp calls them, can also be heard on Bill Monroe, *Bluegrass Time* (MCA-116); for background on "Turkey in the Straw," see my notes to tune no. 31 and Jabbour, *American Fiddle Tunes*, pp. 31–34.

40. "Rubber Dolly Breakdown" played by Charley Hughes on fiddle. Recorded by Robert Sieber at Charley Hughes's home near Milford, New York, 11 April 1973. Hughes shows what he can do on the fiddle by playing off the opening theme of the fiddle tune usually called "Rubber Dolly." He also shows how a phrase or theme of an old fiddle tune can lead to the for-

mation of a variant, a common practice in the evolution of old-time music. Hughes plays a four-measure vamp as a showcase for fancy shuffles and double-string playing. Again he quotes the shuffle from "Orange Blossom Special" on the second variation. "Rubber Dolly" was first collected as a British-American children's singing game with variations of the words "My mommy told me, She's going to buy me a rubber dolly, If I was good, So don't you tell her I kissed a feller (or soldier), Or she won't buy me a rubber dolly." Peter and Iona Opie in *The Singing Game* report versions from England, Ireland, Canada, Australia, and the United States. The Opies make the reasonable guess that the text is based on a music-hall song of the 1890s. Nonetheless, the tune has a relation to an older melody in the British Isles tradition called "Lord Alexander's Reel (or Hornpipe)." See Opie and Opie, *The Singing Game*, pp. 447–49; *One Thousand Fiddle Tunes*, p. 127; Krassen, *O'Neill's Music of Ireland*, p. 193; or listen to "Lord Alexander's Reel" on *25 Great Fiddle Hits* (K-Tel 9110, 1976). "Rubber Dolly" as a fiddle tune was a favorite Texas or western swing number during the 1930s and 1940s, although it has also been collected in the Northeast as a widely travelled folk tune by Bayard in *Dance to the Fiddle*, p. 69, Vance Randolph in Arkansas and Missouri (Archive of Folk Culture, Library of Congress, Vance Randolph Papers, Box 7), by Joe Hickerson in Virginia (Archive of Folk Culture, 26 March 1966), and by Alan Jabbour in North Carolina (Archive of Folk Culture, 16 October 1965, 25 November 1966). For versions of the tune showing great stylistic variety, listen to Uncle Bud Landress's "Rubber Dolly Rag" on *Old-Time Southern Dance Music* (Old Timey LP-101); Harry Choates's "Rubber Dolly" on *Western Swing* (Old Timey LP 105); Woody Guthrie, *Hard Travelin'* (Disc D 110); Johnny Gimble's "Rubber Dolly" on *The Texas Fiddle Collection* (CMH Country Classics 9027, 1981).

41. "Devil's Dream" played by John Dingler on fiddle. Recorded by Simon Bronner at the Newfield Old-Time Fiddlers Contest, Newfield, New York, 2 July 1977. John Dingler learned this tune from his father but in his version he uses variations that employ elaborate phrases and fancy shuffles. Indeed, this is a tune that is often used to show a fiddler's creativity. Tolman and Page in the *Country Dance Book* write, "All fiddlers are jealous of their accomplishments, you know, and it is an absolute impossibility to be accepted into their clan unless one can perform both Devil's Dream and Speed the Plow in a creditable manner, preferably with homemade variations. Old Theophilus (Parse) Ames used to say that a fiddler without his own version of Devil's Dream was of 'as much account as a string of wampum in the Washington mint' " (p. 112). The shuffle on Dingler's first variation has a jazzy feel to it because five accented notes are played over four beats by rocking the bow back and forth over three strings in combination of two and two. The second variation is a standard elaboration of this tune requiring the fiddler to move into the third position, while the third variation uses an unusual repetition of a two-note pattern in the second measure. Dingler's B part differs from most versions of the tune in his use of a droning motif rather than a string-crossing one. According to Bayard in *Dance to the Fiddle*, "Devil's Dream" is "a variant form of a tune called 'The Devil among the Tailors'"—quite common under that name in the British Isles, and often reprinted in commercial tune-books." As "Devil's Dream," the tune is among the best-known in America. For variants, see Bayard, *Dance to the Fiddle*, pp. 314–17; Ford, *Traditional Music in America*, p. 62; Cazden, *Dances from Camp Woodland*, p. 36; Kennedy, *Fiddler's Tune Book*, p. 9; Shaw, *Cowboy Dances*, p. 390; Ryan, *Dances of Our Pioneers*, p. 140; Kraus, *One Thousand Fiddle Tunes*, p. 30; *Square Dances of Today*, p. 52; Adam, *Old Time Fiddlers' Favorite Barn Dance Tunes*, no. 68; Sweet, *Fifer's Delight*, p. 62; Linscott, *Folk Songs of Old New England*, p. 74; *Sym's Old Time Dances*, p. 9; De Ville, *Universal Favorite Contra Dance Album*, no. 77; O'Malley and Atwood, *Seventy Good Old Dances*, p. 12; Tyson, *Twenty-Five Old Fashioned Dance Tunes*, no. 27; Brody, *Fiddler's Fakebook*, p. 85; Gene Lowinger, *Bluegrass Fiddle* (New York: Oak Publications, 1974). For a recording of "Devil's Dream" by another New York State fiddler, listen to Lawrence Older, *Adirondack Songs, Ballads and Fiddle Tunes* (Folk Legacy FSA-15, 1963). "Devil's Dream" also refers to a contra dance that uses the tune as an accompaniment. According to Tolman and Page writing in 1937, "fifty years ago no contry was in more demand than Devil's Dream, which bears a decided resemblance to Old Zip Coon" (p. 112). For other dances to "Devil's Dream" from New York and New England see Linscott, *Folk Songs of Old New England*, pp. 72–74; Cazden, *Dances from Camp Woodland*, p. 36. More general dances to "Devil's Dream" are described in Howe, *Ball-Room Hand Book*, p. 86; Burchenal, *American Country Dances*, pp. 14–15; Ryan, *Dances of Our Pioneers*, p. 141.

42. "Flop Eared Mule" played by Milo Kouf and John Dingler on fiddles. Recorded by

Simon Bronner at picnic grounds in Newfield, New York, 2 July 1977. Kouf and Dingler take this tune at a fast pace. The second fiddle part uses a ♫♫ rhythm on chords using double stops. The variation that occurs in the third measure is a rhythmic alteration that requires a different bowing. Bayard in *Dance to the Fiddle* speculates that the tune hails from the early nineteenth century. Although the tune is often associated with southern playing, I heard northern fiddlers often mention it as an old-time tune for a schottische dance, also called "The Barn Dance," which was popular in New York State before World War II. Lyle Miles and Jehile Kirkhuff knew the tune as "D-A Quadrille" a name also familiar to John Dingler. Kouf explained that the switch from playing in D in the first part to A in the second gives it this common York State name. The use of "quadrille" refers not to the time signature but probably to a dance known as a "Schottische Quadrille" described in Howe, *Ball-Room Hand Book,* pp. 59–60. Ford in *Traditional Music in America* cites the "College Schottische" as a source for "Flop Eared Mule" (p. 121). John Dingler still plays it in performances with his band; it is a favorite "breakdown" duet. For variants of the tune, see Bayard, *Dance to the Fiddle,* pp. 101–7; Kennedy, *The Second Fiddler's Tune Book,* p. 27 (which he calls "Bluebell Polka"); Ford, *Traditional Music in America,* pp. 121, 157; Thede, *The Fiddle Book,* p. 129; Messer, *Down East Fiddlin' Tunes,* no. 24; Adam, *Old-Time Fiddlers' Favorite Barn Dance Tunes,* pp. 25, 34; Christeson, *Old-Time Fiddler's Repertory,* p. 74; Brody, *Fiddler's Fakebook,* p. 108; Reiner, *Anthology of Fiddle Styles,* p. 22. Putney and Flood give a dance to an arrangement of a variant of "Flop Eared Mule," which they simply call "Schottische," in *Square Dancing U.S.A.,* p. 68. They describe it this way: "Couple in open position. Beginning outside foot, walk forward three steps. On count four, hop on outside foot, and swing inside foot slightly forward. Repeat beginning with the inside foot. The true Schottische step is: 'Step, close step, hop.' " They also comment that "early in the century, the Barn dance was popular and is almost exactly like the Schottische but is danced more vigorously and less smoothly" (p. 67).

43. "Wilson's Clog" played by Milo Kouf on fiddle. Recorded by Simon Bronner at the Newfield Old-Time Fiddlers' Contest, Newfield, New York, 2 July 1977. Milo Kouf learned this tune from his father. It is distinguished by a complex slurring pattern in the A part and heavily accented shuffles in the B part. Kouf said that in addition to appealing to old-timers from New York, this tune was a frequent request from Canadians. Bayard in *Dance to the Fiddle* also collected this tune as "Harvest" and "Harvest Home," and traces its probable British-American roots to the early nineteenth century (p. 392). It has also appeared by its dance name, "Cincinnati Hornpipe," "Cliff Hornpipe," and "Brown's Hornpipe." Sometimes, a full name of "Fred Wilson's" is attached to "Clog" or "Hornpipe," although the connection of this name with the tune or dance is uncertain. For variants going under the title "Wilson's Clog," see Bayard, *Dance to the Fiddle* Ford, *Traditional Music in America,* p. 100; Cazden, *Dances from Camp Woodland,* p. 37; Dunham, *Fiddlin' Dance Tunes,* no. 33; O'Malley and Atwood, *Seventy Good Old Dances,* p. 34; *White's Excelsior Collection of Jigs, Reels,* p. 43; *One Thousand Fiddle Tunes,* p. 100; *Gems of the Ball Room,* no. 23. Other versions under different names are found in Krassen, *O'Neill's Music of Ireland,* p. 207; Kennedy, *Fiddler's Tune Book,* p. 3; Jarman and Hansen, *Old Time Dance Tunes,* p. 70; Cazden, *Dances from Woodland,* p. 41; *Jigs and Reels,* II, p. 25; Brody, *Fiddler's Fakebook,* p. 131; Sweet, *Fifer's Delight,* p. 58; Christeson, *Old-Time Fiddler's Repertory, Volume 2,* p. 72; Burchenal, *American Country Dances,* p. 35. You can hear the tune done by Margaret McNiff-Locke's Instrumental Trio (1930) on Spottswood, *Dance Music* and find a list of references on pp. 5–6. The contra dance "Cincinnati Hornpipe" to which "Wilson's Clog" is attached is described in Howe, *Ball-Room Hand Book,* p. 81; Tolman and Page, *Country Dance Book,* p. 124; Briggs, *Thirty Contras from New England,* p. 46. Tolman and Page comment that this dance tune was a specialty of Maine's Mellie Dunham who helped to bring it "back to popularity." Briggs adds that "this dance is easy, great for polishing the right and left movement and serves well to bring out the point about precise timing, for no contra is more precise." For other versions of the dance, see Cazden, *Dances from Camp Woodland,* p. 36; Burchenal, *American Country Dances,* p. 35.

44. "Farmer Had a Dog" played by Milo Kouf on fiddle. Recorded by Simon Bronner at the picnic grounds at Newfield, New York, 2 July 1977. Milo Kouf learned this tune from his father. It is characterized by short or stacatto eighth notes in the A part and contrasting longer or legato eighths in the B part. It is a snappy dance tune that nicely demonstrates the catchy melody and "endless" quality that mark most fiddle-tune performances. The title of this song suggests

that it accompanied the children's play-party game of "Bingo," because of the first line "There was a farmer had a dog." But the simple melody of the game as it is usually reported bears little resemblance to this tune. It is conceivable that Milo's father elaborated on a version of the singing game to produce this dance tune. Milo himself was not sure, and the fact remains that tune is now familiar by the title "Farmer Had a Dog" to Milo's fiddling cronies in Tompkins County. It does seem to be a part of the "Mason's Apron" family of tunes that spawned "Hell on the Potomac" and "Wake Up Susan" (see my tune nos. 2, 14); see the relations to Bayard's variant E in *Dance to the Fiddle,* p. 348, and his discussion on pp. 352–53.

45. "Crockford's Jig" played by Milo Kouf on fiddle. Recorded by Simon Bronner at Newfield Old-Time Fiddlers Contest, Newfield, New York, 2 July 1977. Milo Kouf learned this tune from Robert Crockford, an older fiddler from Groton, New York, Tompkins County. Kouf uses it as a showcase tune to boast his dexterity on the bow and to draw attention to his old-time style. The tune is characterized by four distinct parts that each have different chord structures. As played, the B and C parts are only one-half as long as the A and D parts. Apparently there has been some interconnections made between this tune and "Wilson's Clog" (tune no. 43); they share almost identical second and fourth measures. Still, the first and third measures for the A and B parts differ and make this tune a variant. Milo Kouf clearly distinguishes the tunes, and to be sure, this performance is closer to printed versions of "Cincinnati Hornpipe" and "Harvest Home" than "Wilson's Clog." The distinction probably emerged from the use of the tunes for different dances; Howe in the *Ball-Room Hand Book,* for example, lists both a "Cincinnati Hornpipe" and "Harvest Home" (pp. 81, 88). For background on this family of tunes and the dances that accompany them, see the notes to tune no. 43.

Works Cited

Books and Articles

Abrahams, Roger D., and George Foss. *Anglo-American Folksong Style.* Englewood Cliffs, N.J.: Prentice-Hall, 1968.

Adam, E. F. *Old Time Fiddlers Favorite Barn Dance Tunes for the Violin.* St. Louis: Hunleth Music, 1928.

Agay, Denes. *Best Loved Songs of the American People.* Garden City, N.Y.: Doubleday, 1975.

Aird, James. *A Selection of Scotch, English, Irish and Foreign Airs.* 6 vols. Glasgow: J. Aird, n.d.

"All States Broadcast Except Wyoming." *Literary Digest* (11 November 1922), p. 29.

Allen, Barbara, and Lynwood Montell. *From Memory to History: Using Oral History Sources in Local Historical Research.* Nashville: American Association for State and Local History, 1981.

Allen, N. H. "Old Time Music and Musicians." *Connecticut Quarterly* 1 (1895): 368–73.

Allen, Nelson. "Texas Revisited." *Country Music Magazine* (October 1977), pp. 38–40, 60–61.

Allen, R. Raymond. "Old-Time Music and the Urban Folk Revival." M.A. thesis, Western Kentucky University, 1981.

The American Veteran Fifer. Cincinnati: Fillmore Music House, 1927.

Arkansas Woodchopper. *The Arkansas Wood-Chopper's World's Greatest Collection of Cowboy Songs.* Chicago: M. M. Cole, 1931.

Armstrong, Janice Gray, ed. *Catching the Tune: Music and William Sidney Mount.* Stony Brook, New York: The Museums at Stony Brook, 1984.

Attebery, Louie W. "The Fiddle Tune: An American Artifact." In *Readings in American Folklore,* ed. Jan Harold Brunvand, pp. 324–33. New York: W. W. Norton, 1979.

Atwood, E. Bagby. "Shivarees and Charivaris: Variations on a Theme." *Publications of the Texas Folklore Society* 32 (1964): 64–71.

Averill, Patricia. "Can the Circle Be Unbroken: A Study of the Modernization of Rural Born Southern Whites Since World War I Using Country Music." Ph.D. diss., University of Pennsylvania, 1975.

Babcock, W. H. "Games of Washington Children." *American Anthropologist* 1 (1888): 243–84.

Barry, Philips. *The Maine Woods Songster.* Cambridge: Harvard University Press, 1939.

————— ; Fannie Hardy Eckstorm, and Mary Winslow Smyth. *British Ballads from Maine.* New Haven: Yale University Press, 1929.

Bayard, Samuel Preston. *Hill Country Tunes: Instrumental Folk Music of Southwestern Pennsylvania.* Philadelphia: American Folklore Society, 1944.

————— . "The British Folk Tradition." In *Pennsylvania Songs and Legends,* ed. George Korson, pp. 17–61. Philadelphia: University of Pennsylvania Press, 1949.

————— . "Some Folk Fiddlers' Habits and Styles in Western Pennsylvania." *Journal of the International Folk Music Council* 8 (1956): 15–18.

————— . *Dance to the Fiddle, March to the Fife: Instrumental Folk Tunes in Pennsylvania.* University Park: Pennsylvania State University Press, 1982.

————— . "Foreword." In *Learning the Fiddler's Ways* by Matthew Guntharp, pp. 11–12. University Park: Pennsylvania State University Press, 1980.

Beck, E. C. *Lore of the Lumber Camps.* Ann Arbor: University of Michigan Press, 1948.

Belden, H. M. *Ballads and Songs Collected by the Missouri Folk-Lore Society.* 1940; rpt. ed., Columbia: University of Missouri Press, 1973.

————— , and Arthur Palmer Hudson, eds. *Frank C. Brown Collection of North Carolina Folklore: Folk Songs from North Carolina.* Durham, N.C.: Duke University Press, 1952.

Benes, Peter, and Jane Montague Benes, eds. *American Speech: 1600 to the Present.* Boston: Boston University Scholarly Publications, 1985.

Bernhardt, Jack. "The Hollow Rock String Band." *Bluegrass Unlimited* 21 (December 1986), 74–81.

Bethke, Robert D. "Old-Time Fiddling and Social Dance in Central St. Lawrence County." *New York Folklore Quarterly* 30 (1974): 163–84.

————— . *Adirondack Voices: Woodsmen and Woods Lore.* Urbana: University of Illinois Press, 1981.

————— . "New England Singing Tradition." *Journal of American Folklore* 97 (1984): 466.

Biggar, June. "The Journal of Richard Weston (1836): An Example of Foreign Travel Literature as Source Material in Folklife Studies." M.A. thesis, Cooperstown Graduate Programs of the State University of New York, 1974.

"Bill Knowlton." *Country Music Courier* (May 1986), cover page.

Blaustein, Richard. "Preservation of Old Time Fiddling as a Living Force." *Devil's Box,* no. 13 (September 1970): 6–8.

————— . "Traditional Music and Social Change: The Old-Time Fiddlers Association Movement in the United States." Ph.D. diss., Indiana University, 1975.

Boorstin, Daniel. *The Americans: The Colonial Experience.* New York: Vintage/Random House, 1958.

————— . *The Americans: The National Experience.* New York: Vintage/Random House, 1965.

Bossard, James H. S., and Eleanor S. Boll. *Ritual in Family Living: A Contemporary Study.* Philadelphia: University of Pennsylvania Press, 1950.

Botkin, B. A. *A Treasury of New England Folklore: Stories, Ballads, and Traditions of Yankee Folk.* 1947; rpt. ed., New York: Bonanza Books, 1955.

Braunlein, John H. " 'Is That Hillbilly Enough for You?': The Northern Country Music

Tradition in Madison County." *Madison County Heritage,* no. 10 (July 1981): 14–17.

Briggs, Dudley T. *Thirty Contras from New England.* Burlington, Mass.: Dudley T. Briggs, 1953.

Brody, David. *The Fiddler's Fakebook.* New York: Oak Publications, 1983.

Bronner, Simon J. " 'I Kicked Three Slats Out of My Cradle First Time I Heard That': Ken Kane, Country Music, and American Folklife." *New York Folklore* 3 (1977): 53–81.

———. "John Baltzell: Champion Old Time Fiddler." *Old Time Music* 27 (Winter 1977/78): 13–14.

———. *Chain Carvers: Old Men Crafting Meaning.* Lexington: University Press of Kentucky, 1985.

———, ed. *American Material Culture and Folklife.* Ann Arbor, Michigan: UMI Research Press, 1985.

———. *Grasping Things: Folk Material Culture and Mass Society in America.* Lexington: University Press of Kentucky, 1986.

Brunnings, Florence E. *Folk Song Index: A Comprehensive Guide to the Florence E. Brunnings Collection.* New York: Garland, 1981.

Buechner, Alan C. "Long Island's Early Brass Bands." *Long Island Forum* (June 1982): 106–11.

Burchenal, Elizabeth. *American Country Dances.* New York: G. Schirmer, 1918.

———. *Folk Dances of Germany.* New York: Schirmer, 1938.

Burman-Hall, Linda C. "The Technique of Variation in an American Fiddle Tune: A Study of 'Sail Away Lady' as Performed in 1926 by Uncle Bunt Stephens." *Ethnomusicology* 12 (1968): 49–71.

———. "Southern American Folk Fiddle Styles." *Ethnomusicology* 19 (1975): 47–65.

Campbell, Olive Dame, and Cecil J. Sharp. *English Folk Songs from the Southern Appalachians.* New York: G. P. Putnam's Sons, 1917.

Cantwell, Robert. *Bluegrass Breakdown: The Making of the Old Southern Sound.* Urbana: University of Illinois Press, 1984.

Caplow, Theodore; Howard M. Bahr; Bruce A. Chadwick; Reuben Hill; Margaret Holmes Williamson. *Middletown Families: Fifty Years of Change and Continuity.* New York: Bantam Books, 1983.

Carlson, Avis D. "Cowboy Ballads at Our Own Firesides." In *A History and Encyclopedia of Country, Western, and Gospel Music,* ed. Linnell Gentry, pp. 33–38. 1961; rpt. ed., St. Clair Shores, Mich.: Scholarly Press, 1972.

Cazden, Norman. *Dances from Woodland: Square Dances from the Catskills.* Ann Arbor, Mich.: Cushing-Malloy, 1955.

———. *The Abelard Folksong Book.* New York: Abelard Schuman, 1958.

———; Herbert Haufrecht; Norman Studer. *Folk Songs of the Catskills.* Albany: State University of New York Press, 1982.

———. *Notes and Sources for Folk Songs of the Catskills.* Albany: State University of New York Press, 1982.

Chappell, William. *A Collection of National English Airs,* 2 vols. London: Chappell, 1840.

———. *Popular Music of the Olden Time.* 2 vols. London: Cramer Beale & Chappell, 1855–59.

Christeson, R. P. *The Old-Time Fiddler's Repertory.* Columbia: University of Missouri Press, 1973.

———. *Old-Time Fiddler's Repertory, Volume 2.* Columbia: University of Missouri Press, 1984.

Coes, George H. *Album of Music: Something New for Professional and Amateur Violinists.* Boston: Louis P. Goullaud, 1876.

Coffin, Tristram Potter. *The British Traditional Ballad in North America.* Rev. ed., Austin: University of Texas Press, 1977.

Cohen, Anne, and Norm Cohen. "Folk and Hillbilly Music: Further Thoughts on Their Relation." *John Edwards Memorial Foundation Quarterly* 13 (1977): 50–57.

Cohen, John. "Fiddlin' Eck Robertson." *Sing Out!* 14 (April–May 1964): 55–59.

————, and Mike Seeger. *Old-Time String Band Songbook.* New York: Oak Publications, 1976.

Cohen, Norm. "Anglo-American Music: Field Recorded and Otherwise." *Journal of American Folklore* 100 (1987): 80–88.

Colcord, Joanna C. *Songs of American Sailormen.* New York: W. W. Norton, 1938.

Cole, Arthur C. "The Puritan and Fair Terpsichore." *Mississippi Valley Historical Review* 29 (1942): 3–34.

Combs, Josiah H. *Folk-Songs of the Southern United States,* ed. D. K. Wilgus. Austin: University of Texas Press, 1967.

Cooper, James Fenimore. *The Pioneers, or The Sources of the Susquehanna.* 1859; rpt. ed., New York: New American Library, 1964.

"The Country Fiddler Boom." *Etude* (January 1929): 55.

"Country Music is Big Business and Nashville is its Detroit." In *Encyclopedia of Country, Western, and Gospel Music,* ed. Linnell Gentry, pp. 108–14. 1961; rpt. ed., St. Clair Shores, Mich.: Scholarly Press, 1972.

"Country Musicians Fiddle Up Roaring Business." In *A History and Encyclopedia of Country, Western, and Gospel Music,* ed. Linnell Gentry, pp. 151–53. 1961; rpt. ed., St. Clair Shores, Mich.: Scholarly Press, 1972.

Cox, John Harrington. *Folk Songs of the South.* Cambridge, Mass.: Harvard University Press, 1925.

Creadick, Nowell. "What is Old Time Music?" *Devil's Box,* no. 21 (1 June 1973): 2–3.

Creighton, Helen. *Songs and Ballads from Nova Scotia.* 1932; rpt. ed., New York: Dover, 1966.

Crockett, Johnny. *Log Cabin Songs.* New York: Universal Music, 1930.

Cuthbert, John A. "A Musicological Look at John Johnson's Fiddling." *Goldenseal: West Virginia Traditional Life* 7 (Winter 1981): 16.

Cutting, Edith E. *Lore of an Adirondack County.* 1944; rpt. ed., Elizabethtown, N.Y.: Denton Publications, 1972.

Damon, S. Foster. *The History of Square Dancing.* Barre, Mass.: Barre Gazette, 1957.

Daniel, Wayne W. "Old-Time Fiddling on Early Radio." *Devil's Box* 17 (Spring 1983): 3–9.

————. "George Daniell's Hill Billies: The Band That Named the Music?" *John Edwards Memorial Foundation Quarterly* 19 (1983): 81–84.

————. "Fiddling in North America: A Selected Annotated Bibliography." *Devil's Box* 18 (Fall 1984): 38–39.

Dennison, Sam. *Scandalize My Name: Black Imagery in American Popular Music.* New York: Garland Publishing, 1982.

DeRyke, Delores. "American Old Time Fiddlers Association." *Devil's Box,* no. 18 (1 September 1972): 6–7.

De Ville, Paul. *The Universal Favorite Contra Dance Album.* New York: Carl Fischer, 1905.

Dichter, Harry, and Elliott Shapiro. *Handbook of Early American Sheet Music, 1768–1889.* 1941; rpt. ed., New York: Dover, 1977.

Doerflinger, William Main. *Songs of the Sailor and Lumberman.* New York: Macmillan, 1972.

Dorson, Richard M. *Jonathan Draws the Long Bow.* 1946; rpt. ed., New York: Russell and Russell, 1969.

———. "Yorker Yarns of Yore." *New York Folklore Quarterly* 3 (1947): 5–27.

———. *America in Legend: Folklore from the Colonial Period to the Present.* New York: Pantheon, 1973.

———. *Folklore and Fakelore: Essays Toward a Discipline of Folk Studies.* Cambridge: Harvard University Press, 1976.

———; George List; Neil Rosenberg. "Folksongs of the Maine Woods." *Folklore and Folk Music Archivist* 8 (Fall 1965): 3–33.

Downer, Alan S. *The Memoir of John Durang, American Actor 1785–1816.* Pittsburgh: University of Pittsburgh Press, 1966.

Duggan, Anne Schley; Jeanette Schlottmann; Abbie Rutledge. *Folk Dances of the United States and Mexico.* New York: Ronald Press, 1948.

Dundes, Alan. "Thinking Ahead: A Folkloristic Reflection of the Future Orientation in American Worldview." *Anthropological Quarterly* 42 (1969): 53–71.

Dunham, Mellie. *Mellie Dunham's Fiddlin' Dance Tunes.* New York: Carl Fischer, 1926.

Epstein, Ellen Robinson, and Rona Mendelsohn. *Record and Remember: Tracing Your Roots Through Oral History.* New York: Monarch, 1978.

Evans, James F. *Prairie Farmer and WLS.* Urbana: University of Illinois Press, 1969.

Ewen, David. *All the Years of American Popular Music.* Englewood Cliffs, N.J.: Prentice-Hall, 1977.

Feintuch, Burt. "The Fiddle in North America: Recent Recordings." *Journal of American Folklore* 95 (1982): 493–500.

———. "The Fiddle in the United States: An Historical Overview." *Kentucky Folklore Record* 29 (1983): 30–38.

" 'Fiddlers' Conversation' at Cooperstown." *Quarterly Newsletter of the Center for the Study of North Country Folklife* (Spring 1978): 9.

"Fiddling to Henry Ford." *Literary Digest* 88 (2 January 1926): 33.

Flanders, Helen Hartness. *Ancient Ballads Traditionally Sung in New England.* Philadelphia: University of Pennsylvania Press, 1965.

———; Elizabeth Flanders Ballard; George Brown; Phillips Barry. *The New Green Mountain Songster: Traditional Folk Songs of Vermont.* Hatboro, Pa.: Folklore Associates, 1966.

———, and Marguerite Olney. *Ballads Migrant in New England.* 1953; rpt. ed., Freeport, N.Y.: Books for Libraries Press, 1968.

Flippo, Chet. *Your Cheating Heart: A Biography of Hank Williams.* New York: Simon and Schuster, 1981.

Flood, Jessie B., and Cornelia F. Putney. *Square Dance U.S.A.* Dubuque, Iowa: Wm. C. Brown, 1955.

Foner, Anne. "Age Stratification and the Changing Family." *American Journal of Sociology,* supplement, 84 (1978): 340–66.

Foote, Nelson. "The Old Generation and the New." In *The Nation's Children: Problems and Prospects,* ed. Eli Ginsberg. New York: Columbia University Press, 1960.

Ford, Ira W. *Traditional Music of America.* New York: E. P. Dutton, 1940.

Ford, Mr., and Mrs. Ford. *"Good Morning": Old-Time Dancing Music, Calls and Directions.* 3rd ed., Dearborn, Mich.: n.p., 1941.

Fowke, Edith. *Lumbering Songs from the Northern Woods.* Austin: University of Texas Press, 1970.

Frankenstein, Alfred. *William Sidney Mount.* New York: Harry N. Abrams, 1975.

Fransworth, Charles H., and Cecil J. Sharp. *Folk-Songs, Chanteys and Singing Games.* New York: H. W. Gray, 1909.

"From the Archives: 'The Arkansas Traveller.' " *John Edwards Memorial Foundation Quarterly* 6 (1970): 51–57.

Fuld, James J. *Book of World-Famous Music.* New York; Crown, 1971.

Gainer, Patrick W. *Folk Songs from the West Virginia Hills.* Grantsville, W.Va.: Seneca Books, 1975.

Gardner, Emelyn. *Folklore from the Schoharie Hills, New York.* Ann Arbor: University of Michigan Press, 1937.

———, and Geraldine Jencks Chickering. *Ballads and Songs of Southern Michigan.* 1939; rpt. ed., Hatboro, Pa.: Folklore Associates, 1967.

Garreau, Joel. *The Nine Nations of North America.* Boston: Houghton Mifflin, 1981.

Gentry, Linnell, ed. *A History and Encyclopedia of Country, Western, and Gospel Music.* 1961; rpt. ed., St. Clair Shores, Mich.: Scholarly Press, 1972.

Glassie, Henry. *Pattern in the Material Folk Culture of the Eastern United States.* Philadelphia: University of Pennsylvania Press, 1968.

———. " 'Take That Night Train to Selma': An Excursion to the Outskirts of Scholarship." In *Folksongs and Their Makers,* pp. 3–68. Bowling Green, Ohio: Bowling Green State University Popular Press, 1971.

Glick, Paul C. *American Families.* New York: John Wiley & Sons, 1957.

Gomme, Alice Bertha. *The Traditional Games of England, Scotland, and Ireland,* 2 vols. 1894; rpt. ed., New York: Dover, 1964.

Gordon, Michael, ed. *The American Family in Social-Historical Perspective.* New York: St. Martin's Press, 1978.

Gray, Roland P. *Songs and Ballads of the Maine Lumberjacks.* Cambridge: Harvard University Press, 1924.

Grayson, Esther G. "The Country Dance Goes to Town." In *A History and Encyclopedia of Country, Western, and Gospel Music,* ed. Linnell Gentry, pp. 46–49. 1961; rpt. ed., St. Clair Shores, Mich.: Scholarly Press, 1972.

Green, Alan W. C. " 'Jim Crow,' 'Zip Coon': The Northern Origins of Negro Minstrelsy." *Massachusetts Review* 2 (1970): 385–97.

Green, Archie. "Hillbilly Music: Source and Symbol." *Journal of American Folklore* 78 (1965): 204–28.

Green, Douglas B. *Country Roots: The Origins of Country Music.* New York: Hawthorn Books, 1976.

Grula, N. DeNault. "Jehile Kirkhuff: A Man and His Music." *Bluegrass Unlimited* 18 (February 1984): 18–20.

Guest, Bill. *One Hundred Fiddle Tunes in Down East Style.* Toronto: Gordon V. Thompson Music, 1980.

Guntharp, Matthew. *Learning the Fiddler's Ways.* University Park: Pennsylvania State University Press, 1980.

Guralnick, Peter. *Feel Like Going Home.* New York: Outerbridge & Dienstfrey, 1971.

Hamm, Charles. *Yesterdays: Popular Song in America.* New York: W. W. Norton, 1979.

———. *Music in the New World.* New York: W. W. Norton, 1983.

Harding's All-Round Collection of Jigs, Reels and Country Dances. New York: Harding's Music House, 1905.

"Haste to the Wedding," *Journal of the English Folk Dance and Song Society* 3 (1938): 208–10.

Hatlo, Jim. "Ricky Skaggs: Nashville's Latest Star Paid His Dues in the Trenches of Bluegrass." *Frets* (March 1985): 30–45.

Haufrecht, Herbt, and Norman Cazden. "Music of the Catskills." *New York Folklore Quarterly* 4 (1948): 32–46.

Hedrick, Ulysses Prentiss. *A History of Agriculture in the State of New York.* 1933; rpt. ed., New York: Hill and Wang, 1966.

Henebry, Richard. *A Handbook of Irish Music.* London: Longmans Green & Co., 1928.

Hickerson, Joseph C., and William Thatcher. "A Brief List of Material Relating to New York State Folk Music." Washington, D.C.: Archive of Folk Song, Library of Congress, 1975.

Historical Memories of Otsego County. Second edition, Otsego County Council of Senior Citizens, 1976.

Hodge, Francis. *Yankee Theatre: The Image of America on the Stage, 1825–1850.* Austin: University of Texas Press, 1964.

Hovemeyer, Pauline. *100 Years in the History of Delhi, New York.* Delhi, N.Y.: Delaware Republican-Express, 1960.

"How 'Bub' Cone of Tylerville, Conn., Divulged the Secret of his Violinistic Art to a Gifted Illustrator." *Musical America* (26 October 1912): 19.

Howard, John Tasker. *Our American Music.* New York: Thomas Y. Crowell, 1965.

Howe, Elias. *Howe's School for the Violin.* Boston: E. Howe, Jr., 1851.

———. *Howe's Complete Ball-Room Hand Book.* Boston: Oliver Ditson, 1858.

Howe, Irving. *World of Our Fathers.* New York: Harcourt Brace Jovanovich, 1976.

Hubbard, Lester A. *Ballads and Songs from Utah.* Salt Lake City: University of Utah Press, 1961.

Huntington, E. Gale, ed. *William Litten's Fiddle Tunes 1800–1802.* Vineyard Haven, Mass.: Hines Point Publishers, 1977.

Ives, Edward. *Joe Scott: The Woodsman Songmaker.* Urbana: University of Illinois Press, 1978.

Jackson, George Pullen. *Spiritual Folk Songs of Early America.* New York: J. J. Augustin, 1937.

Jarman, H. and Bill Hansen. *Old-Time Dance Tunes.* New York: Broadcast Music Co., 1951.

Jennings, Jim. "For Woody, It's . . . " *Elmira Star-Gazette* (19 November 1977), p. 16.

Jennings, Paula Tadlock. "One Year Later: NYSCA's Folk Arts Program." *New York Folklore Newsletter* 7 (May 1986): 3–4.

"John A. McDermott, 187, Well Known Conservationist and Old Time Fiddler, Dies Here." *Cortland Standard* (24 June 1957), p. 2.

Johnston, Neil. "Folk Fiddling: Which Direction—Preservation or Development?" *Devil's Box,* no. 21 (1 June 1973): 5–6.

———. "Preservation and Development in the Next Decade." *Devil's Box,* no. 23 (1 December 1973): 17–19.

Jones, Louis C. "Farmers' Museum Folklore Archive." *Folklore and Folk Music Archivist* 2 (Summer 1959): 2.

———. *Three Eyes on the Past: Exploring New York Folk Life.* Syracuse: Syracuse University Press, 1982.

———. "Early Days of the Folklore Renaissance in New York State." *New York Folklore* 11 (1985): 25–36.

Jones, Loyal. *Radio's "Kentucky Mountain Boy" Bradley Kincaid.* Berea, Kentucky: Berea College Appalachian Center, 1980.

Joyce, Patrick Weston. *Old Irish Folk Music and Songs.* London: Longmans Green, 1909.

Karpeles, Maud, and Lois Blake. *Dances of England and Wales.* New York: Chanticleer Press, 1951.

Karpeles, Maud, and Kenworth Schofield. *A Selection of 100 English Folk Dance Airs.* London: English Folk Dance and Song Society, 1951.

Keller, Kate W., and Ralph Sweet. *A Choice Selection of American Country Dances of the Revolutionary Era.* New York: Country Dance and Song Society, 1975.

Keniston, Kenneth. *All Our Children: The American Family Under Pressure.* New York: Harcourt Brace Jovanovich, 1977.

Kennedy, Peter. *The Fiddler's Tune-Book.* New York: Hargail Music Press, 1951.

_____ . *The Second Fiddler's Tune-Book.* New York: Hargail Music Press, 1954.

_____ . *Folk Songs of Britain and Ireland.* London: Cassell, 1975.

Kimball, Marilyn. "George Edwards, Catskill Folksinger." M.A. thesis, Cooperstown Graduate Programs of the State University of New York, 1966.

King, Nelson. "Hillbilly Music Leaves the Hills." In *A History and Encyclopedia of Country, Western, and Gospel Music,* ed. Linnell Gentry, pp. 127–30. 1961; rpt. ed., St. Clair Shores, Mich.: Scholarly Press, 1972.

King, Willis. *Stories of a Country Doctor.* Philadelphia: Hummel and Parmele, 1891.

Kincaid, Bradley. *My Favorite Mountain Ballads and Old-Time Songs.* Chicago: Prairie Farmer Station WLF, 1931.

_____ . *My Favorite Mountain Ballads and Old Time Songs.* Rochester, N.Y.: WHAM, 1940.

Kinkle, Roger D. *The Complete Encyclopedia of Popular Music and Jazz, 1900–1950.* New Rochelle, N.Y.: Arlington House, 1974.

Kirksey, Kelley. "The Future of Old-Time Fiddling." *Devil's Box,* no. 5 (22 July 1968): 8–12.

Knauff, George P. *Virginia Reels.* Baltimore: Geog. Willig, 1839.

Kobbe, Gustav. *Famous American Songs.* New York: Thomas Y. Crowell, 1906.

Kochman, Marilyn, ed. *The Big Book of Bluegrass.* New York: Quill, 1984.

Korson, George, ed. *Pennsylvania Songs and Legends.* Philadelphia: University of Pennsylvania Press, 1949.

Krassen, Miles. *Appalachian Fiddle.* New York: Oak Publications, 1973.

_____ . *O'Neill's Music of Ireland.* New York: Oak Publications, 1976.

Kraus, Richard G. *Square Dances of Today.* New York: Ronald Press, 1950.

Landis, Paul H. *Rural Life in Process.* New York: McGraw-Hill, 1940.

Lasch, Christopher. *Haven in a Heartless World: The Family Besieged.* New York: Basic Books, 1977.

Laws, G. Malcolm. *American Balladry from British Broadsides.* Philadelphia: American Folklore Society, 1957.

_____ . *Native American Balladry.* Rev. ed., Philadelphia: American Folklore Society, 1964.

Leach, MacEdward. *Folk Ballads and Songs of the Lower Labrador Coast.* Ottawa: National Museum of Canada, 1965.

Leary, James P. "Old Time Music in Northern Wisconsin." *American Music* 2 (1984): 71–87.

Leivers, George Kenneth. "Structure and Function of an Old-Time Fiddlers Association." M.A. thesis, California State University-Chico, 1974.

Lewis, David L. "The Square Dancing Master." *Devil's Box,* no. 17 (1 June 1972): 4–16.

Linscott, Eloise Hubbard. *Folk Songs of Old New England.* New York: Macmillan, 1939.

Lloyd, Ruth, and Norman Lloyd. *The American Heritage Songbook.* New York: American Heritage Publishing, 1969.

Lomax, Alan. *The Folk Songs of North America.* 1960; rpt. ed., Garden City, N.Y.: Doubleday, 1975.

Lomax, John A., and Alan Lomax. *American Ballads and Folk Songs.* New York: Macmillan, 1934.

_____ . *Cowboy Songs and Other Frontier Ballads.* New York: Macmillan, 1938.

_____ . *Folk Song U.S.A.* New York: Duell Sloan & Pearce, 1947.

Loomis, Ormond. *Cultural Conservation: The Protection of Cultural Heritage in the United States.* Washington, D.C.: Library of Congress, 1983.

Lowinger, Gene. *Bluegrass Fiddle.* New York: Oak Publications, 1974.

Luther, Frank. *Americans and Their Songs.* New York: Harper and Brothers, 1942.

Mahar, William J. "March to the Music." *Civil War Times* 23 (1984): 41–42.

————. "Black English in Early Blackface Minstrelsy: A New Interpretation of the Sources of Minstrel Show Dialect." *American Quarterly* 37 (1985): 260–85.

Malone, Bill C. *Country Music, U.S.A.: A Fifty Year History.* 1968; rev. ed., Austin: University of Texas Press, 1985.

————. *Southern Music, American Music.* Lexington: University Press of Kentucky, 1979.

Maloy, Frank. "Fiddle Tablature: Soldier's Joy (Traditional South Georgia Version)" *Devil's Box* 20 (Winter 1986): 48–49.

Marks, Edward B. *They All Had Glamour: From the Swedish Nightingale to the Naked Lady.* New York: Julian Messner, 1944.

Massey, Ellen Gray. *Bittersweet Country.* Garden City, N.Y.: Doubleday, 1978.

McCurry, John Gordon. *The Social Harp.* 1855; rpt. ed., Athens: University of Georgia Press, 1973.

McDowell, Lucien L., and Flora L. McDowell. *Folk Dances of Tennessee, Old Playparty Games of the Caney Fork Valley.* Ann Arbor, Mich.: Edwards Brothers, 1938.

McGlashan, Alexander, *A Collection of Reels.* Edinburgh, Scotland: Neil Stewart, n.d.

McIntosh, David S. *Folk Songs and Singing Games of the Illinois Ozarks.* Carbondale: Southern Illinois University Press, 1974.

McKelvey, Blake. *The Urbanization of America, 1860–1915.* New Brunswick, N.J.: Rutgers University Press, 1963.

McNeil, W. K. "Five Pre-World-War-II Arkansas String Bands: Some Thoughts on Their Recording Success." *John Edwards Memorial Foundation Quarterly* 20 (1984): 68–75.

Mendelson, Michael. "A Bibliography of Fiddling in North America." *John Edwards Memorial Foundation Quarterly* 11 (1975): 104–11, 153–60, 201–204, and 12 (1976): 9–14, 158–64.

Messer, Don. *Way Down East Fiddlin' Tunes.* Toronto: Gordon V. Thompson, 1948.

Milligan, Jean. *101 Scottish Country Dances.* Glasgow, Scotland: Collins, 1956.

————. *99 More Scottish Country Dances.* Glasgow, Scotland: Collins, 1963.

Moore, Thurston, ed. *Pictorial History of Country Music, Volume 2.* Denver: Heather Publications, 1969.

Morris, W. H. *Old Time Violin Melodies.* St. Joseph, Mo.: W. H. Morris, 1927.

Moser, Joan. "Instrumental Music of the Southern Appalachians: Traditional Fiddle Tunes." *North Carolina Folklore* 12 (1964): 1–8.

Narvaez, Peter. "Country Music in Diffusion: Juxtaposition and Syncretism in the Popular Music of Newfoundland." *Journal of Country Music* 7 (1978): 93–101.

Nathan, Hans. *Dan Emmett and the Rise of Early Negro Minstrelsy.* Norman: University of Oklahoma Press, 1961.

National Magazine. *Heart Songs.* Boston: Chapple Publishing, 1909.

Neeser, Robert W. *American Naval Songs and Ballads.* New Haven: Yale University Press, 1938.

Nevell, Richard. *A Time to Dance: American Country Dancing from Hornpipes to Hot Hash.* New York: St. Martin's Press, 1977.

Newell, William Wells. *Games and Songs of American Children.* 1883; rpt. ed., New York: Dover, 1963.

Nobley, Robert E. "Old-Time Singing Versus Folk Singing." *Devil's Box,* no. 15 (20 August 1971): 9–10.

———. "What is Old Time Music?" *Devil's Box*, no. 20 (1 March 1973): 19–20.

Nye, Russel Blaine. *Society and Culture in America, 1830–1860*. New York: Harper and Row, 1974.

O'Donnell, Thomas F., ed. *Harold Frederic's Stories of York State*. Syracuse: Syracuse University Press, 1966.

"Old Time Dance Series." *Country Music Courier* (May 1986): 17.

"Old Time Fiddlers to Compete at Fair." *New York Times* (10 July 1927), sec. 2, p. 7.

O'Malley, F., and F. Atwood. *Seventy Good Dances*. Boston: Oliver Ditson, 1919.

One Thousand Fiddle Tunes. 1940; rpt. ed., Chicago: M. M. Cole, 1967.

O'Neill, Francis, and James O'Neill. *O'Neill's Music of Ireland*. Chicago: Lyon & Healy, 1903.

Opie, Iona, and Peter Opie. *The Singing Game*. Oxford, England: Oxford University Press, 1985.

Ord, John. *The Bothy Songs and Ballads of Aberdeen, Banff and Moray, Angus and the Mearns*. Paisley, Scotland: Gardner, 1930.

Owens, Lee, and Viola Ruth. *Advanced Square Dance Figures of the West and Southwest*. Palo Alto, Ca.: Pacific Books, 1950.

Owens, W. A. *Swing and Turn: Texas Play Party Games*. Dallas: Tardy Publishing, 1936.

Pennsylvania Council on the Arts, *Apprenticeships in Traditional Arts*. Harrisburg: Pennsylvania Council on the Arts, 1986.

Petersen, Richard A. "Single-Industry Firm to Conglomerate Synergistics: Alternative Strategies for Selling Insurance and Country Music." In *Growing Metropolis: Aspects of Development in Nashville*, ed. James F. Blumenstein and Benjamin Walter. Nashville: Vanderbilt University Press, 1975.

———, and Russell Davis. "The Fertile Crescent of Country Music." *Journal of Country Music* 6 (1975): 19–27.

Pickett, Robert S. "The American Family: An Embattled Institution." *The Humanist* 35 (May/June 1975): 5–8.

Playford, John. *The English Dancing Master*. 1651; rev. and updated ed., New York: Dance Horizons, 1975.

Proctor, George A. "Old-Time Fiddling in Ontario." *National Museum of Canada Bulletin*, no. 190 (1963): 173–208.

Randolph, Vance. *Ozark Folksongs*, 4 vols. 1946–1950; rpt. ed., Columbia: University of Missouri Press, 1980.

Reiner, David. *Anthology of Fiddle Styles*. Pacific, Mo.: Mel Bay Publications, 1979.

Richardson, Ethel Park. *American Mountain Songs*. Ellioctt City, Md.: Greenberg, 1927.

Richardson, Philip J. S. *The Social Dances of the Nineteenth Century in England*. London: Herbert Jenkins, 1960.

Rivers, Jerry. *Hank Williams: From Life to Legend*. Denver: Heather Enterprises, 1976.

The Robbins Collection of 200 Jigs, Reels, and Country Dances. New York: Robbins Musical Corp., 1933.

Roberson, Don. "Uncle Bunt Stephens: Champion Fiddler." *Old Time Music* 5 (Summer 1972): 4–6.

Roberts, Roderick J. "An Introduction to the Study of Northern Country Music." *Journal of Country Music* 7 (1978): 22–28.

Robison, Carson J. *Carson J. Robison's World's Greatest Collection of Mountain Ballads and Old Time Songs*. Chicago: M. M. Cole, 1930.

Rollinson, T. H. *Favorite Reels, Jigs and Hornpipes For the Violin*. Boston: Oliver Ditson, 1907.

Rosenberg, Neil. " 'Folk' and 'Country' Music in the Canadian Maritimes: A Regional Model." *Journal of Country Music* 5 (1974): 76–83.

_____. *Country Music in the Maritimes: Two Studies.* St. John's: Memorial University of Newfoundland Reprint Series, No. 2, 1976.

_____. *Bluegrass: A History.* Urbana: University of Illinois Press, 1985.

Roy, Fred. "A Pictorial Review of Country Music in Canada, From 1922 to 1965." In *Pictorial History of Country Music, Volume 2,* ed. Thurston Moore, pp. 1–8. Denver: Heather Enterprises, 1969.

Rudnick, Joyce Newberry. "Alice Clemens: Tug Hill Virtuoso." *Bluegrass Unlimited* (August 1986): 62–66.

Rumble, John W. "The Emergence of Nashville as a Recording Center: Logbooks from the Castle Studio, 1952–1953." *Journal of Country Music* 7 (1978): 22–41.

Ryan, Grace L. *Dances of Our Pioneers.* New York: A. S. Barnes, 1939.

Ryan, William Bradbury. *Ryan's Mammoth Collection: 1050 Reels and Jigs . . . And How to Play Them.* Boston: Elias Howe, 1883.

Sacks, Howard L. "John Baltzell, A Country Fiddler from the Heartland." *Journal of Country Music* 10 (1985): 18–24.

Sandburg, Carl. *The American Songbag.* New York: Harcourt, Brace, 1927.

Sandvik, Ole. *Folke-Musik i Gudbrandsdalen.* 1919; rpt. ed., Oslo: Johan Gundttanum, 1948.

Scherman, Tony. "A Man Who Mined Musical Gold in the Southern Hills." *Smithsonian* 16 (April 1985): 173–96.

Schinhan, Jan Philip, ed. *Frank C. Brown Collection of North Carolina Folklore: The Music of the Ballads.* Durham, N.C.: Duke University Press, 1957.

Schoenberg, Mark. "The Plum Creek Boys: College Bluegrass in the Early Sixties." *Bluegrass Unlimited* 21 (December 1986): 28–32.

Schwartz, H. W. *Bands of America.* Garden City, N.Y.: Doubleday, 1957.

Scott, Donald M., and Bernard Wishy, eds. *American's Families: A Documentary History.* New York: Harper and Row, 1982.

Scott, John Anthony. *The Ballad of America.* New York: Bantam Books, 1966.

Seemann, Charlie. "Review of *Country Music, U.S.A.*" *Journal of American Folklore* 99 (1986): 356–58.

Shapiro, Henry D. *Appalachia on Our Mind: The Southern Mountains and Mountaineers in the American Consciousness, 1870–1920.* Chapel Hill: University of North Carolina Press, 1978.

Sharp, Cecil J. *Country Dance Tunes.* London: Novello, 1909.

_____. *The Country Dance Book.* Rev. ed., London: Novello, 1934.

Shaw, Lloyd. *Cowboy Dances.* Caldwell, Id.: Caxton Printers, 1952.

Shelton, Robert. "Old Time Fiddlers." *New York Times* (9 April 1961), sec. 2, p. 13.

Shoemaker, Henry W. *Mountain Minstrelsy of Pennsylvania.* Rev. ed., Philadelphia: Newman F. McGirr, 1931.

Shorter, Edward. *The Making of the Modern Family.* New York: Basic Books, 1975.

Shumway, Larry V., and Tom Carter. "The History and Performance Style of J. W. 'Babe' Spangler, The 'Old Virginia Fiddler.' " *John Edwards Memorial Foundation Quarterly* 14 (1978): 198–207.

Smith, Andrew. "The New Lost City Ramblers." *Country and Western Spotlight,* n.s., no. 15 (June 1978): 6–8.

Smith's Collection of Mountain Ballads and Cowboy Songs. New York: Wm. J. Smith Music, 1932.

Smithyman, Kendrick. "Little Mohee." *New York Folklore Quarterly* 25 (1970): 64–70.

Smyth, Mary Winslow. *Minstrelsy of Maine.* Boston: Houghton Mifflin, 1927.

Solomon, Jack, and Olivia Solomon. *Zickary Zan: Childhood Folklore.* University: University of Alabama Press, 1980.

Spaeth, Sigmund. *Read 'Em and Weep: The Songs You Forgot to Remember.* Garden City, N.Y.: Doubleday, Page and Co., 1926.

———. *Weep Some More My Lady.* New York: Doubleday, Page and Co., 1927.

———. *A History of Popular Music in America.* New York: Random House, 1948.

Spielman, Earl V. "The Fiddling Traditions of Cape Breton and Texas: A Study in Parallels and Contrasts." *Yearbook for Inter-American Musical Research* 8 (1972): 39–47.

———. "The Texas Fiddling Style." *Devil's Box* 14 (1 September 1980): 24–32.

Spitzer, Nicholas. " 'Bob Wills is Still the King': Romantic Regionalism and Convergent Culture in Central Texas." *John Edwards Memorial Foundation Quarterly* 11 (1975): 191–96.

Stekert, Ellen. "Cents and Nonsense in the Urban Folksong Movement: 1930–1966." In *Folklore and Society: Essays in Honor of Benj. A. Botkin,* ed. Bruce Jackson. Hatboro, Pa.: Folklore Associates, 1966.

Stilgoe, John R. *Common Landscape of America, 1580–1845.* New Haven: Yale University Press, 1982.

Studer, Norman. "Grant Rogers: Folksinger of the Delaware Valley." *Sing Out!* 12 (Summer 1962): 30.

"Sunrise in Memphis." *Country Music Magazine* (March 1977): 26.

Susman, Warren. *Culture as History: The Transformation of American Society in the Twentieth Century.* New York: Pantheon, 1984.

Sweet, Ralph. *The Fifer's Delight.* Hazardville, Ct.: Powder Mill Barn, 1964.

Sym's Old Time Dances. New York: G. T. Worth, 1930.

Thede, Marion. "Traditional Fiddling." *Ethnomusicology* 6 (1962): 19–24.

———. *The Fiddle Book.* New York: Oak Publications, 1967.

Thomas, Jean, and Joseph A. Leeder. *The Singin' Gatherin': Tunes from the Southern Appalachians.* New York: Silver Burdett, 1939.

Thompson, Harold W. *Body, Boots and Britches: Folktales, Ballads and Speech from Country New York.* 1939; rpt. ed., Syracuse: Syracuse University Press, 1979.

———. *A Pioneer Songster: Texts from the Stevens-Douglass Manuscripts of Western New York, 1841–1856.* Ithaca: Cornell University Press, 1958.

Thompson, John H., ed. *Geography of New York State.* Syracuse: Syracuse University Press, 1966; rev. ed.,

Thompson, Sally. "Plymouth Old-Time Dance Orchestra." *Vermont History* 40 (1972): 185–89.

Thurston, H. A. *Scotland's Dances.* London: G. Bell and Sons, 1954.

Toll, Robert C. *Blacking Up: The Minstrel Show in Nineteenth-Century America.* New York: Oxford University Press, 1974.

Tolman, Beth, and Ralph Page. *The Country Dance Book.* New York: A. S. Barnes, 1937.

Tolman, Newton F. *Quick Tunes and Good Times.* Dublin, N.H.: William L. Bauhan, 1972.

Townsend, Charles R. *San Antonio Rose: The Life and Music of Bob Wills.* Urbana: University of Illinois Press, 1976.

Trachtenberg, Alan. *The Incorporation of America: Culture and Society in the Gilded Age.* New York: Hill and Wang, 1982.

Tribe, Ivan M. "The Hillbilly Versus the City: Urban Images in Country Music." *John Edwards Memorial Foundation Quarterly* 10 (1974): 41–50.

———. *Mountaineer Jamboree: Country Music in West Virginia.* Lexington: University Press of Kentucky, 1984.

———. "The Economics of Hillbilly Radio: A Preliminary Investigation of the 'P.I.' System in the Depression Decade and Afterward." *John Edwards Memorial Foundation Quarterly* 20 (1984): 76–83.

Truxal, Andrew G., and Francis E. Merrill. *The Family in American Culture.* New York: Prentice-Hall, 1947.

Tudor, Dean, and Nancy Tudor. *Grass Roots Music.* Littleton, Col.: Libraries Unlimited, 1979.

Tyson, James C. *Twenty-Five Old Fashioned Dance Tunes for Piano Solo.* New York: Belwin, n.d.

Vlach, John Michael, and Simon J. Bronner, eds. *Folk Art and Art Worlds.* Ann Arbor, Mich.: UMI Research Press, 1986.

von Schmidt, Eric, and Jim Rooney. *Baby Let Me Follow You Down.* Garden City, N.Y.: Doubleday, 1979.

Walker, J. Herbert. "Lumberjacks and Raftsmen." In *Pennsylvania Songs and Legends,* ed. George Korson, pp. 326–53. Philadelphia: University of Pennsylvania Press, 1949.

Walsh, Jim. "John H. Kimmel, 'The Irish Scotchman.' " *Hobbies* (February 1958): 34.

Warner, Anne. *Traditional American Folk Songs from the Anne and Frank Warner Collection.* Syracuse: Syracuse University Press, 1984.

Watts, Jim, and Allen F. Davis. *Generations: Your Family in Modern American History.* New York: Knopf, 1978.

Welker, Martin. *Farm Life in Central Ohio Sixty Years Ago.* Wooster, Ohio: Clapper's Print, 1892.

Wells, Paul. "Mellie Dunham: 'Maine's Champion Fiddler.' " *John Edwards Memorial Foundation Quarterly* 12 (1976): 112–18.

Whisnant, David E. *All That Is Native & Fine: The Politics of Culture in an American Region.* Chapel Hill: University of North Carolina Press, 1983.

White's Unique Collection of Jigs, Reels, Etc. New York: White-Smith Music, 1896.

White's Excelsior Collection of Jigs, Reels, Etc. New York: White-Smith Music Publishing, 1907.

Wiggins, Gene. "Popular Music and the Fiddler." *John Edwards Memorial Foundation Quarterly* 15 (1979): 144–56.

Wilgus, D. K. *Anglo-American Folksong Scholarship since 1898.* New Brunswick, N.J.: Rutgers University Press, 1959.

———. "Introduction to the Study of Hillbilly Music." *Journal of American Folklore* 78 (1965): 195–204.

———. "Country-Western Music and the Urban Hillbilly." In *The Urban Experience and Folk Tradition,* ed. Américo Paredes and Ellen J. Stekert, pp. 137–59. Austin: University of Texas Press, 1971.

———. "Bradley Kincaid." In *The Stars of Country Music,* ed. Bill C. Malone and Judith McCulloh, pp. 93–102. New York: Avon, 1975.

Wilkinson, Winston. "Virginia Dance Tunes." *Southern Folklore Quarterly* 6 (1942): 1–10.

Williams, Roger M. *Sing a Sad Song: The Life of Hank Williams.* Garden City, N.Y.: Doubleday, 1970.

Winch, Robert F. *The Modern Family.* New York: Holt, Rinehart and Winston, 1964.

Winslow, David. "The Rural Square Dance in the Northeastern United States: A Continuity of Tradition." Ph.D. diss., University of Pennsylvania, 1972.

Wolfe, Charles K. "That Old-Time Music." *Devil's Box,* no. 22 (1 September 1973): 6–9.

———. "Early Nashville Media and Its Response to Old Time Music." *Journal of Country Music* 4 (1973): 2–16.

———. "Toward a Contextual Approach to Old-Time Music." *Journal of Country Music* 5 (1974): 65–75.

———. "Uncle Jimmy's Repertoire." *Devil's Box* 9 (1 September 1975): 53–54.

———— . *The Grand Ole Opry: The Early Years.* London: Old-Time Music, 1975.

———— . *Tennessee Strings: The Story of Country Music in Tennessee.* Knoxville: University of Tennessee Press, 1977.

———— . *Kentucky Country: Folk and Country Music of Kentucky.* Lexington: University Press of Kentucky, 1982.

Wolford, Leah Jackson. *The Play Party in Indiana.* Indianapolis: Indiana Historical Commission, 1916.

Work, Henry Clay. *Songs of Henry Clay Work.* 1884; rpt. ed., New York: Da Capo Press, 1974.

Yates, Mike, and Tony Russell. "Tracing the Arkansas Traveler." *Old Time Music.* no. 31 (Winter 1978/79): 14.

Zeitlin, Steven J.; Amy J. Kotkin; Holly Cutting Baker. *A Celebration of American Family Folklore.* New York: Pantheon, 1982.

Zelinsky, Wilbur. "Selfward Bound? Personal Preference Patterns and the Changing Map of American Society." *Economic Geography* 50 (1974): 144–79.

Zolotow, Maurice. "Hillbilly Boom." *Saturday Evening Post* (12 February 1944): 22–23, 36, 38.

Records

Arm and Hammer String Band. *Stay on the Farm.* Fretless 136.

Beer Parlour Jive. String 801.

Blake, Norman. *Rising Fawn String Ensemble.* Rounder 0122.

Botkin, B. A., ed. *Play and Dance Songs and Tunes.* Music Division, Library of Congress, Album AAFS L9.

Boys of the Lough. *Second Album.* Rounder 3006.

Brave Boys: New England Traditions in Folk Music. New World Records NW 239, 1977.

Byrd, U.S. Senator Robert, *Mountain Fiddler.* County 769.

Carawan, Guy. *Jubilee.* June Appal JA 029, 1979.

Carignan, Jean. *French Canadian Fiddle Songs.* Legacy 120.

———— . *Jean Carignan rend hommage à Joseph Allard.* Philo FI-2012.

Collins, Earl. *That's Earl Collins Family Fiddling.* Briar 0798.

Cyr, Albert. *Old Time Fiddling.* Century 36464, 1969.

Double Decker Stringband. *Giddyap Napoleon.* Fretless FR 144, 1980.

Douglas, Wilson. *The Right Hand Fork of Rush's Creek.* Rounder 0047.

Franklin, Major. *Texas Fiddle Favorites.* County 707.

Galax 73. Tennvale TV-002.

Great Big Yam Potatoes: Anglo-American Fiddle Music from Mississippi. Mississippi Department of Archives and History AH-002, 1985.

Gimble, Johnny. *The Texas Fiddle Collection.* CMH Country Classics 9027, 1981.

Guthrie, Woody. *Hard Travelin'.* Disc D110.

Hunter, Tommy. *Deep in Tradition.* June Appal 007, 1976.

Instrumental Dance Music 1780s–1920s. New World Records NW 293, 1978.

Jabbour, Alan, ed. *American Fiddle Tunes from the Archive of Folk Song.* Music Division, Library of Congress, Album AFS L62, 1971.

Kessinger, Clark. *Sweet Bunch of Daisies.* County 747.

Lamb, Grant. *Tunes from Home.* Voyager 312-S.

Lundy, Emmett W.: Fiddle Tunes from Grayson County, Virginia. String 802.

McDonald, John A. *Marches, Strathspeys, Reels and Jigs of the Cape Breton Scot.* Rodeo RLP 75.

McGuire, Sean. *Ireland's Champion Traditional Fiddler.* Outlet 1031.

McMillan, Roma. *Old Time Fiddling 1976.* Fretless 122.

Michael, McCreesh & Campbell. *The Host of the Air.* Front Hall FHR-023.

Monroe, Bill. *Bluegrass Instrumentals.* Decca 74601.

———. *Bluegrass Time.* MCA 116.

Monroe, Charlie. *On the Noonday Jamboree.* County 538.

New England Contra Dance Music. Kicking Mule 216.

Old Time Fiddle Classics. County 514.

Old-Time Southern Dance Music. Old Timey LP-101.

Older, Lawrence. *Adirondack Songs, Ballads and Fiddle Tunes.* Folk-Legacy FSA-15, 1963.

Perkins, J. T. *Fiddle Favorites Perkins Style.* David Unlimited DU 33017.

The Pride of America: The Golden Age of the American March. New World Records 266, 1976.

Rogers, Grant. *Songmaker of the Catskills.* Folk-Legacy FSA-27, 1965.

———. *Ballads and Fiddle Tunes.* Kanawha 313.

Seems Like Romance to Me: Traditional Fiddle Tunes from Ohio. Gambier Folklore Society GFS 901, 1985.

Spottswood, Richard, ed. *Dance Music: Reels, Polkas, & More.* Library of Congress, Music Division, Folk Music in America Series, vol. 4, LBC 4, 1976.

Summers, John W. *Indiana Fiddler.* Rounder 0194.

Thomasson, Benny, and Jerry Thomasson. *A Jam Session with Benny & Jerry Thomasson.* Voyager VRLP 309.

Townsend, Graham. *Le Violon/The Fiddle.* Rounder 7002.

———. *Down Home Fiddlin'.* Audat 477-9048.

25 Great Fiddle Hits. K-Tel 9110, 1976.

Wanzer, Lloyd. *Plain and Fancy Fiddlin'.* American Heritage 19A.

Wells, Paul, ed. *New England Traditional Fiddling, 1926-1975.* John Edwards Memorial Foundation JEMF-105, 1978.

Western Swing. Old Timey LP 105.

The Wonderful World of Old Time Fiddlers, 2 vols. Vetco 104, 106.

Yankee Brass Band: Music from Mid-Nineteenth-Century America. New World Records 312, 1981.

Yankee Ingenuity. *Kitchen Junket.* Fretless 200A.

Index

THIS INDEX covers subjects, figures, organizations, songs and tunes, and locales discussed in the text. Locales in New York are listed together under the entry for "New York"; locales outside of New York are listed separately. If a tune is transcribed in the text, I indicate this by citing its tune number and adding an asterisk (*) to the page number on which the transcription appears and a dagger (†) to the page number on which any note to the tune is found. One can find cross-references to the tune numbers by consulting the list of musical transcriptions on pages viii–ix.

OLD-TIME MUSIC MAKERS OF NEW YORK STATE

was composed in 12 on 13 Garamond No. 3 on a Linotron 202
by Partners Composition;
with display type in Largo Light provided by Jōb Litho Services;
printed by sheet-fed offset on 50-pound, acid-free Glatfelter Antique Cream,
and Smyth sewn and bound over binder's boards in Joanna Arrestox B,
by Maple-Vail Book Manufacturing Group, Inc.;
with dust jackets printed in 2 colors by New England Book Components, Inc.;
designed by Mary Peterson Moore;
and published by

SYRACUSE UNIVERSITY PRESS
SYRACUSE, NEW YORK 13244-5160